Daddy! hope you enjoy this Daily Champion! You are my Champion Love you! [illegible]

FIVESTARMAN

The Daily Champion

365 Daily Proverbs to Provide Positive Change and a Champion's Mentality

By Neil Kennedy

FivestarMan.com

THE DAILY CHAMPION
365 Daily Proverbs to Provide Positive Change and a Champion's Mentality

FivestarMan, Inc.
8729 East 98th Place
Tulsa, Oklahoma 74133
FivestarMan.com

Editor: Linda A. Schantz
Cover & Layout Design: Peppermedia

Printed in the United States of America

FIVESTARMAN™

Champions do daily
what the average
do occasionally.

FIVESTARMAN™

The Daily Champion

The Daily Champion

SIMPLY THE BEST WAY TO START YOUR DAY.

Champions do daily what the average do occasionally. ***The Daily Champion*** email is your FREE source for positive change and encouraging a champion's mentality.

Now that you have the book, take advantage of receiving ***The Daily Champion*** in your inbox with the added convenience of reading, listening, or watching each day.

To signup for daily email delivery of ***The Daily Champion,*** visit

thedailychampion.com

In the back of this book is a very special offer exclusively for you valued at $50. It's our gift to you, absolutely FREE.

Also, ***The Daily Champion*** is worth sharing with your family, friends, and co-workers. Invite them to join you in the pursuit of authentic manhood.

Day 1: Wisdom For Living Successfully

PROVERBS 1:1-2 (MSG)

These are the wise sayings of Solomon,
David's son, Israel's king—
Written down so we'll know how to live well and right,
to understand what life means and where it's going.

PRINCIPLE

Proverbs are universal principles that contain wisdom for living a successful and abundant life.

When I was a desperate, young, and naïve man about to embark on life, and more than a little nervous about what I was going to do and where I was going to go, I picked up a copy of a book entitled, ***See You At The Top*** by Zig Ziglar.

Zig recommended reading one chapter of Proverbs a day for each day of the month. Doing so, he said, would help a simple person gain wisdom to be successful.

Well, that was an attractive concept for me. I was a simple guy, who was eager and excited about life, but I was ignorant and poorly educated. My only advantage was that I knew I didn't know anything. The pattern of living that had been modeled before me was failure—drug abuse, alcoholism, adultery, jealousy, fits of rage—I wanted something more in life.

I invite you to adventure with me on this journey. Every day, we will read a chapter of Proverbs and gain wisdom to immediately apply it our lives. It's only a commitment of about five minutes a day, and the rewards of consistency could be amazing.

REMEMBER

Champions do daily what average men do occasionally.

READ PROVERBS CHAPTER 1

fivestarman.com/day-1

Day 2: Even Champions Need A Coach

PROVERBS 2:1-5 (NIV)

My son, if you accept my words
and store up my commands within you,
turning your ear to wisdom
and applying your heart to understanding—
indeed, if you call out for insight
and cry aloud for understanding,
and if you look for it as for silver
and search for it as for hidden treasure,
then you will understand the fear of the Lord
and find the knowledge of God.

PRINCIPLE

Proverbs is a man's book—written by a man to a man. It is the greatest compilation of manly wisdom, and we should devour it.

Taking advice is sometimes a difficult task for men. We're notorious when it comes to asking for directions, largely because we believe we have a natural sense of direction. However, when it comes to life and how to live it successfully, we need to get wisdom. We can gain wisdom either through experience and pain or through a mentor. I recommend a mentor.

Even champions need a coach. Every successful player has a coach—or even a team of coaches and trainers to help make his game a success. That's what the book of Proverbs is for us. It is a team of mentors who help us win in the game that matters and where the score counts—the game of life.

REMEMBER

Even champions need a coach.

READ PROVERBS CHAPTER 2

fivestarman.com/day-2

Day 3: Prolonged Life, Peace, And Prosperity

PROVERBS 3:1-2 (NIV)

My son, do not forget my teaching,
but keep my commands in your heart,
for they will prolong your life many years
and bring you peace and prosperity.

PRINCIPLE

Prolonged life, peace, and prosperity: These three benefits are promised to the one who stores up wisdom.

Think about how amazing these three promises are. I can't think of anything that people want more. The promise of prolonged life, peace, and prosperity is a pretty amazing promise; yet, that's the promise of hearing and keeping the commands of wisdom in your heart.

Why the heart? Because it is with the heart that you believe, and out of it flow the issues of life. What you store in your heart is what will be expressed. When you're under pressure, you're going to want to express wisdom.

P.S. The word *prosperity* doesn't equate to a dollar amount. It simply means, *your journey will go well with you.*

REMEMBER

Wisdom's by-products are prolonged life, peace, and prosperity.

READ PROVERBS CHAPTER 3
fivestarman.com/day-3

Day 4: Fatherly Advice

PROVERBS 4:1-2 (MSG)

Listen, friends, to some fatherly advice;
sit up and take notice so you'll know how to live.
I'm giving you good counsel;
don't let it go in one ear and out the other.
When I was a boy at my father's knee,
the pride and joy of my mother,
He would sit me down and drill me:
"Take this to heart. Do what I tell you—live!"

PRINCIPLE

Wisdom has a generational track. It has the ability to become an inheritance.

A father sits down and shares his life lessons with his son, hoping to spare him some of life's challenges. As that son sits atop the knee of the "old man," he seldom values the tremendous blessing he is receiving; however, once he becomes a father, things come full circle as he then calls his son to climb up and sit at the seat of his experience.

Some of us never experienced that kind of fathering. What are we to do? That's one of the great benefits of reading the book of Proverbs. It is the wisdom of a father speaking to his son.

You may not have inherited generational wisdom, but you can become the patriarch of it. Learn wisdom. Call your son to sit at the seat of your experience.

REMEMBER

Wisdom is generational. Give and receive fatherly advice.

READ PROVERBS CHAPTER 4

fivestarman.com/day-4

Day 5: Protect Your Purpose

PROVERBS 5:1-2 (NIV)

My son, pay attention to my wisdom,
turn your ear to my words of insight,
that you may maintain discretion
and your lips may preserve knowledge.

PRINCIPLE

Wisdom gives you the discretion to maintain your purpose.

We identify ourselves as ***FivestarMen*** because of the five purposes of authentic manhood. Solomon, our adviser, instructs us to listen to wisdom so that we may "maintain discretion."

Maintaining discretion means we preserve and protect our purpose. As men, we have an enemy who is devising schemes and crafting seductions for us to surrender our manhood. By being discreet, we're able to avoid most of these traps in life. Being discreet is different from being secretive. Our goal is to have discernment and appropriate wisdom for every occasion.

Wisdom will also give us a filter on our language. Discretion causes us to weigh carefully what we say and how we say it.

REMEMBER

Wisdom gives you the discretion to maintain your purpose.
Protect your purpose with discretion.

READ PROVERBS CHAPTER 5
fivestarman.com/day-5

Day 6: Gazelle Intensity

PROVERBS 6:1-5 (NLT)

My child, if you have put up security for a friend's debt
or agreed to guarantee the debt of a stranger—
if you have trapped yourself by your agreement
and are caught by what you said—
follow my advice and save yourself,
for you have placed yourself at your friend's mercy.
Now swallow your pride;
go and beg to have your name erased.
Don't put it off; do it now!
Don't rest until you do.
Save yourself like a gazelle escaping from a hunter,
like a bird fleeing from a net.

PRINCIPLE

Don't get caught in a bad contract.

We're advised to free ourselves from obligations we have made without serious thought and consideration. The language is meant to be alarming. He is saying, "Don't get caught in a bad contract!"

Famed money coach, Dave Ramsey, calls this "gazelle intensity." The visualization is that of a gazelle bursting off its hooves and into an escape at full speed. Gazelles can run up to sixty miles per hour and maintain a speed of thirty miles per hour for an extended amount of time.

The point here is, don't enter into contracts or obligations you can't control. It's good advice.

REMEMBER

Have gazelle intensity!

READ PROVERBS CHAPTER 6

fivestarman.com/day-6

Day 7: Bound By Covenant

PROVERBS 7:3 (NIV)

Bind them on your fingers;
write them on the tablet of your heart.

PRINCIPLE

The Word of God is a relational covenant.

Our advisor in the book of Proverbs tells us the words and commands he is giving us are to be considered a covenant of relationship—a binding agreement between two parties. God's character backs up His Word. He personally watches over the Word to see it fulfilled (Jeremiah 1:12). He guarantees it.

We have a role in this covenant as well. For the Word of God to be performed in our lives, we must put ourselves in agreement with the covenant relationship. How do we do that?

We do it in the same manner in which we agree in marriage. We bind our fingers as a sign of covenant, and we write the covenant or vows on our hearts. Then we openly speak what we believe (Romans 10:8).

The heart is the seat of our appetites. It is the place from where we choose our cravings. When we are married, we have expressed that we will be faithful to crave our spouse exclusively. When we are in covenant with the Word of God, we choose the appetite of the Word over the flesh, believing that relationship is worth protecting and honoring.

This understanding will help us approach our relationship with the Word of God seriously and nurture that covenant to see it mature.

REMEMBER

The Word of God is a relational covenant. Keep covenant with God's Word.

READ PROVERBS CHAPTER 7
fivestarman.com/day-7

Day 8: Wisdom Raises Her Voice

PROVERBS 8:1 (NIV)

Does not wisdom call out?
Does not understanding raise her voice?

PRINCIPLE

Wisdom is personified as the attention-grabbing, attractive voice of a woman. Wisdom raises her voice.

It is interesting that our advisor personifies wisdom in the feminine voice. This chapter tells us how aggressive Wisdom is to get our attention—even positioning herself in the most obvious place: at the gate of the city. She is attractive and wanting our attention. In the Greek, Wisdom is named *"Sophia."*

At times, we tend to think of Wisdom as illusive and secretive. Some act as if Wisdom is hiding in the shadows or that only a few select people have access to her. But Wisdom is actually raising her voice and calling out to *all* men.

That's good news for us. We are summoned to hear what she has to say. However, it needs to be noted that wisdom and education are two different things. Education is important, but wisdom is the most important thing. Wisdom gives us special insight that helps us know what to do. She gives us principles, solutions, and action steps to get things done.

REMEMBER

Give your attention and listen to Wisdom.

READ PROVERBS CHAPTER 8

fivestarman.com/day-8

Day 9: Leave Your Simple Ways

PROVERBS 9:6 (NIV)

Leave your simple ways and you will live;
walk in the way of insight.

PRINCIPLE

God relates to men in the daily commute.

Adam walked with God in the cool of the day. Enoch walked with God, and he was no more, for God took him. Noah walked in favor with God in the midst of a wicked culture. Abraham walked with God even when he didn't know where God was leading. Moses walked barefooted with God on the Holy Mountain. David walked with God in the valley of the shadow of death. Jesus, God with us, walked with man.

One of the greatest lessons I've learned is that God directs our steps. As you go to work today, realize that God wants to commune with you. He will give you insight for the day. He can help you with the challenges you face.

When you leave work to go home, commune with God again. Ask Him about your family. What do they need from you? How can you be an encouragement to them and draw out the gifts each of them has?

Don't waste your time listening to "talking heads" on the radio about nothing that matters—take the time to commune with God and gain insight.

REMEMBER

Commune with God as you come and go today.

READ PROVERBS CHAPTER 9

fivestarman.com/day-9

Day 10: A Father's Joy

PROVERBS 10:1 (NIV)

A wise son brings joy to his father
but a foolish son brings grief to his mother.

PRINCIPLE

Wisdom solves problems; foolishness causes them.

Is there any greater joy to a father than knowing his son makes wise decisions?

Recently, my son faced a life decision. A big one. The decision involved relocating to another city to accept a job with an up-and-coming corporation. I can't tell you how much joy it gave me to see my son process the decision with wisdom.

Equip your son to be a problem solver, and not a problem causer. To do this, teach him wisdom.

Keys to Problem Solving:

- Look for the natural gifting your son possesses. His gift may be similar to yours or completely opposite. Don't box him in to do only what you like.
- When he operates in his gifts, doors will open, and momentum will occur for him. It will seem supernatural.
- Your son will be compensated in proportion to the problems he solves. He will be penalized for the problems he causes.
- Your son cannot solve every problem. He needs you to mentor him.

Don't allow your own insecurity to keep you from helping your son. If you don't know what to do or how to do it, find a resource for him. Find a coach, a tutor, or another mentor. Helping your son grow in wisdom will make you joyful and will win him favor.

REMEMBER

Teach your son how to solve problems, not cause them.

READ PROVERBS CHAPTER 10

fivestarman.com/day-10

Day 11: Set The Standard

PROVERBS 11:1 (NIV)

The Lord detests dishonest scales,
but accurate weights find favor with him.

PRINCIPLE

The standard you use to measure with is the weight you should use for everyone else.

In the business culture corruption is epidemic. Bureaucrats impose laws upon others which they have exempted themselves from observing. Street-market thieves have moved from alleyways to marbleized offices, but they're common thieves nonetheless.

We should not measure our success by what we gain in dishonest transactions. We should hold ourselves to a higher standard. Was the deal equitable? Did both parties receive mutual benefit?

This is especially true in dealing with people who are in the weaker position. The manner in which we treat the weakest among us is the true measure of our character.

There will be transactions when you will be the weaker person. How do you want and expect to be treated?

You set the standard. The measure that you use will be measured back to you.

REMEMBER

You set the standard.

READ PROVERBS CHAPTER 11
fivestarman.com/day-11

Day 12: Leaders Are Readers

PROVERBS 12:1 (NLT)

To learn, you must love discipline;
it is stupid to hate correction.

PRINCIPLE

Leaders are readers.

Advertisers have mastered the art of making men look stupid. A man is seen as the butt of the joke. Men have shown good humor by laughing at our own expense, but it's an old and worn out strategy. The laughter is over. In fact, I am embarrassed that, as men, we have allowed ourselves to be the fodder of foolishness.

The word for *stupid* in our advisor's language refers to men being *brutish*. It's the sad imagery of mindless and meaningless men with the herd mentality of cattle. A man who isn't willing to learn or be corrected is a brute. He lacks rational thinking. He is aimlessly going with the flow—traveling the same trails and grazing the same fields. The only excitement in the routine of cattle is butting heads with each other. That's the picture painted to describe mindless men who don't think.

As men, we need to think. We must continue to learn and grow. We need to explore by reading. We must have the discipline not just to take care of our bodies, but also to take care of our minds.

Expand your conversations beyond the surface of things. Don't have a herd mentality. Leaders are readers. Distinguish yourself from the crowd.

REMEMBER

Don't be a brute.

READ PROVERBS CHAPTER 12

fivestarman.com/day-12

Day 9: Leave Your Simple Ways

PROVERBS 9:6 (NIV)

Leave your simple ways and you will live;
walk in the way of insight.

PRINCIPLE

God relates to men in the daily commute.

Adam walked with God in the cool of the day. Enoch walked with God, and he was no more, for God took him. Noah walked in favor with God in the midst of a wicked culture. Abraham walked with God even when he didn't know where God was leading. Moses walked barefooted with God on the Holy Mountain. David walked with God in the valley of the shadow of death. Jesus, God with us, walked with man.

One of the greatest lessons I've learned is that God directs our steps. As you go to work today, realize that God wants to commune with you. He will give you insight for the day. He can help you with the challenges you face.

When you leave work to go home, commune with God again. Ask Him about your family. What do they need from you? How can you be an encouragement to them and draw out the gifts each of them has?

Don't waste your time listening to "talking heads" on the radio about nothing that matters—take the time to commune with God and gain insight.

REMEMBER

Commune with God as you come and go today.

READ PROVERBS CHAPTER 9
fivestarman.com/day-9

Day 10: A Father's Joy

PROVERBS 10:1 (NIV)

A wise son brings joy to his father
but a foolish son brings grief to his mother.

PRINCIPLE

Wisdom solves problems; foolishness causes them.

Is there any greater joy to a father than knowing his son makes wise decisions?

Recently, my son faced a life decision. A big one. The decision involved relocating to another city to accept a job with an up-and-coming corporation. I can't tell you how much joy it gave me to see my son process the decision with wisdom.

Equip your son to be a problem solver, and not a problem causer. To do this, teach him wisdom.

Keys to Problem Solving:

- Look for the natural gifting your son possesses. His gift may be similar to yours or completely opposite. Don't box him in to do only what you like.
- When he operates in his gifts, doors will open, and momentum will occur for him. It will seem supernatural.
- Your son will be compensated in proportion to the problems he solves. He will be penalized for the problems he causes.
- Your son cannot solve every problem. He needs you to mentor him.

Don't allow your own insecurity to keep you from helping your son. If you don't know what to do or how to do it, find a resource for him. Find a coach, a tutor, or another mentor. Helping your son grow in wisdom will make you joyful and will win him favor.

REMEMBER

Teach your son how to solve problems, not cause them.

READ PROVERBS CHAPTER 10

fivestarman.com/day-10

Day 13: Intelligent Parenting

PROVERBS 13:1 (MSG)

Intelligent children listen to their parents;
foolish children do their own thing.

PRINCIPLE

Intelligent Parenting: Never discipline whom you have not discipled.

One of the biggest mistakes parents make is assuming that children know something they haven't been taught. I've seen parents speak with harsh tones and curse words to berate their children, while the children stood there in total confusion.

Constant correction without explanation will exasperate your child. To *exasperate* means *to arouse anger as a form of punishment.* It is an insidious treatment that causes deep and bitter emotional wounds.

Don't assume your children know what you know. Teach them. Train them up. Instruct them how to do things and why.

Intelligent children listen to their parents because they have intelligent parents who speak to them. Foolish children do their own thing because their parents are absent teachers.

REMEMBER

Never discipline whom you have not discipled.

READ PROVERBS CHAPTER 13

fivestarman.com/day-13

Day 14: Cowboys Wear Boots For A Reason

PROVERBS 14:4 (NLT)

Without oxen a stable stays clean,
but you need a strong ox for a large harvest.

PRINCIPLE

You can have a clean barn, or you can get something done.

I grew up on a small ranch with cattle, horses, pigs, and chickens. One thing you learn when you're raising animals is that they're messy. There's a full array of odors to fill your senses. The day to clean out the stables is not a particularly fun day. I quickly learned that cowboys wear boots for a reason.

I also learned in order to have the benefits, you have to put up with the manure.

The same is true for any other job. Along with the benefits of having workers and the strengths that they bring to your table, you must also put up with their messes.

When you are dealing with people, they're going to have the residue of their lives on them. Some of it may not be pleasant. Here's the choice you'll have to make: Do you want a very clean environment, or do you want the strength that comes with messy people?

REMEMBER

In order to have the benefits, you must deal with the messes.

READ PROVERBS CHAPTER 14

fivestarman.com/day-14

Day 15: Control Wild Fires

PROVERBS 15:1 (MSG)

A gentle response defuses anger,
but a sharp tongue kindles a temper-fire.

PRINCIPLE

Calm words control wild fires.

We've all seen the disastrous repercussions of hot-tempered words. I recall being asked to mediate a confrontation between two men that very quickly got out of hand when one of them brandished a pistol. A quick call to 911 intervened in this disaster waiting to happen. In order for the charges to be dropped, I was asked to help resolve the issue.

Unbelievably, the two men were practicing Christians, brothers in Christ, yet anger aroused a murderous spirit in one of them. As the meeting started, the words that spewed out of their mouths were as heated as flames of a fire.

It wasn't going well. I turned and calmed the entire conversation with a gentle, whispering voice. "Gentlemen, this is dishonoring as followers of Christ. You are not living up to the standard of authentic manhood. We're better than this."

My calmness seemed to be like water on the fire. It doused the embers that were ready to explode. We should be very careful of our words and temper them for each circumstance and situation.

REMEMBER

Calm words control wild fires.

READ PROVERBS CHAPTER 15

fivestarman.com/day-15

Day 16: Don't Be Confused

PROVERBS 16:1 (NLT)

We can make our own plans,
but the Lord gives the right answer.

PRINCIPLE

If your plans do not agree with God's purpose you will enter into confusion.

God's original intent for Man was to "be fruitful and increase in number; fill the earth..." (Genesis 1:28 NIV). Nomads began to move eastward and discovered the beautiful and plentiful plain of Shinar. The Bible says that the men settled there.

The settlers began to engineer and make preparations to build a city. They developed new technologies, including the uniformity of bricks and the invention of tar for a sealant. Their elaborate plans involved a centerpiece of architectural wonder called the Tower of Babel.

God came down to see the city and the tower. After surveying their progress, He exclaimed, "If... they have begun to do this, then nothing they plan to do will be impossible for them" (Genesis 11:6 NIV).

God's answer to their plans was to confuse their ability to speak and understand one another. This caused clusters of people to unite and scatter across the Earth, resulting in a return to God's original intent and purpose for mankind.

When we make plans contrary to God's purpose, we invite confusion.

REMEMBER

Align your plans with your purpose.

READ PROVERBS CHAPTER 16

fivestarman.com/day-16

Day 17: Protect Your Home From Evil

PROVERBS 17:1 (NIV)

Better a dry crust with peace and quiet,
than a house full of feasting, with strife.

PRINCIPLE

Where there is strife, every evil is at work.

Atmosphere matters. It is vitally important that we protect the atmosphere of our homes and places of work. Our advisor in the book of Proverbs recommends chewing on morsels rather than feasting where there is strife. Why is this important?

"Wherever there is jealousy (envy) and contention (rivalry, selfish ambition, strife), there will also be confusion (unrest, disharmony, rebellion) and all sorts of evil and vile practices" (James 3:16, AMP).

My wife and I have made it an absolute rule that our residence is a home of peace. We do not allow strife in our home—not through family members, guests, the television, or the internet. We guard our home as if strife is an invasion of evil.

Abraham's wife, Sarah, was so concerned about strife that she recommended her husband banish Hagar and Ishmael from their home. Ishmael was a mocker and full of strife. He was jealous and threatened Isaac's future. The Bible says, "drive out the mocker, and out goes strife" (Proverbs 22:10 NIV).

Men, you're the gate of authority to your home. Don't allow strife to take up residence.

REMEMBER

Protect your home from evil.

READ PROVERBS CHAPTER 17

fivestarman.com/day-17

Day 18: Not Every Voice Should Be Heard

PROVERBS 18:2 (MSG)

Fools care nothing for thoughtful discourse;
all they do is run off at the mouth.

PRINCIPLE

When you don't know what you're talking about it's hard to know when you're finished.

Throughout Proverbs, our advisor calls people who are arrogant, dull-minded, unteachable, simpletons, and fools. Fools are everywhere: in government, media, the arts, education, sports, and even in churches.

How To Recognize Fools:

- They deny the existence of God (Psalm 53:1).
- They spew godless chatter (Proverbs 10:8).
- They slander other people (Proverbs 10:18).
- They have uncontrolled anger (Proverbs 14:16).
- They reject parental discipline (Proverbs 15:5).
- They are not teachable (Proverbs 17:7).
- They quickly enter into quarrels (Proverbs 20:3).
- They are unreliable (Proverbs 26:6).
- They are unemployable (Proverbs 26:10).
- They talk incessantly (Ecclesiastes 5:3).

REMEMBER

Just because someone has a voice, that doesn't mean they should be heard.

READ PROVERBS CHAPTER 18

fivestarman.com/day-18

Day 19: Don't Be Stupid

PROVERBS 19:3 (MSG)

People ruin their lives by their own stupidity,
so why does God always get blamed?

PRINCIPLE

"Life is hard. It's even harder when you're stupid." –John Wayne

The word for *ruin* in this verse actually indicates someone who twists, turns, and falls. It has the imagery of someone slipping and sliding on thin ice. They run on unsafe foundations, and, when they crash through, instead of accepting the blame for their stupidity, they turn their anger toward God.

It's similar to the television shows that entertain the stupidity of people caught on camera. You marvel and ask, "What were they thinking?"

The truth is, they *weren't* thinking. That's the problem.

As a young man, I worked seven nights a week in a coal mine in southeastern Oklahoma. I was responsible for managing the water pumps to keep the strip mine open. One frigid night, the water had frozen. To manage the pump, I had to walk out to the platform it was stationed upon. As I walked, the ice began to crack, and I plummeted into the water.

My life was in danger from my stupidity. I disobeyed the voice of wisdom to walk on the ice.

We've all done things we could describe as stupid. God is not to blame. Life is hard. Let's not make it more difficult by being stupid.

REMEMBER

Don't blame God for your stupidity.

READ PROVERBS CHAPTER 19
fivestarman.com/day-19

Day 20: Wine And Strong Drink Are Deceptive

PROVERBS 20:1 (AMP)

Wine is a mocker, strong drink a riotous brawler;
and whoever errs or reels because of it is not wise.

PRINCIPLE

One night of drunkenness can expose your family to generational curses.

Here's my confession: I do not drink alcohol. You may be surprised that my decision is not based upon a religious conviction. I choose not to drink because of experiences I've had and my exposure to good people who were ruined by its deception.

I grew up surrounded by drunkenness and drug abuse. My personal objection to alcohol is the indignity that it brings upon men. Our advisor, Solomon, gives the same warning. He warns that those who are led astray or deceived by drink lose their ability to think rationally and conduct themselves with integrity.

Noah was a man of great faith, who received a prophetic warning of the global flood and labored for decades to build the ark to save his family. When the waters receded Noah planted a vineyard. After drinking heavily, he lost his integrity and exposed his son Ham to a generational curse.

Lot was considered a righteous man, who escaped the meteoric annihilation of Sodom and Gomorrah; however, during a night of drunkenness he allowed his daughters to commit incestuous acts with him, again, resulting in a generational curse.

Our mission is to protect our families, and, as such, we carry the responsibility to protect them from our own appetites. To do so, we must be sober-minded and vigilant. We must think in terms of generations and not simply our own immediate gratification.

REMEMBER

Don't be deceived by wine and strong drink.

➜ READ PROVERBS CHAPTER 20

fivestarman.com/day-20

Day 21: God Speaks Through Leadership

PROVERBS 21:1 (NLT)

The king's heart is like a stream of water directed by the Lord;
he guides it wherever he pleases.

PRINCIPLE

God places you *under* authority so that you can manage what He places you *over*.

It is a hard pill to swallow at times—the concept that God directs the heart of leaders. Throughout Scripture, there are examples of men who were placed under harsh leaders, yet they still purposed to do the will of God.

Joseph served as the Prime Minister of Egypt under Pharaoh; yet, it was evident God's hand directed Pharaoh to favor Joseph. Daniel served the dictator of Persia and suffered persecution for his faith from his peers; yet, Daniel was established as a respected counselor to the throne. Mordecai honorably served King Xerxes and played a significant role in averting the annihilation of the Jews.

We must remember we serve *through* leadership and not *around* it. Paul tells us, "Work with enthusiasm, as though you were working for the Lord rather than for people" (Ephesians 6:7 NLT).

Don't excuse yourself from service by judging the righteousness of those whom you serve. "For the one in authority is God's servant for your good" (Romans 13:4a NIV).

REMEMBER

God speaks through leadership, not around it.

READ PROVERBS CHAPTER 21
fivestarman.com/day-21

Day 22: Teach Your Children Well

PROVERBS 22:6 (MSG)

Point your kids in the right direction—
when they're old they won't be lost.

PRINCIPLE

As fathers, we have the responsibility to give our children intentional direction and teach them well.

Did you know Abraham was chosen to be in covenant with God because of his teaching ability? That's right, God chose him because he would "direct his children and his household after him to keep the way of the Lord by doing what is right and just" (Genesis 18:19 NIV).

Children are insatiable learners. If we do not teach our children, they will get their wisdom from someone else. Unfortunately, they may go to the unknowing for knowledge. The knowledge that children receive from the world and their friends is often the knowledge of good and evil. It can be sinful and wicked.

Notice: Abraham's teaching would ensure God's promises. God said, "I will bring about for Abraham what I have promised to do" (Genesis 18:19 NIV).

Great men of faith are men who believe for something that requires more than their own lifetime to achieve it. Do you have faith for something beyond your lifetime? If you do, direct your children toward it.

The greatest compliment a father can receive is to hear his children tell their children, "We serve the God of my father."

REMEMBER

Protect your children by pointing them in the right direction. Teach them well.

READ PROVERBS CHAPTER 22

fivestarman.com/day-22

Day 23: Leading The Way To Influence

PROVERBS 23:1-3 (MSG)

When you go out to dinner with an influential person, mind your manners:
Don't gobble your food, don't talk with your mouth full.
And don't stuff yourself; bridle your appetite.

PRINCIPLE

Respect yourself by your conduct; respect others through good manners.

We live in a very casual time. The workplace's "Casual Friday" has turned into casual *every* day. However, there are occasions that require men to conduct themselves with decorum, and rightly so. One of the passions of a ***FivestarMan*** is to be gallant in relationships. Knowing how to conduct ourselves with good manners is part of being a gallant man.

Table Manners of a Gallant Man:

- He washes his hands before coming to the table.
- He is properly groomed and appropriately dressed.
- He never tilts his chair at the table.
- He does not overload his plate. He bridles his appetite.
- He eats slowly and chews with his mouth closed.
- He treats those who serve him with dignity, saying, "Thank you."
- He keeps his voice at a respectable level, not dominating a conversation.
- He never answers his phone or is distracted by it at the table. If he must answer in a true emergency, he will step outside and take the call.
- He does not reach across the table.
- He is seated with good posture and does not slouch.
- He does not clean his fingernails with a fork or use a toothpick at the table.

If your profession requires you to dine with influential people, I recommend that you invest in an etiquette coach.

REMEMBER

Represent yourself with dignity. Lead the way to influence.

READ PROVERBS CHAPTER 23
fivestarman.com/day-23

Day 24: Avoid Unnecessary Conflict

PROVERBS 24:1-2 (NLT)

Don't envy evil people
or desire their company.
For their hearts plot violence,
and their words always stir up trouble.

PRINCIPLE

Some battles are a distraction from a worthy cause.

As men, we often have a warrior mentality. This is good when it comes to having the courage and zeal to fight for a worthy cause; however, there are times when we are confronted by contentious people and become distracted.

Nothing of great value is ever achieved without facing violent opposition from mediocre minds. If you're in pursuit of a cause, you will face opposition. The challenge becomes knowing how to focus your attention toward the objective without being sideswiped by those who oppose you.

"Don't envy evil people or desire their company." The word *envy* seems obvious; however, let's look deeper into the meaning. It gives the picture of *someone who burns with zeal or becomes a rival with another.* We should not change the zeal from our cause and turn it toward our rivals.

When David inquired about the cause to fight the giant Goliath, his elder brother, Eliab attempted to rival him and send him home. He belittled him in front of others out of jealousy, but David remained focused on the cause and dismissed his distraction (1 Samuel 17:28).

On the way toward your cause, don't be distracted by unnecessary conflict.

REMEMBER

Some battles are a distraction from a worthy cause.

READ PROVERBS CHAPTER 24

fivestarman.com/day-24

Day 25: The Heart Of God Is To Conceal A Matter

PROVERBS 25:2 (NLT)

It is God's privilege to conceal things
and the king's privilege to discover them.

PRINCIPLE

God doesn't keep secrets *from* you. He keeps secrets *for* you.

Jesus taught this principle: "Ask and it will be given to you; seek and you will find; knock and the door will be opened to you" (Matthew 7:7 NIV). One of the things I like most about God's character is that He keeps things close to the vest. In other words, God is not flippant or trivial when it comes to His plans for us.

The Apostle Paul said, "No eye has seen, no ear has heard, and no mind has imagined what God has prepared for those who love him" (1 Corinthians 2:9 NLT).

God already has plans for you; however, He has concealed the plans—not to hide them *from* you, but to hide them *for* you. Don't copy what you see others doing. Don't scheme to devise your own plans. You can't dream a bigger dream than God has already dreamed for you.

Our advisor tells us, "It's the king's privilege to discover them." Dig deep and discover what God has prepared for you.

REMEMBER

God has a plan for you, and you're going to love it.

READ PROVERBS CHAPTER 25
fivestarman.com/day-25

Day 26: Don't Fear the Reaper

PROVERBS 26:2 (MSG)

You have as little to fear from an undeserved curse
as from the dart of a wren or the swoop of a swallow.

PRINCIPLE

Don't allow birds to make a nest in your hair.

Some men are very superstitious. They have omens, lucky charms, and forebodings, or they mix a little religion with it, and they have dead saints. You don't need any of that.

Our advisor tells us we have little to fear when it comes to superstition and witchcraft. We don't have to light candles, pray to statutes, or crawl on our knees to protect us from swooping birds.

Men have authority, and we're not subject to demonic activity and witchcraft. Don't allow yourself to be confused or fearful. You're a man! Stand up, put your shoulders back, and face your fears.

Recently, I traveled to the town of San Christobal, Mexico. It is a tourist mecca for people from all over the world, especially Europeans who come there primarily for a type of new-age spiritualism mixed with ancient Mayan culture. I was amazed at the way superstition exercised control over people.

Our superstitions may not be as overt, but we still should be in control of our belief systems. We have faith in God, and Christ has redeemed us from the curse (Galatians 3:13). So, don't fear the reaper.

REMEMBER

Fears, curses, and magic spells have no place in our lives.

READ PROVERBS CHAPTER 26

fivestarman.com/day-26

Day 27: Learn As You Go

PROVERBS 27:1 (NLT)

Don't brag about tomorrow,
since you don't know what the day will bring.

PRINCIPLE

We don't know what we don't know.

At first this seems to suggest that we shouldn't make plans or have goals; yet, in the balance of other scriptures, we know that our advisor in the book of Proverbs must be focusing on the very specific issues of bragging about what we're going to do.

The word *brag* is used in the negative sense, denoting something that *madly and arrogantly raises its voice for a show.*

In contrast, we certainly should have a vision for the future and faith to motivate us to take the necessary steps to accomplish it. Our plans are submitted to the will of God; meaning, we're not arrogantly swaying about telling everyone what we're doing. Our plans align with God's purposes. Our confidence is in Him, not in ourselves.

Our advisor continues, "You don't know what the day will bring." As we are pressing toward the mark, we may have to pivot our plans because there are things we don't know, but we will learn more as we're in the pursuit of God's purpose.

REMEMBER

You don't know what you don't know, but you will learn as you go.

READ PROVERBS CHAPTER 27
fivestarman.com/day-27

Day 28: Is There Not A Cause?

PROVERBS 28:1 (NLT)

The wicked run away when no one is chasing them,
but the godly are as bold as lions.

PRINCIPLE

Men fear what they know about themselves.

Our advisor makes the object of fear or the absence of it something that a man knows about himself. The wicked man runs while no one is chasing him. In contrast, the godly man stands firm, regardless of the opposition.

Men fear what they know about themselves. The wicked have an unrighteous cause, and the godly have a righteous one.

King Saul led the Israeli army to the battle lines against his nemesis Goliath. When the undefeated warrior-giant came out to mock the Israelites and blaspheme God, Saul cowered in his tent. He offered a reward along with the king's armor to the man who would face the giant.

David boldly stepped forward and asked the question, "Is there not a cause?" (1 Samuel 17:29 NKJV)

The word for *godly* in today's Proverb speaks of a man with a righteous cause. David's assurance came from what he knew about himself. He had a cause. He had fought a lion and a bear, and the giant was just another obstacle in the pursuit of his cause.

When you know your purpose, opposition is simply a hurdle on the way to your destiny.

REMEMBER

Is there not a cause?

READ PROVERBS CHAPTER 28

fivestarman.com/day-28

Day 29: Don't Be Stiff-Necked

PROVERBS 29:1 (NIV)

Whoever remains stiff-necked after many rebukes
will suddenly be destroyed—without remedy.

PRINCIPLE

If you keep heading in this direction, you'll get to where you're going.

Have you argued with someone who was completely wrong about a subject, yet they would not yield their argument no matter how much evidence you had to prove the case?

If you read the Bible often, you'll see a recurring theme: God makes His case for people to follow Him, worship Him only, trust His character, live under His blessing, etc.; yet, people regularly turn away from Him to follow worthless leaders, pursue unhealthy relationships, and worship false gods. This is a constant theme in Scripture: People fail, God corrects, people are stiff-necked, God rebukes, people suffer, people repent, and God forgives.

The word-picture for *stiff-necked* is one of someone who will not turn. They resist change. They're difficult people to deal with. They perversely adhere to their own opinion, course, or purpose, in spite of reason, argument, or persuasion.

Don't be the kind of person who refuses to take a warning. God is merciful. He sees the outcome of our obstinate ways and warns us of impending danger.

REMEMBER

If you have a stiff neck, you need to loosen it up.

READ PROVERBS CHAPTER 29

fivestarman.com/day-29

Day 30: Skeptics Swear To Themselves

PROVERBS 30:1–2 (MSG)

The skeptic swore, "There is no God! No God!
I can do anything I want!
I'm more animal than human;
so-called human intelligence escapes me."

PRINCIPLE

Skeptics swear to themselves. Intelligent men give praise to God.

This kind of swearing is pretty common in our day. We've had a few decades of absent-minded people exclaiming that we're really just a link in the chain of animal evolution. The theory, as weak as it could be, has this primary goal: to claim the absence of God and assert the animalistic nature of man.

What does this kind of reasoning achieve? It gives men two things to believe: first, without a God, all behavior is excusable; second, man's behavior is rational, since man is merely carnal.

The fallout of this kind of thinking has detrimental effects. It denies the existence of God, even though the evidence of created design and intellectual order is in everything in the Earth and universe. Paul tells us futile thinking is the seed of all kinds of perversion, including sexual perversions (Romans 1).

This brutish thinking also eliminates purpose from the equation of humanity. Without divine creation, there is simply no meaning, no law, no reason, no order, no justice, no intelligence, no morality, and no love.

REMEMBER

Don't listen to the skeptic. He's brutish and ignorant of the things of God.

READ PROVERBS CHAPTER 30

fivestarman.com/day-30

Day 31: The Proverbs 31 Man

PROVERBS 31:1 (NLT)

The sayings of King Lemuel contain this message,
which his mother taught him.

PRINCIPLE

A champion receives a prophecy from his mother.

The book of Proverbs is a man's book. It is life's little instruction book for men. The primary source for the book of Proverbs is Solomon, and he passes on the wisdom he gained from his father, David. But Proverbs 31 takes a turn. It's Lemuel's opportunity to share wisdom—the wisdom his mother taught him.

Jewish and Christian women have claimed Proverbs 31 as the lofty standard for biblical womanhood. The etymology of the name *Lemuel* literally means *man of God, mighty man, or champion.* So, this chapter is for champions!

Yet, it's even better. The Hebrew word for *message* or *teaching* actually means *prophecy*. Lemuel's mother prophesies to her son the kind of woman she desires for him. You can hear the kind of direct language that can only come from a mother.

So, listen up son. You're a champion. Here are some things you need to know. Here are warnings you should hear from a concerned mother. She is speaking spiritually, and we need to listen up.

As you read Proverbs 31, don't brush it off and think it's a chapter for women, thinking the burden is on them to measure up to an elite standard.

This mother is serious. She's raising a ***FivestarMan***—a champion!

REMEMBER

Listen to a wise mother's advice.

READ PROVERBS CHAPTER 31

fivestarman.com/day-31

Day 32: A Manual For Living

PROVERBS 1:3 (MSG)

A manual for living,
for learning what's right and just and fair;
To teach the inexperienced the ropes
and give our young people a grasp on reality.

PRINCIPLE

Everything created has a manual.

We have manuals for everything. When you buy an appliance, a car, or a child's toy, it comes with an owner's manual. It only makes sense that man comes with a manual, as well.

The book of Proverbs is like an owner's manual for men—written by a man to men. If you don't read it, you won't know the ins and outs of living successfully.

Men can be hard-headed when it comes to reading manuals. We open up boxes and start assembling with only a glance at the instructions. Just when we think we have it all together, we look down to see extra pieces and screws we failed to use. We finally give up and read the manual. We find things that would have saved us time and effort, if only we had read the instructions to begin with.

That sums up the experience of young men venturing out only to find there are missing pieces to the puzzle of life. Society tends to educate children with knowledge but fails to give them wisdom.

That's not the case for us. We seek wisdom for living successfully: knowing how to discern right from wrong, having a sense of direction, judging fairly, and making smart decisions.

REMEMBER

Don't try to assemble your life without the instructions.

READ PROVERBS CHAPTER 1

fivestarman.com/day-32

Day 33: A Thousand Sacrifices

PROVERBS 2:6 (MSG)

. . . God gives out Wisdom free,
is plainspoken in Knowledge and Understanding.

PRINCIPLE

God scholarships Wisdom.

When King David died, the household was in chaos. Alliances were formed. Servants jockeyed for position. David's sons gathered political cohorts. Israel's palace was thrown into confusion. The treasury was an attractive prize for the next king. The building fund for the Temple was enormous, estimated to be in the trillions. Personal ambition distracted family members from mourning their patriarch-king.

Solomon, the son of David and Bathsheba, emerged as the selected and anointed heir to the throne. The task was far out of reach for his naïveté. Either he gained wisdom quickly, or his kingship would soon be overthrown.

Upon securing the throne Solomon offered a thousand burnt offerings to God. In return, God granted Solomon the opportunity to request anything he wanted—wealth, fame, long life, or military dominance.

Solomon asked for a discerning heart to govern—the skill of knowing right from wrong. God's response? Since Solomon asked for wisdom, God gave him all of the above, plus wisdom (1 Kings 3:11–12).

God gives wisdom freely. He doesn't discriminate or show favoritism. If you ask for it, He gives it generously without judgment (James 1:5). He doesn't require a thousand sacrifices or $1,000 gift to a tele-evangelist. He simply awaits your need for wisdom above your selfish motivations.

REMEMBER

You need wisdom more than anything.

➲ READ PROVERBS CHAPTER 2
fivestarman.com/day-33

Day 34: Earn A Reputation

PROVERBS 3:4 (MSG)

Earn a reputation for living well
in God's eyes and the eyes of the people.

PRINCIPLE

A reputation is the shadow your character casts.

Our advisor tells us to earn a reputation. That's a great way of phrasing it. Henry Ford once said, "A man can't build a reputation on what he is going to do."

We live in a time of masterful marketing; however, when we peel back the curtains, we often find that the marketing is a cover for flawed character. Few realize the value of character and how it affects a man's reputation.

But here's what Jesus said: "But when you pray, go into your room, close the door and pray to your Father, who is unseen. Then your Father, who sees what is done in secret, will reward you" (Matthew 6:6 NIV).

A good friend asked me to meet with his son and give him some advice. I gave the young man this admonishment, "Don't try to do something public. You're not ready for that. Instead go find everything you can do secretly so no one knows you've done it. In other words, clean your closet. What you do in secret will gain you momentum in public."

He followed my advice and within months had seen incredible growth in his efforts.

REMEMBER

What you do in secret is what moves you in public.

READ PROVERBS CHAPTER 3

fivestarman.com/day-34

Day 35: Get A Promotion

PROVERBS 4:8 (AMP)

Prize Wisdom highly and exalt her,
and she will exalt and promote you;
she will bring you to honor when you embrace her.

PRINCIPLE

Wisdom is the prize.

Wisdom is personified in the feminine. She is descriptively attractive to men. The relationship with Wisdom is often contrasted with the relationship of a brazen woman called the Adulteress.

The Adulteress is a nemesis for man—lurking, seducing, devouring men as objects of her wrath. She constantly prowls to bring down great men.

Antithetical to the Adulteress, Wisdom is our greatest ally—always looking for the good of man, extending life, adding value, and bringing promotion. If you embrace a relationship with Wisdom, she will add enormous benefits to your life. One of those benefits is promotion.

Promotion means *to be lifted up, exalted, to be elevated,* and *to be made high.* In other words, Wisdom knows how to celebrate you.

This is a lesson that requires some effort to think about. Take time to contemplate what the relationship with Wisdom can bring into your life.

REMEMBER

Wisdom will bring you honor.

READ PROVERBS CHAPTER 4

fivestarman.com/day-35

Day 36: The Sweet Sauce Of Sin

PROVERBS 5:3 (AMP)

For the lips of a loose woman drip honey as a honeycomb,
and her mouth is smoother than oil.

PRINCIPLE

Not everything that tastes sweet is good.

As I write this, today's headline news is, "Too Much Sugar Can Kill You." A new study warns that America's love affair with sugary food and drinks doubles the risk of a heart-related, premature death. The takeaway is this: Not everything that tastes sweet is good for you.

In Proverbs, you'll find repeated warnings about the Adulteress. Our advisor warns us of the honey of the harlot. If we're not careful, we'll think he is obsessive and nagging; however, he warns us because she is a true enemy of authentic manhood.

Her lips drip honey. Her opened mouth and seductive eyes have a sweetness about them. Her look of love and the sweet sauce of sin are appealing to the appetites of men.

Listen to Peter's description, "They have eyes full of harlotry, insatiable for sin. They beguile and bait and lure away unstable souls. Their hearts are trained in ... lust ... children of a curse ..." (2 Peter 2:14 AMP).

The trap of authentic manhood is the honey of a harlot. If you eat her sugar, it will kill you. You will suffer a heart-related, premature death.

REMEMBER

The sweet sauce of sin is deadly.

READ PROVERBS CHAPTER 5

fivestarman.com/day-36

Day 37: Lazy Bones

PROVERBS 6:6 (NLT)

Take a lesson from the ants, you lazybones.
Learn from their ways and become wise!

PRINCIPLE

God gave man a job before He gave man a woman.

Contrary to popular belief, work is not a curse. In fact, it's the opposite. Work is a blessing from God.

God created a system of supply: "The Law of Seed." This law is housed within each and every seed. A seed holds its potential until it is sown into the ground. God gave seed to mankind so we could determine our diets. God's amazing gift of seed gives man the ability to satisfy his cravings.

But God does not do the work for man. It's up to us to arise each and every morning with a plan and then work the plan. It's a fantasy to expect a future for which you haven't sown a seed.

Our advisor tells us to learn the ways of ants. It's in their DNA to work. They don't have to think about it. It's their nature.

It's in the DNA of man to work. God created Man in His own image and likeness. The Bible is very clear that God works. So, in His likeness, we must work to satisfy our cravings and to fulfill our purposes.

REMEMBER

Seed gives you the ability to satisfy your cravings.

READ PROVERBS CHAPTER 6
fivestarman.com/day-37

Day 38: Twilight Years

PROVERBS 7:4 (AMP)

In the twilight, in the evening;
night black and dense was falling [over the young man's life].

PRINCIPLE

Don't allow a dark period to envelop you.

You can almost hear the sigh of anxiety in our advisor's voice as he tells the story of a young man strolling toward sin. He wants to open the shutters and yell, "Don't go there! You're too valuable. You have too much potential. Don't waste it!"

There appears to be a season in men between the teenage years and maturity when innocence explores naïve abandonment. It's such a volatile time. A young man's simple-mindedness can have devastating consequences.

I didn't have the luxury of a seasoned advisor when I was younger. I made so many mistakes and have a lifetime of regrets from those transitional years. I could have done things so much better and saved myself and others a lot of pain.

That is one of my motivations for writing. ***The Daily Champion*** is my way of peering through the window, shouting to young men passing by on their way to the black of night and the dense fog of naïveté, "Don't go there! God has a better plan for you!"

Seasoned men should go out of our way to speak wisdom to the young. Young men should knock on the doors of seasoned men for advice.

REMEMBER

Never underestimate the destruction of simple-mindedness.

READ PROVERBS CHAPTER 7

fivestarman.com/day-38

Day 39: Speak The Truth In Love

PROVERBS 8:7 (NIV)

My mouth speaks what is true,
for my lips detest wickedness.

PRINCIPLE

When a man's entire life is built upon lies, telling the truth is not an option nor his moral code.

Our grandfathers lived in a time when there was a "man code"—a baseline of understanding that a man's word was his bond. If a man said it, you could bank on it. Now, it seems very few men operate with this moral code.

That's so unfortunate. It makes us approach every conversation with suspicion. We look for signs of deceit—body language, nuances, facial expressions—anything that can clue us in to whether a speaker is honest.

Now, mendacity is the norm. Some politicians spin their news conferences with double-speak, saying the complete opposite of what they're actually doing. Some businessmen have mastered manipulation. Some elite athletes have been caught creating elaborate schemes to deceive. Each seared conscience would argue that it is for the higher good that they lie. As Jack Nicholson's character in the movie, ***A Few Good Men***, famously yelled, "You can't handle the truth!"

But Wisdom speaks truthfully. It is wise for us to watch over our words. Honesty is a moral code that will guard us against deception—not just the deception of others, but our own deception, as well.

REMEMBER

Speak the truth in love.

READ PROVERBS CHAPTER 8
fivestarman.com/day-39

Day 40: Shin Kickers

PROVERBS 9:7 (NLT)

Anyone who rebukes a mocker will get an insult in return.
Anyone who corrects the wicked will get hurt.

PRINCIPLE

Don't waste your breath correcting mockers and shin kickers.

When you were a kid, did you ever get in an argument with someone and, rather than debate, the other kid tried to kick you in the shins? That's the strategy of those with no solid argument.

The dull-witted are too stubborn to listen to reason. Our advisor suggests that we avoid arguing with a cynic, an arrogant man, or a mocker. The word *mocker* describes someone who stammers and repeats your words in an argument.

A mocker doesn't focus on issues but returns personal attacks against you. You see this when politicians slander their opponents, hoping to divert attention away from the issues at hand. All too often it works.

The second warning from our advisor is an attempt to correct the wickedness in our culture. Often the wicked not only turn from the issue and mock you, they become violent, as well.

We're seeing more and more wicked protesters becoming physically violent toward our moral standards in society. It's more than a kick in the shins. It's the spirit of Cain, who murdered his brother out of jealousy.

Some people can't be reasoned with, and others should be avoided all together.

REMEMBER

Don't answer a fool.

READ PROVERBS CHAPTER 9

fivestarman.com/day-40

Day 41: Live A Legacy

PROVERBS 10:7 (MSG)

A good and honest life is a blessed memorial;
a wicked life leaves a rotten stench.

PRINCIPLE

The greatest compliment you can receive is to hear your children tell their children, "We serve the God of my father."

Solomon said God placed eternity in the heart of man (Ecclesiastes 3:11). In other words, we have the concept of endless time. That alone is an amazing principle that should guide and guard our lives.

At the end of our days, each of us will perform an internal audit, examining our lives, reviewing our decisions, and surveying whether we will be remembered. I've had the opportunity to sit down on the porch with seasoned men and heard them muse on their lives. Amazingly, each man did not brag or list their assets. They didn't inventory what they had purchased. Interestingly, these men had one concern. It was how they would be remembered.

We should consider this as we live our lives. How will our decisions determine our legacy? What will this do to further our cause? Will our children be enriched by our lives? Will our children point to us as examples to follow?

We must make daily decisions with a legacy mindset.

REMEMBER

Make decisions to leave a legacy.

READ PROVERBS CHAPTER 10
fivestarman.com/day-41

Day 42: Tumbling Down—Pride

PROVERBS 11:2 (NLT)

Pride leads to disgrace,
but with humility comes wisdom.

PRINCIPLE

Pride may get the position, but lack of performance will bring disgrace.

First, know that pride doesn't mean being self-assured. A prideful man takes on a different demeanor than someone who is assured of who they are in Christ. Self-assurance isn't pride when it's properly measured by your calling.

Pride acts presumptuously. It's assumes a position without securing it with proven ability. You may get the position, but your lack of performance will disgrace you.

Secondly, humility is not self-abasement. Casting disparaging remarks upon yourself is not only unbecoming, it's a type of pride in reverse. Seeking affirmation and accolades from men has proven to be a snare to many.

Humility is honing your skill set to achieve the purposes for which you've been called. In fact, pursuing excellence isn't prideful. It's a form of humility.

When David stepped forward to challenge the giant-warrior Goliath, Eliab accused him of being prideful. David wasn't prideful; he was self-assured because he had a proven track record against the lion and the bear, and he knew his cause was God's.

On the other hand, Goliath arrogantly assumed mastery because of his size and strength. His boasting brought him to a swift beheading.

REMEMBER

Don't confuse pride with self-assurance. Don't confuse humility with self-abasement.

READ PROVERBS CHAPTER 11

fivestarman.com/day-42

Day 43: Your Wife Is Your Crown

PROVERBS 12:4 (NIV)

A wife of noble character is her husband's crown,
but a disgraceful wife is like decay in his bones.

PRINCIPLE

Draw strength from your wife.

There is no greater asset for a man than a strong wife beside him. There is no greater weakness for a man than to have a shameful wife.

Job's wife is an example of a woman who shamed her husband at a time when he needed her most. Job was suffering from a series of satanic attacks—thieves, fire, raiding parties, tornadoes, and disease—disaster upon disaster. And his wife prodded him to curse God and die (Job 2:9).

You can imagine Job's disappointment with the mother of his ten children. Job languished that his "crown was removed from his head" (Job 19:9). His wife was a disgrace.

As men who are striving to be authentic, there are some who are struggling. You may be going through something disastrous or facing tragic events. You may have even suffered betrayal by your wife. If that is the case, don't give up. Keep your integrity, and God will see you through.

And if you do have a strong wife with noble character, celebrate her. The fact that she will endure hardship with you makes her a prized possession—a crown to adorn your head.

REMEMBER

When disaster strikes, draw strength from one another.

READ PROVERBS CHAPTER 12
fivestarman.com/day-43

Day 44: Careful Words, Careful Life

PROVERBS 13:3 (MSG)

Careful words make for a careful life;
careless talk may ruin everything.

PRINCIPLE

Some men lack a partition between their vacuous minds and their flippant tongues.

Very few men realize the potential effect words can have, especially regarding those who have the positional authority of a husband or father. As a young man, I didn't realize how potent my words were to those whom I loved. Once I discovered this principle, I began to weigh carefully my choice of words and the manner in which I spoke them.

Jesus spoke about the incredible potential of words. "The words that I speak to you aren't mere words. I don't just make them up on my own. The Father who resides in me crafts each word into a divine act" (John 14:10 MSG).

It's pretty overwhelming when you think about that kind of potential and emphasis on words; yet, Solomon warned, "The tongue has the power of life and death" (Proverbs 18:21 NIV).

"Think twice before you speak, because your words and influence will plant the seed of either success or failure in the mind of another." —Napoleon Hill

REMEMBER

Engage your mind before you speak it.

READ PROVERBS CHAPTER 13

fivestarman.com/day-44

Day 45: The Test Of Friendship

PROVERBS 14:10 (MSG)

The person who shuns the bitter moments of friends
will be an outsider at their celebrations.

PRINCIPLE

Friends show their love in times of trouble, not just happiness.

As you go through life, there will be times of trial. Everyone faces bumps in the road. It's in those times that you'll need to take notes. You'll gain wisdom through the pain, if you seek God. You will also be able to test your relationships.

Job discovered this the hard way. We saw how shamefully his wife responded to his troubles. Now, let's consider how his friends responded to them.

At Job's bedside, his "friends" gathered around him and began to speak harsh and untruthful words about God and condemning words to Job.

When you go through difficult times—and we all do—that's the time when you discover the list of your true friendships. Unfortunately that list is usually a short one.

Correspondingly, when Job was healed and his wealth was restored, his celebration had a short list of invitations, but it was a great time to honor good friends.

REMEMBER

When I was young and naïve I trusted. When I became mature I tested.

READ PROVERBS CHAPTER 14

fivestarman.com/day-45

Day 46: The Closet Principle

PROVERBS 15:3 (NIV)

The eyes of the Lord are everywhere,
keeping watch on the wicked and the good.

PRINCIPLE

God pays attention to what is done in secret chambers.

The kingdom of God operates very differently from the world's system. The world acknowledges the famous—even if they're only famous for being famous.

In the kingdom of God, that which is done in secret is acknowledged. I call it "The Closet Principle." God pays attention to what is done in secret chambers. Remember: What we do in secret is what moves us in public.

"When you pray, go into your room, close the door and pray to your Father, who is unseen. Then your Father, who sees what is done in secret, will reward you" (Matthew 6:6 NIV).

If you look at the pattern of Jesus' life, you'll see He created a rhythm between isolation and public ministry. Amazingly, even though Jesus knew He only had a short window of time upon the Earth, He often withdrew to the wilderness to pray.

The secret to your future is hidden in the daily routine of what you do in secret.

REMEMBER

"The Closet Principle" will work *for* you, or *against* you.

READ PROVERBS CHAPTER 15

fivestarman.com/day-46

Day 47: Rolling Stones

PROVERBS 16:3 (NIV)

Commit to the Lord whatever you do,
and he will establish your plans.

PRINCIPLE

Put God in charge of your work, and your plans will come to pass.

We previously looked at how to avoid making plans that disagree with God's purpose so we can be free from confusion. Here, we see that when we commit our plans to the Lord, they will be established.

The Hebrew word for *commit* in this verse is interesting, because the word-picture used to describe it means *to roll something, as if it were stones.* This connotation paints the picture of someone struggling to get a stone to roll but then inertia is overtaken, and the stone no longer requires help to move. A seemingly invisible force takes over—the force of momentum.

When you commit what you're doing—your work, life, marriage, etc.—to the Lord, He will step up the velocity, and momentum will take over.

You may be working to establish a business, a new venture, or a product. Commit your plans to the Lord, and let Him help you with the supernatural inertia and get things "rolling."

Jesus said it this way, "I tell you the truth, if you had faith… you could say to this mountain, 'Move from here to there,' and it would move. Nothing will be impossible" (Matthew 17:20 NLT).

REMEMBER

Commit your work to God, and enjoy His momentum.

READ PROVERBS CHAPTER 16
fivestarman.com/day-47

Day 48: Prosper In Friendships

PROVERBS 17:9 (NLT)

Love prospers when a fault is forgiven,
but dwelling on it separates close friends.

PRINCIPLE

Don't be a fault finder.

I saw a family member take offense. You could see the change in his appearance. Bitterness became a heavy burden to bear. It was a moment that changed his life and devastated relationships he once held dear. He has since lived his life distancing himself from anyone and everyone. Now, he is a lonely, sad person with a hardened heart and a downcast countenance.

I witnessed a daughter take offense when her father restricted her from eating a second helping of birthday cake. I'm sure he didn't mean to cause such an emotional wound, but she assumed one that wreaked havoc upon her life, plunging her into a cycle of addiction and eating disorders.

Our advisor in the book of Proverbs warns us not to dwell on the faults of others. Don't allow them to occupy your mind. When you do, your thoughts become delusional, crafting all kinds of false scenarios. Offense causes us to forfeit friends and lose dear relationships.

However, if we forgive, we actually prosper in our relationships. Our friendships become stronger and better when we overlook offense.

REMEMBER

Forgive, and it will be forgiven.

READ PROVERBS CHAPTER 17
fivestarman.com/day-48

Day 49: Vandalism

PROVERBS 18:9 (MSG)

Slack habits and sloppy work
are as bad as vandalism.

PRINCIPLE

You will never have an excellent life with eighty-percent effort.

During the decades of the 60's, 70's, and 80's, New York City fell into disrepair, with rampant violence, economic decline, and disorder. The streets became violent. It wasn't looking good for Gotham.

Three men led NYC into a cultural change. Evangelist David Wilkerson planted Times Square Church and began to change the spiritual climate. Michael Eisner, CEO of Disney, led an economic resurgence at Times Square. And Mayor Rudy Giuliani dramatically brought down the crime rate with a unique program targeting vandalism and petty crimes. Focusing on small crimes reduced the larger, more violent ones. Vandalism was simply a manifestation of the deeper issue of disorder.

Our advisor tells us slack habits and sloppy work are as bad as vandalism. In other words, if you want to have a resurgence in your own life, focus on the small things that make big differences. Some men want to have excellent results with minimal efforts. When your work is sloppy and your habits are slack, your presentation to the world is like graffiti. It signals that your life is in disorder.

Your future is hidden in your daily routine. How is your work ethic? If you're slack in your work, it won't be long before you're out of work.

REMEMBER

You know what to expect from the average guy. A champion exceeds all expectations.

READ PROVERBS CHAPTER 18

fivestarman.com/day-49

Day 50: Champion A Cause

PROVERBS 19:6 (MSG)

Lots of people flock around a generous person;
everyone's a friend to the philanthropist.

PRINCIPLE

"What we've done for ourselves alone dies with us; what we have done for others and the world remains and is immortal."
– Albert Pike

A few years ago, while at lunch, a particularly generous friend exhaled frustration and handed me a pledge card. It was small, with minimal graphics and effect, promising an annual gift of $5, $10, or $25. As I looked it over, I couldn't help but wonder what caused his frustration.

Then my friend said, "Neil, I gave this charity a half a million dollars last year. This year, I am sending them $5 dollars because that's what they expect from me!"

I'm sure the charity didn't purposely offend their generous friend, but they did not speak to him with the respect his generosity deserved. He dreamed big dreams and worked hard to give. They offended him by asking for pennies.

Some men live at subsistence level. Others reach success, meeting their personal needs and achieving a measure of self-indulgence. However, authentic manhood seeks significance. That's a level of philanthropy where needs are not even a consideration. Self-indulgence is easily achieved, but authentic men focus on transferring their wealth for the benefit of others.

A ***FivestarMan*** uses his entrepreneurial hand to gather wealth so his philanthropic hand can scatter it. He leaves his mark on the present and transfers his influence into eternity.

REMEMBER

Champion a cause.

READ PROVERBS CHAPTER 19

fivestarman.com/day-50

Day 51: Mad-Dog Leaders

PROVERBS 20:2 (MSG)

Quick-tempered leaders are like mad dogs—
cross them and they bite your head off.

PRINCIPLE

When a leader loses control of himself, he forfeits inspirational influence.

If you intimidate people to lead them, you will not attract strong, creative people. You will not maintain an inspirational atmosphere in the workplace and will forfeit long-term success for your company or organization.

Conflict often begins with an issue but very quickly turns personal through a breakdown of communication. Quick-tempered leaders resort to personal attacks and threatening language to seize control. This never solves the problem, but actually exacerbates it.

Conflict distracts you from your goals. It breaks your focus. It destroys relationships and crushes creativity. If you aren't inspired, don't expect your followers to be.

I know a man who is by all measures a genius. He has one of the best minds I've ever seen in many regards. He has incredible ability; yet, as smart as he is, his leadership borders on abuse. He occasionally has delusional thoughts and crafts tests for employees to check their loyalty. He is extremely suspicious and overbearing in control. The collateral damage of his leadership is a sad commentary on an otherwise inspirational man.

As men, we should be careful to build our leadership skills beyond positional intimidation and into purposeful inspiration.

REMEMBER

Don't bite people's heads off.

READ PROVERBS CHAPTER 20

fivestarman.com/day-51

Day 52: Appearance Or Motive

PROVERBS 21:2 (MSG)

We justify our actions by appearances;
God examines our motives.

PRINCIPLE

Men look on the outward appearance. God looks at the heart.

King Saul, the first king of Israel, had succumbed to the fear of men. He rejected God's Word and thought he could keep up appearances, but the anointing had departed and demons had come to torment him.

The prophet Samuel was commissioned to anoint the second King of Israel. When he arrived at the house of Jesse, he saw the good-looking elder son, Eliab, and thought to himself, "Here he is! God's anointed!"

God responded to Samuel, "Looks aren't everything. Don't be impressed. I've eliminated him. Keep looking." (See 1 Samuel 16.)

Our culture is deceived by appearances. With glossy photos and makeup, we cover up blemishes. We dress the bony skeletons, all for the sake of an image of the ideal.

Our God doesn't justify us on the bathroom scales, nor by which designer's fashions we're wearing. God examines our hearts. He checks motives. Our thoughts are before Him, and He knows them.

We're justified by a completely different standard than men use. As men, we should find a quiet place in the pasture where we can worship Him alone and ask God for His approval.

REMEMBER

The fear of man is a snare, trapping those who desire approval.

READ PROVERBS CHAPTER 21

fivestarman.com/day-52

Day 53: Inequality

PROVERBS 22:2 (MSG)

The rich and poor shake hands as equals—
God made them both!

PRINCIPLE

The wealth of humanity is not measured by bank accounts.

I recently spent a week in a small town in Chiapas, Mexico, to build a school for *ChildHope*. Laboring with some of the local men was a privilege and will be a memory I'll take into my old age. These men were dedicated to their craft, they were devoted husbands, protective fathers, and followers of Christ. We were equals.

When you read Proverbs, you discover Wisdom treats those who are suffering in poverty with respect, dignity, and generosity. We're not to look down on the poor, as if something they've done has caused their subsistence living.

It is wrong to have an attitude of inequality between the poor and the rich—believing the poor deserve their poverty and the rich deserve their riches. All mankind deserves dignity, regardless of their financial holdings or lack thereof.

Spend some time with the poor, and you'll soon discover they're just like you. They're concerned about their daily needs. They have dreams for their lives and hopes for their children's futures. We're equals.

Whenever I've asked God to meet a need in my life, He has shown me someone for whom I can meet the need in their life.

REMEMBER

Don't look down on the poor. God is the maker of us all.

READ PROVERBS CHAPTER 22

fivestarman.com/day-53

Day 54: Don't Jump Fences

PROVERBS 23:10–11 (NIV)

Do not move an ancient boundary stone
or encroach on the fields of the fatherless,
for their Defender is strong;
he will take up their case against you.

PRINCIPLE

Never move a fence without knowing why it was put up.

Every relationship is governed by a line between respect and familiarity. Familiarity breeds contempt. When someone acts with familiarity they don't hesitate to cross established boundaries. They have a lawless attitude toward established "stones."

If a government official doesn't respect ancient and foundational documents, he flippantly dismisses them as old ideas irrelevant to our times, and he'll twist the true meaning of words. This person is arrogantly moving ancient boundaries.

As a society, we must resist flippant changes to our foundations. For an example, the argument to redefine marriage has fundamental and transformational repercussions on our society. Moving this ancient boundary stone will encroach on and replace established guidelines for relationships.

Our advisor in the book of Proverbs lays out a warning that we should heed: Moving boundary stones and taking advantage of what seems defenseless is dangerous because God steps up to defend. He will take up the case.

REMEMBER

Be careful before you jump. Some fences are guardrails.

READ PROVERBS CHAPTER 23

fivestarman.com/day-54

Day 55: Extreme Home Makeover

PROVERBS 24:3–4 (NIV)

By wisdom a house is built,
and through understanding it is established;
through knowledge its rooms are filled
with rare and beautiful treasures.

PRINCIPLE

Turn your house into a home with wisdom, knowledge, and peace.

My wife and I enjoy watching shows that transform old, outdated, and often damaged houses into remodeled and renewed structures with new furnishings into "dream homes."

As beautiful as these houses are, there is another makeover that needs to happen for our homes: the makeover of the atmosphere within it.

I've had the opportunity to be a guest in some pretty remarkable homes and even mansions. These homes were filled with very costly furnishings; yet, I've also noticed the atmosphere of the homes. Some were incredibly depressing and filled with strife. You could feel the tension when you walked into the foyer.

What good are all of the treasures in a house, if there isn't any true value there?

The greatest treasures you can furnish your home with are wisdom, knowledge, and peace. When a house is filled with these, it becomes a home.

REMEMBER

Make your house a home.

READ PROVERBS CHAPTER 24

fivestarman.com/day-55

Day 56: Don't Jump To Conclusions

PROVERBS 25:8 (MSG)

Don't jump to conclusions—there may be
a perfectly good explanation for what you just saw.

PRINCIPLE

Seeing something is not the conclusion of a matter.

A man noticed that his neighbor's Harley was put up for sale. He realized he had not seen his neighbor in a while. Then his boat went up for sale… later his truck. He concluded to his wife, "He must have left her. They must be getting a divorce." All of the signs were there. Other neighbors came to the same conclusion, and they chatted about it, each sharing their version of speculation and assumptions.

Then came the truth.

The man was gone. His wife and son were left alone—but not for the reason the neighbors imagined. Their neighbor had died.

When my embarrassed friend and his wife realized the error of their impromptu conclusion they were saddened they had been so callous and cynical.

They walked over to the widow's home, repented for their judgment and asked what they could do to help. She was gracious.

One day, my friend noticed the leaves of fall. He immediately began to rake the widow's leaves. During the winter months, he made sure the snow was removed from her driveway and sidewalks. Other neighbors began to jump in and help. Neighbors became true friends.

Eyes give us the ability to see, but we must also have the ability to perceive.

REMEMBER

Don't believe everything that you see.

READ PROVERBS CHAPTER 25

fivestarman.com/day-56

Day 57: Don't Bring Me Down

PROVERBS 26:4 (MSG)

Don't respond to the stupidity of a fool;
you'll only look foolish yourself.

PRINCIPLE

Don't answer the fool.

Have you ever had a conversation with someone who simply will not listen to reason? They talk in circles. They go around and around a subject, never comprehending a solution. They raise their voices to command attention. They lean forward, point fingers, and slap tables. They air their stupidity for all to see. They are foolish.

It's so tempting to try to persuade them out of their vacuous thinking, but it won't do any good. They simply can't reason with rational minds. They're "know-it-alls."

What should you do?

Nothing. Don't answer the fool. Don't respond. Doing so only brings you down to their level.

REMEMBER

When you try to talk sense to a fool, he will call you foolish.

READ PROVERBS CHAPTER 26
fivestarman.com/day-57

Day 58: Self-Promotion

PROVERBS 27:2 (MSG)

Don't call attention to yourself;
let others do that for you.

PRINCIPLE

If you've done something special, it will get the attention of others. You won't need to tell everyone.

Self-promotion has become an art form in modern culture. Social media has all the trappings for the narcissist; yet, it also provides an incredible opportunity for us. It's pretty clear a lot of people think the world revolves around them. The social networking platform has many negatives, but it also has many positives. It gives us the ability to connect globally, as if we're all local neighbors having coffee and bumping into one another on a downtown street.

Courtesy, ethics, and good manners should govern our conversations and connections on the social media platform as well as in our public lives.

Jesus rebuked the Pharisees because they demanded prominent places and wore attention-drawing clothes. "Woe to you Pharisees, because you love the most important seats in the synagogues and respectful greetings in the marketplaces" (Luke 11:43 NIV).

Drawing attention to ourselves is not the goal. We should work to live commendable lives but refrain from lavishing praise upon ourselves and our good works. Let's leave that for others.

REMEMBER

Don't break your arm patting yourself on the back.

READ PROVERBS CHAPTER 27

fivestarman.com/day-58

Day 59: Moral Rot Destroys A Nation

PROVERBS 28:2 (NLT)

When there is moral rot within a nation,
its government topples easily.
But wise and knowledgeable leaders bring stability.

PRINCIPLE

The stability of a nation rests upon the moral fiber of its people and the wisdom and knowledge of its leaders.

Any student of history knows a nation's greatest enemy is the moral rot of its own people. When a nation is facing the violence of a foe, it rallies to the cause with purpose and resolve. However, when that nation enjoys peace and comfort, its boredom draws moral decline and self-indulgence.

Everything rises and falls on leadership. As someone so aptly said, "The people have voted; now they must be punished." Or, as another has spoken, "The people elect the leadership they deserve." If a nation elects a person for selfish gain, they will soon find their leader enjoys gain at their expense.

The nation of Israel murmured against God and wanted a king like all of the nations around them. God warned them that a king would be an expensive entitlement. And it proved to be true. The nation rose and fell on the leadership that served Israel. Some kings were good; yet, others were wicked, and the nation of Israel paid for their decision.

REMEMBER

Pray for your nation, its people, and its leaders.

READ PROVERBS CHAPTER 28

fivestarman.com/day-59

Day 60: Start With God

PROVERBS 1:7 (NLT)

Fear of the Lord is the foundation of true knowledge,
but fools despise wisdom and discipline.

PRINCIPLE

The beginning of wisdom is to respect God's existence and supremacy.

To gain an understanding of a concept, go to the source or the seed of it. The spiritual "Law of Seed" demonstrates that within any seed is the ability to produce after its own kind. By examining the seed, you discover the original intent.

The Bible starts with the announcement, "In the beginning, God…." The Gospel of John speaks of the same genesis this way, "In the beginning was the Word…."

The beginning of *ALL* things is the Word. The Word was with God. The Word was God. Through the Word, all things have been made. Nothing has been made except through the Word. The Word is the verbal expression of God (John 1:1–3).

Our advisor tells us that if we want to gain wisdom, we should start with God. Society has lost reverence and respect for the Word of God. The Bible is no longer generally accepted as sacred. Ignorant people with the brevity of a few decades of life and a few hours of study conclude they know more than the Eternal Word. They're foolish in their futile thinking and clumsy in their darkened, calloused minds.

We need to reverently bow, and have a fear of the Lord. It is the beginning of wisdom.

REMEMBER

If you're going to begin anything, begin with the Word.

READ PROVERBS CHAPTER 1

fivestarman.com/day-60

Day 61: Treasure Common Sense

PROVERBS 2:7–8 (NLT)

He grants a treasure of common sense to the honest.
He is a shield to those who walk with integrity.
He guards the paths of the just
and protects those who are faithful to him.

PRINCIPLE

"Common sense is as rare as genius." –Ralph Waldo Emerson

God gives the treasure of common sense to those who are honest. Honesty is a foundational pillar of wisdom. No man will ever leave a lasting legacy who has not lived with integrity. History has a way of bringing out the truth of a man's life and isn't kind to the man who did not deal honestly.

I had a relative that wasn't an honest man. In fact, he was a liar. He would make up stories, not for the sake of humor or in jest—he simply would not tell the truth. I don't know his motivations, but I know it was embarrassing because the truth would eventually be revealed. He was a pretender.

Our advisor tells us that integrity serves as a shield. God has a protection plan for those who are just and faithful to Him.

Job said, "Let God weigh me on the scales of justice, for he knows my integrity" (Job 31:6 NLT).

Job went through a rough time but held onto his integrity through it all. Even after his wife mocked him, "Are you still holding onto your integrity? Curse God and die," Job held onto his integrity and established his legacy.

REMEMBER

It makes sense to be honest.

READ PROVERBS CHAPTER 2

fivestarman.com/day-61

Day 62: Hearing God

PROVERBS 3:6 (MSG)

Listen for God's voice in everything you do, everywhere you go;
he's the one who will keep you on track.

PRINCIPLE

God still speaks to men.

I was playing a round of golf with a couple of guys, enjoying the course, having a great time, and engaged in conversation. One of the men asked me directly, "Neil, you said earlier that God spoke to you. What do you mean by that?"

He looked at me as if I were strange to say that God had spoken to me. Yet, I looked at him as equally strange in thinking that he hadn't heard the voice of God.

God still speaks to men; however, God's voice no longer thunders and booms from Heaven. When did God's voice become quiet?

"When the people heard the thunder and the loud blast of the ram's horn, and when they saw the flashes of lightning and the smoke billowing from the mountain, they stood at a distance, trembling with fear. And they said to Moses, 'You speak to us, and we will listen. But don't let God speak directly to us, or we will die!'" (Exodus 20:18-19 NLT)

Men asked God to be silent. His voice was so overwhelming that they begged Moses to speak with God on their behalf.

However, now we have the Holy Spirit. He speaks *to* us and *through* us. We can still hear the voice of God. Jesus said those who follow Him would hear His voice, and the voice of a stranger they would not follow (John 10:4–5).

You can hear from God.

REMEMBER

Listen to the voice of God.

READ PROVERBS CHAPTER 3

fivestarman.com/day-62

Day 63: The Good Life

PROVERBS 4:10 (NLT)

My child, listen to me and do as I say,
and you will have a long, good life.

PRINCIPLE

Your Father has some good advice for you.

I've met thousands of men, and not one of them has said to me that they want to live a destructive and disastrous life. Yet, there are countless men who are roaming aimlessly through life with destructive habits, causing collateral damage among their families and friends. It doesn't have to be that way.

God wants to speak to you as He would speak to His son because that's the way He regards you. Jesus said, "In that day you will ask in my name. I am not saying that I will ask the Father on your behalf. No, the Father himself loves you because you have loved me . . . ." (John 16:26 NIV).

Jesus clearly says that the Father wants a direct relationship with you. He desires that you listen to Him and do what He says so that you may have a long and good life.

The Apostle Paul tells us that a child honoring a father brings a promise, "... That it may go well with you and that you may enjoy long life on the earth" (Ephesians 6:3 NIV). How much more will we be blessed for honoring God as our Father?

REMEMBER

If you want a long and good life, listen to your Father.

READ PROVERBS CHAPTER 4
fivestarman.com/day-63

Day 64: Proximity

PROVERBS 5:8 (NIV)

Keep to a path far from her,
do not go near the door of her house.

PRINCIPLE

All sin is a failure of proximity.

You can avoid a lot of pain simply by protecting your zone. There is a line between respect and familiarity, and governing that line protects your relationships. In other words, sin is caused by a failure in proximity.

Knocking on the wrong door will lead you to places you don't want to end up. Unfortunately, I've helped men face the fallout of crossing this line. The devastation is unimaginable. The pain is unbearable.

All of it can be avoided simply by keeping your distance—from the path, from the door, from the woman. Respect this line and you're safe. Cross it, and the grip of familiarity will take hold of you.

Three Keys to Respect (Rejecting Familiarity):

- **Make a covenant with your eyes.** Job made a covenant with his eyes not to look upon a woman. It's much like the discipline of a diet. You promise your stomach that you're going to refrain from certain foods which are damaging to your health. Make a covenant with your eyes that you will not look at women inappropriately.
- **Don't go down that road.** Every city—every Internet site—every store has a path to destruction. Recently, I was in Alaska, and one thing you learn quickly there is to stay on safe trails to avoid danger.
- **Keep your distance.** The only way to regain respect is to create distance. Familiarity breeds contempt. As you get close to something, you lose its value, or, in this case, the fear of it.

REMEMBER

Don't go down that path.

READ PROVERBS CHAPTER 5

fivestarman.com/day-64

Day 67: Don't Twist My Words

PROVERBS 8:8 (MSG)

You'll only hear true and right words from my mouth;
not one syllable will be twisted or skewed.

PRINCIPLE

What you repeatedly hear, you will eventually believe.

Seven Reasons to Listen to the Word of God:

- The Word of God is the truth. God doesn't lie or twist truth (2 Timothy 3:16).
- The Word of God supplies faith. Faith comes by hearing the Word (Romans 10:17).
- The Word of God cleanses and changes your mind (Psalm 119:9).
- The Word of God gives you stability of mind (Proverbs 3:2).
- The Word of God gives you direction (Psalm 37:31).
- The Word of God gives you warnings and promptings concerning the future (Psalm 19:11).
- The Word of God helps during stressful times (Psalm 119:49–50).

REMEMBER

God is not a man that He can lie.

READ PROVERBS CHAPTER 8

fivestarman.com/day-67

Day 68: Leaders Are Readers

PROVERBS 9:9 (NIV)

Instruct the wise and they will be wiser still;
teach the righteous and they will add to their learning.

PRINCIPLE

The more you learn, the more your capacity to know.

I was shocked when the publisher generally dismissed men as non-readers. He may have some selective evidence to support his claim, but I refuse to believe men are buffoons and imbecilic.

"The average millionaire reads one non-fiction book a month." —Dave Ramsey

Charlie Jones states, "You are the same today as you will be five years from now, except for two things: the books you read and the people you meet." Your world expands by traveling and reading. I recommend doing both.

As a young man, I didn't enjoy reading, primarily because my mind wasn't in the habit of it. I was slow to comprehend and stumbled over the words. I was embarrassed and considered myself slow to learn.

In desperation, I picked up the book, ***See You At The Top,*** by Zig Ziglar. In it, he advised to develop the habit of reading one chapter of Proverbs each day of the month. After committing myself to this discipline, not only did I develop an insatiable appetite for reading, but also my mind enlarged its capacity to learn.

Our advisor tells us, "Instruct the wise and they will be wiser still." In other words, as you learn, your capacity to learn grows. There's unlimited potential in the ability to learn and retain knowledge.

REMEMBER

Leaders are readers.

READ PROVERBS CHAPTER 9

fivestarman.com/day-68

Day 69: The Centurion Principle

PROVERBS 10:8 (MSG)

A wise heart takes orders;
an empty head will come unglued.

PRINCIPLE

God speaks through leadership.

One of the greatest principles that can be discovered is the protocol of authority. It is a hallmark of ***FivestarMan*** and the foundation for understanding proper leadership. I call it, "The Centurion Principle."

In Matthew 8:5, a centurion approached Jesus with a request, "... My servant lies at home, suffering terribly" (NIV). Jesus offered to go to the home and heal the servant. The centurion's reply caused Jesus to marvel at his demonstration of faith, he said, "I have not found anyone in Israel that understands faith like this man."

The centurion's secret? "For I also am a man subject to authority, with soldiers subject to me. And I say to one, Go, and he goes; and to another, Come, and he comes; and to my slave, Do this, and he does it" (Matthew 8:9 AMP).

The centurion knew how to receive orders and how to pass those orders to others. That is the protocol of authority. The wise understand authority.

REMEMBER

The wise take orders.

READ PROVERBS CHAPTER 10

fivestarman.com/day-69

Day 70: Integrity

PROVERBS 11:3 (MSG)

The integrity of the honest keeps them on track;
the deviousness of crooks brings them to ruin.

PRINCIPLE

Integrity will keep you from a crash.

An entrepreneur called me to seek some feedback on a difficult situation he faced. He had stepped into a business needing a radical turnaround or it would face foreclosure. Although he did not create the debt, he felt the load of it. The pressure began to cause him sleepless nights. As he described the situation, I responded, "I know you to be a man of integrity. Hold on to your integrity, and it will see you through this situation. God will give you wisdom to manage it."

Later, he shared with me that the advice encouraged him. Not only had he received wisdom for the financial situation, but he was also completely at peace with handling it.

Job faced pressure like very few people have been subjected to, he "held onto his integrity" and came through it all (Job 27:5).

David prayed, "May integrity and uprightness protect me, because my hope, Lord, is in you" (Psalm 25:21 NIV).

When you face a season of hardship, hold onto your integrity, it will see you through.

REMEMBER

Integrity is the wheel to keep you on track.

READ PROVERBS CHAPTER 11
fivestarman.com/day-70

Day 71: Your Purposes Are Reliable

PROVERBS 12:5 (AMP)

The thoughts and purposes of the [consistently] righteous are honest and reliable, but the counsels and designs of the wicked are treacherous.

PRINCIPLE

An authentic man has integrity with his purposes.

The foundational concept of ***FivestarMan*** is that within men are five purposes: an adventurous spirit, an entrepreneurial drive, gallant relationships, faithful character, and philanthropic in a cause. When a man gains an understanding of his purposes, his life becomes a passionate pursuit of authentic manhood.

When you draw upon your purposes, you will discover a passion that you've not known any other way. It truly becomes an empowering force for living with integrity.

Integrity in this case means, *the quality and state of being complete.* Men who gain an understanding of their purposes feel completion, a wholeness in their purposes. They have a sense of personal assurance.

REMEMBER

Your purposes are reliable.

READ PROVERBS CHAPTER 12

fivestarman.com/day-71

Day 72: Satisfy Your Cravings

PROVERBS 13:4 (AMP)

The appetite of the sluggard craves and gets nothing,
but the appetite of the diligent is abundantly supplied.

PRINCIPLE

God gave man the gift of seed to satisfy his cravings.

Before God created Man, He prepared a place of residence for the Man. It was built upon an agrarian system of supply: seed, time, and harvest. It was a place of abundance. However, God did not release the system until he created Man so that the place could be worked. That was the Man's vocation—to work the Garden. He was to sow seeds, harvest them, and scatter them upon the entire Earth. Unlimited seed—abundant harvest.

After God pronounced the blessing upon Man, He presented him with the gift of seed. "Then God said, 'I give you every seed-bearing plant on the face of the whole earth and every tree that has fruit with seed in it. They will be yours for food'" (Genesis 1:29 NIV).

With seed, Man has an exceptional ability to satisfy his cravings. With it, Man has the ability to sow a seed for a determined harvest.

We still operate by this principle; however, if we're lazy and are unwilling to work, then we will have constant cravings without satisfaction.

REMEMBER

The man who understands the principle of planting seed will have abundant supply.

READ PROVERBS CHAPTER 13

fivestarman.com/day-72

Day 73: The Tent Called "Flourish"

PROVERBS 14:11 (NIV)

The house of the wicked will be destroyed,
but the tent of the upright will flourish.

PRINCIPLE

Life isn't about cars, clothes, and cottages. It's about a cause.

There was a time that the "American dream" of owning a home was the equivalent of being prosperous. Sadly, that "dream" became a nightmare for millions of people who had been enticed to enter into financial loans that didn't make budgetary sense for their incomes.

Many lenders used unscrupulous tactics and even wicked strategies to trick people into disastrous loans that were doomed to fail. The housing bubble was a disaster.

Interestingly, if you read the eleventh chapter of Hebrews (also known as the "hall of faith"), you discover that many people of faith saw what they believed for from a distance but did not take possession of it. "...They wandered in deserts and mountains, living in caves and in holes in the ground" (Hebrews 11:38 NIV).

It is clear that these people are noted for their faith, yet they also were nomadic. Their tents flourished.

Don't confuse cars, clothes, and cottages for your life purpose. You're living a life of faith for a cause.

REMEMBER

Have faith for a cause.

READ PROVERBS CHAPTER 14
fivestarman.com/day-73

Day 74: Kind And Comforting Words

PROVERBS 15:4 (MSG)

Kind words heal and help;
cutting words wound and maim.

PRINCIPLE

Speak kind and comforting words.

As men, we cannot underestimate the power of our words. This is one of the most important lessons I've ever discovered. Words matter.

We need to build a partition between our minds and our tongues to allow a filter to inspect and approve the words we speak. They should be words that heal and help, rather than wound and disfigure.

The prophet Zechariah was speaking with the Lord in a vision. After explaining a coming event upon the Earth, the Lord turned to speak kind and comforting words to the angel who was accompanying him (Zechariah 1:13).

This is so characteristic of the Lord to be concerned with a lower-ranking angel who needed to be comforted.

I grew up in an atmosphere of harsh, hurtful, and haunting words. Curses, cussing, and disparagement were the norm. My relative was maimed by those words. He has a deep wound of bitterness within him because of them. Decades later, those words still ring within his ears, as if he had just heard them yesterday.

Our words can have the opposite effect as well. I recall words that my high school principal spoke to me upon graduation. His words have continued to be a lasting encouragement to me.

We should be considerate to those who are within our hearing.

REMEMBER

Words matter.

READ PROVERBS CHAPTER 15

fivestarman.com/day-74

Day 75: Don't Kick Against The Pricks

PROVERBS 16:4–5 (NLT)

The Lord has made everything for his own purposes,
even the wicked for a day of disaster.
The Lord detests the proud;
they will surely be punished.

PRINCIPLE

It's hard to kick against the pricks.

At ***FivestarMan,*** we talk a lot about purposes. We know that men make plans, but God's purposes prevail.

Amazingly, there are those who have positioned themselves as adversaries of God's purposes. An old Greek proverb says, "It's hard to kick against the pricks."

Farmers used a stick with a pointed piece of iron on its tip to prod the oxen when plowing. The farmer used it to steer the ox in the right direction. If the animal rebelled by kicking at the prick, it would be driven deeper into his flesh—causing even more pain.

A religious zealot named Saul "kicked against the pricks" of God's purposes by opposing believers in Christ—that is until Jesus interrupted his pursuit on the road to Damascus. After the prodding of Jesus, Saul aligned with God's purposes and became a great apostle for the Church.

When a prideful person rebels against the direction of God's purposes, he suffers.

There are men who are opposing God's purposes to their own destruction; however, if they realign their lives in the right direction, God can use them for greatness.

REMEMBER

Don't rebel against the direction of God's purposes.

READ PROVERBS CHAPTER 16

fivestarman.com/day-75

Day 76: Living A Legacy

PROVERBS 17:6 (NLT)

Grandchildren are the crowning glory of the aged;
parents are the pride of their children.

PRINCIPLE

It takes three generations to establish a legacy.

The distinguishing mark of Abraham's character that captured the attention of God was that Abraham would direct his household and command his children after him. In this way, the covenant promise would be established in three generations as a lasting legacy: Abraham, Isaac, and Jacob.

Solomon said, "A righteous man leaves an inheritance to his children's children" (Proverbs 13:22a NKJV).

Remember: the greatest compliment that could be received is to hear your children tell their children, "We serve the God of our father."

Living with this goal in mind will help you deny a temporary appetite for a more effective future.

REMEMBER

We should think in terms of generations when we make decisions. How will your life reflect living a legacy?

READ PROVERBS CHAPTER 17

fivestarman.com/day-76

Day 77: The Name Of The Lord

PROVERBS 18:10 (NLT)

The name of the Lord is a strong fortress;
the godly run to him and are safe.

PRINCIPLE

The name is representative of the person.

Have you ever explored the etymology of your name? It's an interesting process. Discovering the root and history of your name can be revealing. For example, my name, "Neil" comes from the old Irish/Gaelic word for "champion." Thus the title of this book, ***The Daily Champion.***

Our advisor tells us, "The name of the Lord is a strong fortress." The Hebrew word for *name* ("shem") means *reputation, signature, mark, or fame.* The Name represents the Person.

The use of a person's name invokes all that the person is and represents. That's why God was so strong on the misuse of His Name. "They speak of you with evil intent; your adversaries misuse your name" (Psalm 139:20 NIV).

Jesus directs us to use His Name when approaching the Father in prayer. "In that day you will no longer ask me anything. Very truly I tell you, my Father will give you whatever you ask in my name" (John 16:23 NIV).

The use of His Name is representative of Him approaching the Father Himself.

REMEMBER

The Name of the Lord is a strong tower.

READ PROVERBS CHAPTER 18

fivestarman.com/day-77

Day 78: Difficult Times Reveal Authentic Friends

PROVERBS 19:7a (NIV)

The poor are shunned by all their relatives—
how much more do their friends avoid them!

PRINCIPLE

During difficult times you discover true friendships.

I've lived long enough to see that every man goes through difficult times. In fact, I read a lot of biographies and have found a common thread in the stories of great men. They all faced difficult seasons. The lessons they learned during their trials are what they value most and unselfishly pass on to those interested in their stories.

One of the most surprising and disappointing truths discovered during a downturn in life is the retreat of those previously considered valuable friends. If you want to discover authentic friends, go through a difficult time. You will see many people whom you trusted run to the exits.

You will also be able to make a list of those who proved true.

Recently, a man I had recommended for a job sent me a note of thanks. He said, "When I went through the most challenging period of my life, others stopped calling. I had nothing to offer. However, you started calling me."

Make no mistake. Everyone faces a blow up in life. It's during these times that you will make two lists of people: those who ran to the exits and those who ran to help and encourage you.

REMEMBER

Take note of those who walk away during tough times.

READ PROVERBS CHAPTER 19

fivestarman.com/day-78

Day 79: Procrastinated Dreams

PROVERBS 20:4 (NLT)

Those too lazy to plow in the right season
will have no food at the harvest.

PRINCIPLE

It's a fantasy to expect a future for which you haven't sown seed.

Solomon advised, "To everything there is a season, A time for every purpose under heaven" (Ecclesiastes 3:1 NKJV).

Have you ever missed a very important business appointment? It's frustrating because you know that, no matter what happens, you may never recover the loss of that moment. Even if you are able to reschedule, there may be lingering doubt about you going forward.

Our advisor warns us that there is a right season—an appointed time to get things done. Miss that appointment, and you will not have the income or reward that could come from it.

When I was a young man, I stood in the office of a successful businessman. As he was telling me his story, I looked at a rendering of a spectacular building. I exclaimed, "Wow! Where is this building?" As I turned to hear his reply, I noticed a forlorn look on his face.

He exhaled a sigh of sadness, "That building is only in my dreams. I missed the opportunity to build it." The opportunity had slipped by. He no longer had the resources to build his dream.

How many guys spend their lives waiting for the right season only to look back and see they lived through it without recognizing the moment?

REMEMBER

Don't procrastinate your dreams.

READ PROVERBS CHAPTER 20
fivestarman.com/day-79

Day 80: Religious Performance

PROVERBS 21:3 (MSG)

Clean living before God and justice with our neighbors mean far more to God than religious performance.

PRINCIPLE

You won't impress God with religious performance.

During the days of Jesus, the religious men were divided primarily into two groups: the Pharisees and Sadducees. Each had their own political, social, and spiritual emphasis. One thing is for sure about them: they performed religious duties. The name, *Pharisee,* means, *set apart.* The name, *Sadducee,* means, *to be right, just.*

As well as their outward appearances reflected their religion, they could not façade the deadness of their faith. Jesus exclaimed about them, "Watch out! ... Beware of the yeast of the Pharisees and Sadducees" (Matthew 16:6 NLT).

One of the real dangers of striving to be "men of God" is creating a system of performance, rather than changing our hearts before God. A lot of efforts toward reaching men have been performance based—completing studies, making personal sacrifices, and becoming "sanctified" saints. These efforts fail because they do not change the heart of a man.

FivestarMan communicates to the five purposes that reside within the heart of man. When a man gains understanding of these purposes, his life becomes a passionate pursuit of authentic manhood.

REMEMBER

Clean living and justified lives are better than performance.

READ PROVERBS CHAPTER 21

fivestarman.com/day-80

Day 81: Be Aware

PROVERBS 22:3 (NLT)

A prudent person foresees danger and takes precautions.
The simpleton goes blindly on and suffers the consequences.

PRINCIPLE

Be aware and take precautions.

The tenth generation of mankind was busy with eating, drinking, romantic intrigue, marrying, and giving in marriage. Along with these distractions, they also corrupted business. When they didn't get what they wanted, they became violent. These people became simpletons—silly people, easily distracted, enticed, and deceived (Matthew 24:38; Luke 17:28-30; Genesis 6:11).

Noah was a prudent man (meaning *aware, alert, crafty*). He walked with God in the daily commute and was warned about the coming cataclysmic judgment. The Earth would experience a water baptism—a cleansing from the wickedness of man. Noah was able to take necessary precautions to save his family (Hebrews 11:7).

As I travel each week, I have noticed that travelers are often unaware. They do not walk with determined steps and purposeful direction. They look like cattle—simple-minded and following the herd on the trail.

When I walk through the corridors of airports, drive interstates, fly to new cities, eat at restaurants, and enter stores, I am constantly aware of my surroundings. My eyes are taking in the room. I survey those who are around me. I am alert.

A ***FivestarMan*** is faithful. We walk with God in the daily commute. Doing so, the Spirit of God gives us foresight of danger. We're aware and alert to what is happening around us.

REMEMBER

Be alert. Be aware.

READ PROVERBS CHAPTER 22

fivestarman.com/day-81

Day 82: Discipline Correctly

PROVERBS 23:13 (NIV)

Do not withhold discipline from a child;
if you punish them with the rod, they will not die.

PRINCIPLE

It requires discipline to discipline correctly.

The purpose of discipline is to teach children that doing wrong will cause pain in life. There is a raging debate on whether children should be disciplined. Raising children in a disciplined environment would seem to be common sense, but there is much argument against any form of corporal punishment.

My wife and I raised three children. Interestingly, we had to use physical punishment on only a few occasions. Our children knew I would not hesitate to correct them so they consistently obeyed and respected our leadership.

My goal in discipline was to demonstrate that they could live under my rewards, or they could lose those rewards by disobedience. It was their choice. I would continue to meet their basic needs—food, shelter, etc., but they would not have privileges and my gracious rewards. It was pretty simple, yet it proved to be an effective process.

I learned early on that most of the strong personality traits that could cause misbehavior were positive traits which were undisciplined. For example, stubbornness was often a conviction misdirected. Rebellion could be creative thinking without guidance.

This process helped my children understand God's reward system of grace and truth. Too much law, and children will never live up to your rules and demands. Too much grace, and they will run wild without restraint.

REMEMBER

Punishment is temporary pain to avoid permanent judgment.

READ PROVERBS CHAPTER 23

fivestarman.com/day-82

Day 83: Mentally Stronger

PROVERBS 24:5 (NLT)

The wise are mightier than the strong,
and those with knowledge grow stronger and stronger.

PRINCIPLE

Intelligence outranks muscle.

The Daily Champion is designed to lead men into the habit of reading one chapter of Proverbs every day of the month (the chapter that corresponds to the day of the month). Habits are the seeds of purpose sown daily. This habit makes you mentally stronger.

Solomon is notably the smartest man who ever walked on Earth (with the exception of Jesus Himself). Reading a chapter of Proverbs each day is the equivalent of sitting down with Solomon over coffee each morning and gleaning from his incredible mind, letting him advise us on the strategies of life, business, and family.

I can't emphasize enough the empowering impact of this daily practice. If you commit to it, I assure you that you will gain mental ability, discernment, prudence, knowledge, and wisdom.

REMEMBER

Habits are the seeds of purpose sown daily.

READ PROVERBS CHAPTER 24

fivestarman.com/day-83

Day 84: Clouds Without Rain

PROVERBS 25:14 (AMP)

Like clouds and wind without rain is a man who boasts of gifts [he does not give.]

PRINCIPLE

We should carefully watch over our promises to deliver them.

Have you ever been promised something, but didn't receive it? Sure you have. Do you remember the disappointment—the bitter taste it left in your mouth?

Our advisor compares it to a farmer who sees clouds and has hopeful expectation for rain, needing its nourishment for his crops, only to feel the brisk winds bring in clouds that fail to release their abundance.

If you're a businessman expecting a client to place a big order that will turn around a failing quarter, or an entrepreneur who is promised the venture capital needed to launch a new product or service, you know the sting that farmer feels.

I could complain about the times I've been promised something only to feel the sting of disappointment, but *more embarrassing* are the times that I've failed to fulfill a promise I've made to someone else.

In my prayer time a few weeks ago, I was reminded of a promise I made to give a sum of money to a friend who was building a new facility. I had advised him on numerous occasions free of charge, but this was a financial promise, and I failed to pay it.

I immediately called him and apologized. Since then I have taken necessary steps to fulfill my pledge. To be perfectly honest, he may not have remembered the promise, yet it was important to me to watch over my word to fulfill it.

REMEMBER

Don't disappoint.

READ PROVERBS CHAPTER 25

fivestarman.com/day-84

Day 85: Bullseye

PROVERBS 26:10 (NIV)

Like an archer who wounds at random
is one who hires a fool or any passer-by.

PRINCIPLE

Have a target before you shoot.

I recently had the privilege to speak at the "Top Shot Men's Conference" in Wasilla, Alaska. At this event last year, I competed in the archery competition. Even though I had never pulled a bow, I made it to the final with one other competitor. Obviously, that experience gave me a hunger to take up archery.

I now have an amazing *Matthews Helim* outfitted to perfection. It is a work of art, but it is also a deadly weapon. I am enjoying learning the skill of archery.

Our advisor recommends, when it comes to hiring, you had better have a target. Hiring just anyone or someone who is not vetted is like shooting arrows without eying a target. He considers it randomly dangerous.

I have made this mistake on a few occasions. Flippantly hiring someone is destructive and usually turns into disaster.

REMEMBER

Know what the target is before you shoot your arrows. You'll hit the bullseye every time.

READ PROVERBS CHAPTER 26
fivestarman.com/day-85

Day 86: The Four Faces Of Anger

PROVERBS 27:4 (NIV)

Anger is cruel and fury overwhelming,
but who can stand before jealousy?

PRINCIPLE

Do not allow the day to pass without ridding yourself of anger.

Anger digs deep into the soul of man. It can draw out buried emotions from years past in an instant. It is very important that we distinguish the different types of anger and extinguish the harmful emotions.

The Four Faces of Anger:

- **RAGE**—Anger that causes us to flurry about with over-expressed gestures, clinched jaws, or boisterous words, even calling down curses. Expressing rage causes people to stare at you in disbelief, confusion, or embarrassment.
- **FURY**—A much stronger, destructive emotion of rage, often leading to a depraved mind and delusional violence. Fury is motivated by evil. This often results in physical harm to others, sometimes even murder.
- **INDIGNATION**—Indignation is a righteous anger caused by witnessing or experiencing injustice, shame, or evil done to the innocent. Indignation motivates men to protect and risk their lives for the cause of others.
- **WRATH**—Wrath is the godliest form of anger. Wrath is what causes a man to correct a wrong and to rid the Earth of evil.

Some men have been taught to sequester their anger, to be stoic in emotions, yet anger has a role to play in our lives if our motivations are pure and our response is disciplined.

Jealousy is the extreme energy of anger expressed by an envious person. Our advisor says jealousy is the most destructive of all forms of anger. It is the motivation of innumerable murders, robberies, and other violent crimes.

REMEMBER

In your anger, do not sin.

READ PROVERBS CHAPTER 27

fivestarman.com/day-86

Day 87: Don't Storm Into Your Home

PROVERBS 28:3 (NIV)

A ruler who oppresses the poor
is like a driving rain that leaves no crops.

PRINCIPLE

Poor leadership can cause storms.

The weather in Oklahoma, where I was raised, plays a significant role in life—especially in the spring. The winters can be difficult, but the spring brings the storm season. Thunderstorms, hail, and tornadoes are a part of life. The storms can bring much needed rain that serves as a blessing for farmers and greening the landscape, but they can also bring disasters. Hail can destroy cars, roofs, and wipe out entire crops.

That's the warning our advisor gives us regarding leaders who have the opportunities and hope of being a blessing but actually cause disasters with their leadership.

I've traveled in Central and South American countries that had incredible opportunities and resources available to them, yet their people struggled in poverty because their leadership caused disasters rather than developing economic opportunities for their people.

Let's bring this closer to home. When you come home, does your family see your coming leadership as a blessing, or are they frightened that you will cause a storm? Do you oppress your family, or do you draw out the deposit of resources within them?

REMEMBER

Don't storm into your home. Bring nourishment and refreshing.

READ PROVERBS CHAPTER 28

fivestarman.com/day-87

Day 88: Can You Handle Truth?

PROVERBS 29:12 (NIV)

If a ruler listens to lies,
all his officials become wicked.

PRINCIPLE

If a man values lies, he will never hear the truth.

It is an iconic moment in the movie, ***"A Few Good Men,"*** when the ideal of military manhood is on trial. Soldiers who were issued an order from the commander to kill a fellow soldier (a "code red") was supposedly to protect the "idea" of loyalty and of the commander. The moral judgment of the "code red" was all based upon a lie.

When a leader values lies, all of his men become wicked. It starts at the top and works through the organization, the nation, or the home. The value set becomes *mendacity (given to or characterized by deception or divergence from truth).* Mendacity has become an art form in modern-day politics. Unfortunately, politicians justify their lying articulations with the claim of a moral high ground; however, lying does not have a moral high ground.

When a man's entire life is mendacious, telling the truth is not an option.

REMEMBER

Lying does not have a moral high ground.

READ PROVERBS CHAPTER 29

fivestarman.com/day-88

Day 89: Shake, Rattle, And Roll

PROVERBS 30:21 (MSG)

Three things are too much for even the earth to bear,
yes, four things shake its foundations—
when the janitor becomes the boss,
when a fool gets rich,
when a whore is voted "woman of the year,"
when a "girlfriend" replaces a faithful wife.

PRINCIPLE

The sin of man shakes the Earth.

The charlatan, apocalyptic, eco-evangelists blame man for global warming. Their thesis is that we're the problem of the planet. I do agree that Earth experiences repercussions from man. That is a biblical concept and is evident; however, the cause/effect of climate change is the result of man's sin—his narcissistic, flippant attitude toward the principles of godliness.

Here are four things that cause the Earth to tremble under our feet:

- **When a janitor becomes the boss.** This isn't speaking against those who start out in a position of servanthood and grow into leadership. This is speaking of someone who hasn't qualified himself through faithfulness. The Earth trembles at a novice in leadership.
- **When a fool gets rich.** Wealth should be the byproduct of productive and intelligent people. There are many who have means without meaning. They're disasters.
- **When a whore is voted "woman of the year."** It's repulsive to the Earth when brazen and whorish women are celebrated.
- **When a girlfriend replaces a faithful wife.** The Earth moves under the feet of a husband who breaks covenant with the wife of his youth and replaces her with sexual flings.

REMEMBER

If you really care about the well-being of the Earth, live a godly life.

READ PROVERBS CHAPTER 30

fivestarman.com/day-89

Day 90: My Son, The Answer To My Prayers!

PROVERBS 31:2 (NIV)

Listen, my son! Listen, son of my womb!
Listen, my son, the answer to my prayers!

PRINCIPLE

A son is the answer to a mother's prayers.

Many people have speculated who King Lemuel is—the son who is being addressed in Proverbs 31. Most scholars have concluded *Lemuel,* which means *for God,* is indeed one of the names of Solomon. Thus, this is most likely a desperate cry from Bathsheba to her son.

Bathsheba's voice is raised, intense, and emphatic. The desperation comes from the pain of her life—the seduction of David, her whorish betrayal of her righteous husband Uriah, and the death of her bastard child. Her emotions are too much to withhold.

"Listen, my son, the answer to my prayers!" She had prayed in desperation for Solomon. He was a product of God's grace! In spite of all of her sins, God had forgiven her. Imagine! Her son was in the lineage of the Savior! Wow! Can you shout, "Grace!"

Recently, I examined the circumstances of my own mother's pain—betrayal, adultery, alcoholism, etc., yet I know my mother prayed for me. She desperately wanted to see her son live a purposeful and rewarding life.

(***FivestarMan*** has released a book entitled, ***A Mother's Guide to Raising A FivestarMan.*** This book will help mothers who face the daunting task of raising a boy into authentic manhood. I am sure you know a mother who is facing this painful challenge. Why don't you purchase a copy, and give it to her?)

REMEMBER

The son of a promise is God's grace.

READ PROVERBS CHAPTER 31

fivestarman.com/day-90

Day 91: Sinful-Minded Men

PROVERBS 1:10 (NIV)

My son, if sinful men entice you,
do not give in to them.

PRINCIPLE

Never underestimate the destructive power of sinful-minded men.

A few days ago, I watched a disturbing video. Christian men were lined up kneeling with their hands tied behind their backs. Other men lined up behind them with handguns placed at the back of the captives' heads. Someone was rallying the crowd with strong, boastful rhetoric claiming that the Christians were blasphemers of "the prophet" and deserved death. There would be no trial, no court of appeals, no justice—just mob violence enticed by fanatics.

Suddenly, one man pulled the trigger. The first Christian man slumped forward. Although he was obviously dead, the gunman unloaded the remaining bullets into his body. Then, the other gunmen followed. Twelve men were killed within seconds, each receiving a volley of bullets.

My heart ached for the Christian brothers who were martyred that day, but I also was disgusted by the cowardly acts of murder by the mob of men.

Evil is insidious. It is unjustifiable and indefensible. Evil motivated these gunmen, but there is more to the irrational behavior behind mob violence. It is the dynamic of collaborative craziness. It's a well-documented phenomenon that mobs of men do things individual men would never do.

Never underestimate the destructive power of sinful-minded men.

REMEMBER

A mob mentality does not suffer intelligence.

READ PROVERBS CHAPTER 1

fivestarman.com/day-91

Day 92: The Three Amigos

PROVERBS 2:9 (NLT)

Then you will understand what is right, just, and fair,
and you will find the right way to go.

PRINCIPLE

If you keep heading in a certain direction, you'll end up at the end of the line.

I continue to be amazed by men who want or expect different results without making any changes in their decisions. It's the definition of insanity to do the same thing repeatedly and expect a different outcome. As West Texas humor asks, "How's that working out for ya?"

Our advisor tells us that making decisions based on what is right, just, and fair will point us in the right direction.

***Right, Just,* and *Fair* are the three friends of destiny:**

- **RIGHT**—means to *have just cause.* It also means to go *straight.* In other words, you can't take two trails at once. You can't be double-minded.
- **JUST**—means to have a *forensic cause.* That means you're able to dissect how making a decision will result in the end. You're able to see the end before you begin.
- **FAIR**—means to have a *balanced cause.* We are able to accurately measure and make a level decision. It is much like using a level to draw a straight line. When we have wisdom, we're able to keep things straight.

REMEMBER

The three amigos, *Right, Just,* and *Fair,* are for making wise decisions.

READ PROVERBS CHAPTER 2

fivestarman.com/day-92

Day 93: Don't Be A Know-It-All

PROVERBS 3:7 (MSG)

Don't assume that you know it all.
Run to God! Run from evil!

PRINCIPLE

Don't assume that you know it all.

I was embarking on life as a young man. I had a poor education, no prospects of a future, and I was as lost as most eighteen-year olds. I was on my own and trying to make a living. I was young, naïve, and desperate.

A book sat on my shelf for months. It was given to me, yet I hadn't broken the binding on the cover. Who reads a free book? There it was unopened, holding advice and wisdom awaiting my discovery.

When I finally opened it, I couldn't put it down. Zig Ziglar's book, ***See You At The Top,*** changed the course of my daily routine, thus changing my life. After reading Zig's book, I developed an insatiable appetite for knowledge and optimistic goal setting. His southern drawl and idiosyncratic humor appealed to me.

His book also taught me to run to God. He kindled a fire for me to know God's Word.

REMEMBER

You don't know what you don't know.

READ PROVERBS CHAPTER 3
fivestarman.com/day-93

Day 94: Sure Footed

PROVERBS 4:12 (NIV)

When you walk, your steps will not be hampered;
when you run, you will not stumble.

PRINCIPLE

God wants you to have a smooth course for your feet so you can be surefooted.

A few months ago I had an injury from my workout routine. The arches in my feet were strained from the high-impact movements. The pain became excruciating, shooting up my leg. It was difficult to walk, especially going up and down stairs. I used this proverb as a confession of faith. When I would take a step and experience pain, I would speak this out loud, "My steps are not hampered, and I will not stumble."

Pain is a messenger. It alerts us to trouble so that we can take the necessary action to avoid even more destruction.

Men at times will have a philosophy to "work through the pain." That may sound manly, but it isn't always wise, especially when it comes to the pain of bad decisions.

The benefits of reading Proverbs each day is that we gain skill and godly wisdom so that we can comprehend the purposes and ways of God. In that, we are able to have a clear direction, avoid pain, and run without stumbling.

REMEMBER

God doesn't place stones in your path to cause you to stumble.

READ PROVERBS CHAPTER 4

fivestarman.com/day-94

Day 95: Money-Grubbers

PROVERBS 5:10 (NLT)

Strangers will consume your wealth,
and someone else will enjoy the fruit of your labor.

PRINCIPLE

"The disingenuous voices are making their noise, coming out of the shadows, and profiting off the death of authentic manhood." –George Sawyer

Have you noticed that there are entire industries devoted to profiteering off the failure of authentic manhood? They prey on the weaknesses of men. They're money-grubbers—bent on consuming your wealth and taking advantage of your hard work.

In his book, ***The Resurrection of Authentic Manhood***, George Sawyer talks about the mourners who were at the tomb of Lazarus. They were professionals—people paid to be at funerals to wail and tear their clothing. George says, "Just because someone shouts the loudest does not mean his words carry truth."

I heard of a divorce attorney who represented wealthy women who were divorcing unfaithful husbands. Unbeknownst to the divorcing parties, the unscrupulous lawyer hired women to entrap the husbands. The lawyer swirled around like a vulture waiting for the moment to swoop down, represent the heartbroken wives, and take all the money he could gather.

There's no excuse for the husband who betrays his marriage; however, he should have been proactive to avoid his entrapment. Remember, there are money-grubbers looking for weaknesses to take full advantage of you. They will not hesitate to take all you have, leaving you a broken wreck of a man.

REMEMBER

Who is making a living off of the death of authentic manhood?

READ PROVERBS CHAPTER 5
fivestarman.com/day-95

Day 96: The Dirty Seven

PROVERBS 6:16 (NLT)

There are six things the Lord hates—
no, seven things he detests.

PRINCIPLE

God is repulsed by the dirty seven.

You can tell a lot about a person's character by what they like and are attracted to. You can also know a person's character by what they hate and are disgusted by.

Here are the "dirty seven" God hates:

1. **Haughty eyes**—This person looks down on others. He thinks he is better, smarter, and more important, and he shows his disdain.
2. **Lying tongue**—This person makes false claims and promises with the intent of deceiving.
3. **Hands that kill the innocent**—With no regard for the value of life, he takes upon himself the appetite of murder.
4. **Hearts that plot evil**—Out of the heart flow the issues (purposes) of a man. This man purposes evil.
5. **Feet that race to do wrong**—There are men who run toward destruction and feast on causing calamity. They are terrorists.
6. **A false witness**—He uses mendacity to make false claims against another, causing irreparable harm to reputation and influence. He is slanderous.
7. **A person who sows discord in a family**—This is the worst of evils—the person who divides families. This man schemes and manipulates strife. Strife is the manifested presence of Satan.

REMEMBER

You can tell a lot about a man by who his friends are and who they aren't.

READ PROVERBS CHAPTER 6

fivestarman.com/day-96

Day 97: Don't Lose The Dignity Of Your Manhood

PROVERBS 7:15 (NLT)

You're the one I was looking for!
I came out to find you, and here you are!

PRINCIPLE

You will never find love in relationship with adultery.

A ***FivestarMan*** is gallant—which means he shows special attention and respect toward women in an honorable way. Treating older women as our own mothers and the young as our own daughters, we treat our peers as we would our own sisters. The only women who receive the intimacy of our eyes and the passion of our loins are our wives.

This standard of authentic manhood is in sharp contrast to the decadence on display in our media.

The writer of this proverb pulls no punches and develops a high-definition picture of how the spirit of adultery entices and entraps a young, naïve man. She approaches him with a unique ploy, "You're the one I was looking for!" She wants him to feel special. There is something about him—and only him—that distinguishes him from all others. Many have fallen into her snares.

Our goal at ***FivestarMan*** is to raise the standard of conduct toward women. We want to demonstrate dignity and be strong men—men who are stronger than temporary temptation and an appalling appetite of seduction.

REMEMBER

Don't misrepresent yourself as an authentic man.

READ PROVERBS CHAPTER 7
fivestarman.com/day-97

Day 98: Better Than Gold!

PROVERBS 8:10–11 (NIV)

Choose my instruction instead of silver,
knowledge rather than choice gold,
for wisdom is more precious than rubies,
and nothing you desire can compare with her.

PRINCIPLE

Wisdom is the Principal Thing.

Almost everything has an exchange rate. Gold, at this moment, is worth $1,303 per ounce. My weight in gold would be worth $4.1 million. At times in history, gold has been used as a currency. Silver also. However, our advisor tells us that there is something greater than silver, gold, and even rubies. It is instruction, knowledge, and wisdom from God. It's God's currency.

That phrase can trip people up but it really describes the manner in which God deals with mankind. God doesn't deal with us in our currency directly. He deals with us in His currency, which is a superior currency to ours. His currency is Wisdom. In fact, Wisdom is called the Principal Thing (Proverbs 4:7). In the Bible, the Principal Thing is also called the "tithe"—or the first of the tenth. So, God's tithe is Wisdom.

When we ask God for provision, His response is always dealt to us in His currency—wisdom, knowledge, insight, witty inventions, favor, or work.

There is a lot more to say on this matter. In fact, I wrote a book on it titled ***God's Currency***. You can get it at ***FivestarMan.com***.

REMEMBER

Wisdom is better than gold.

READ PROVERBS CHAPTER 8

fivestarman.com/day-98

Day 99: Fear Or Familiarity?

PROVERBS 9:10 (NIV)

The fear of the Lord is the beginning of wisdom,
and knowledge of the Holy One is understanding.

PRINCIPLE

Familiarity breeds contempt.

The pendulum has swung to the extreme. A few years ago, the general theme of religious people could have been summed up with Jonathan Edwards' sermon, "Sinners in the Hands of an Angry God." Now, the counterbalance has appeared, and many Christians seem to have become way too familiar with God. From fear to familiarity, both positions are extreme. You can err by emphasis. For every mile of road, there are two miles of ditch.

Our advisor's use of the phrase, "the fear of the Lord," establishes the genesis of wisdom. Without the respectful posture of awe toward God, we're fools. Familiarity breeds contempt.

The prophet Ezekiel described his response to seeing the glory of the Lord. "I fell facedown!" (Ezekiel 1:28) The byproduct of seeing the shadow of the Lord caused Moses' face to radiate glory for days. Others describe falling as "dead men." It is an overwhelming moment to see the glory of God. We should fear Him. Not to fear Him is asinine.

We need to have a respectful fear—not the terror of the murderous maniac god of the Gnostics, recently portrayed in the movie, ***Noah***. Nor should we have a flippant familiarity that He is the "Man upstairs." We should never trivialize the awesomeness of our Father.

REMEMBER

The man who fears God will avoid all extremes (Ecclesiastes 7:18).

READ PROVERBS CHAPTER 9

fivestarman.com/day-99

Day 100: The Evasive Eye—Wink, Wink

PROVERBS 10:10 (NIV)

Whoever winks maliciously causes grief,
and a chattering fool comes to ruin.

PRINCIPLE

Empty words and winking of the eye are signs of fraud.

A wink can be extremely offensive in some cultures. It is a type of secret communication. For example, in India and some Latin American countries, a wink is a sexual invitation. In business, a wink can signal deception regarding a contract or a fraudulent business deal. The word for *wink* in this proverb actually means *tearing, to cut off,* or *to destroy.*

We're advised that a wink causes grief. A wink is rarely appropriate outside of a humorous situation. As men, we should be very keen as to what our gestures communicate.

Similarly, our advisor warns us of a "chattering fool." This is someone who only gives "lip service." Their words don't mean anything. We find an abundance of this on social media.

Paul tells Timothy to turn away and avoid godless chatter (1 Timothy 6:20; 2 Timothy 2:16). Much like a ventriloquist who provides a voice and speaks through a dummy, a chatterer spews words he has heard others say that don't truly represent anything of himself.

Both of these types of communication are fraudulent and should be avoided.

REMEMBER

An evasive eye is a sign of trouble. A chattering fool is to be avoided.

READ PROVERBS CHAPTER 10

fivestarman.com/day-100

Day 101: What Money Can't Buy

PROVERBS 11:4 (NIV)

Wealth is worthless in the day of wrath,
but righteousness delivers from death.

PRINCIPLE

Money is a shelter for trouble but not for the day of wrath.

Make no mistake. Money is a necessity. You know it is, and so does God. One of the purposes that an authentic man draws upon is the entrepreneurial drive. It motivates you to meet your needs, grant the desires of your family, and finance your purpose.

We're living in difficult times. The financial foundations of the United States, thus the world, have trembled from the strain of a financial bubble in the housing market. ("Financial bubble" is an old financial term dating back to the early 1700's.) The Federal Reserve responded by what they called, "quantitative easing," (the massive pumping of capital into the system). This had an immediate effect of relaxing the crisis and a long-term effect of hyper-inflation.

Pumping money into the system may ease the pain of a financial crisis, but it will not help in the day of wrath. The "day of wrath" is a particular day on the eschatological calendar of the Lord. On that day, wealth will not help us. There are some things money can't buy. Righteousness will be required to deliver one from death.

We should not only take care of our families today, but we should also prepare them for the day when only righteousness will deliver them from death.

REMEMBER

Money is a tool, but it doesn't fix everything.

READ PROVERBS CHAPTER 11
fivestarman.com/day-101

Day 102: God Gave Man A Zoo

PROVERBS 12:10 (NIV)

The righteous care for the needs of their animals,
but the kindest acts of the wicked are cruel.

PRINCIPLE

We have a responsibility to properly care for what we have rulership over.

In modern culture, there is propaganda circulating that Christians are hostile toward the environment and have antipathy toward animals. There is nothing further from the truth.

When God gave Man rule over all creatures, it came with a responsibility to properly care for them. God went into great detail to describe ethical and legal governance for an owner's behavior and responsibilities toward animals.

In the errant storyline of the recent movie, ***Noah***, the Creator wills to destroy all of humanity so that the animals of Earth will repopulate, creating a utopia without man. The anti-man spirit is communicated throughout this movie. The only reasonable conclusion is that all men are cruel and deserving of death, and the highest good of the Earth is the extinction of humanity.

Our advisor says that the kindest acts of the wicked are cruel. Yes, there is a relationship between Man and the Earth, but that relationship is based upon the righteousness of mankind or the lack thereof. When men sin, the Earth recoils, trembles, and bursts out of frustration (Romans 8). A righteous man is a steward of the land and is also kind to animals.

REMEMBER

A righteous man is the best caretaker of animals.

READ PROVERBS CHAPTER 12

fivestarman.com/day-102

Day 103: Haste Leads To Waste

PROVERBS 13:11 (NIV)

Dishonest money dwindles away,
but whoever gathers money little by little makes it grow.

PRINCIPLE

Haste leads to poverty. Contentment keeps investments.

It's a sad reality, but within forty-eight months, most lottery winners are completely bankrupt. Can you imagine the overwhelming disappointment they must feel? They were granted a fantasy. They were awarded free money, yet they saw it dwindle or get swindled away.

Wealth not earned but won in haste or generated unjustly from the production of things for vain or detrimental use will dwindle away, but he who gathers little by little will increase his riches.

Recently, I read about a man who had left his fortune to charity. The most surprising truth about his story was that the man had worked his entire life as a high school janitor. No one knew that the wisest man in the room was the one who dumped the trash.

REMEMBER

Chasing fantasies doesn't pay off.

READ PROVERBS CHAPTER 13
fivestarman.com/day-103

Day 104: You Can't Get There From Here

PROVERBS 14:12 (NIV)

There is a way that appears to be right,
but in the end it leads to death.

PRINCIPLE

Purpose determines direction; direction determines destiny.

We joke about it, but it is often true that men do not want to ask anyone for directions. Now we have GPS systems and maps built within our cars so that we can avoid the embarrassing gas station question, "How do I get there from here?"

I've had a similar conversations with a lot of men. It's not about taking a vacation or a business trip. It's much more important. It's about their destiny. They may have a vision—a glimpse of a picture to pursue that represents whom they want to become and what they want to accomplish in life. However, very few men are smart enough to ask for directions.

We need to be smart. We should read biographies of men who've paved the way for us. We need to seek out direction from those who are well ahead. We need to look for mentors who can speak into our lives about the warnings and pitfalls of the particular road we're on.

REMEMBER

The road less traveled is often not as smooth as we would like, but the view will be amazing.

READ PROVERBS CHAPTER 14

fivestarman.com/day-104

Day 105: Pious Posers

PROVERBS 15:8 (MSG)

God can't stand pious poses,
but he delights in genuine prayers.

PRINCIPLE

God does not entertain lies in our prayers.

Despite the popular notion to the contrary, men are overwhelmingly spiritual. In fact, nine out of ten say they believe in God; however, only two of six attend church.

Part of the disconnect is that, for the most part, men have an aversion toward church. I think men's distance from the church is primarily because most men have experienced or have the notion that the church is irrelevant, ineffective, or even irreverent. Yes, irreverent. Not because the church doesn't have its established religious liturgy, but because men have a natural antipathy for pious posing.

Men do not speak piously but practically. Men do not worship with liturgy, but in the language of the common man. Men relate to God in the daily commute.

The good news for us is that God delights in the genuine, as well. He values the practical prayer. He enjoys the daily commute with man. God is not moved by the hypocritical worship of men, nor is He entertained by sacrificial lip service. The prayers we speak, exhaled with true and genuine emotion from our hearts, are the fragrance of authentic manhood that God admires.

REMEMBER

God will take delight in your genuine prayers.

READ PROVERBS CHAPTER 15

fivestarman.com/day-105

Day 106: No Unsettled Claim

PROVERBS 16:7 (AMP)

When a man's ways please the Lord,
He makes even his enemies to be at peace with him.

PRINCIPLE

When you please the Lord, you're at peace with men.

Reading the stories of the kings of Israel is very similar to the drama of a reality show. God would graciously deliver the people out of trouble, for them only to follow the lead of a disobedient king. The king would erect symbols and memorials for other gods. The people would fall prostrate before idols and prostitute themselves spiritually. God's hand of favor and protection would withdraw. Enemies would rise up against the people and overcome and defeat them. The collateral damage would be massive. Then the people would cry out to God and ask why He had abandoned them.

Reading these stories from the cheap seats, we can be pretty hard on the examples of their failures; however, we need to be aware that the same cycle may be repeating itself in our own lives.

When we live to please the Lord, God makes our enemies to settle down and be at peace with us.

"It is God's will that your honorable lives should silence those ignorant people who make foolish accusations against you" (1 Peter 2:15 NLT).

REMEMBER

There are no unsettled claims against you.

READ PROVERBS CHAPTER 16

fivestarman.com/day-106

Day 107: Lies From Our Leaders

PROVERBS 17:7 (MSG)

We don't expect eloquence from fools,
nor do we expect lies from our leaders.

PRINCIPLE

Two things that we should not expect are eloquence from fools and lies from leaders.

In the 16th century, a political theorist, writer, and philosopher named Niccolo Machiavelli wrote, ***The Prince***, in which he analyzed and revealed many political strategies that are still in use today. The term, *Machiavellian* has become synonymous with political gaming, manipulation, and ruthless imperium. He taught leaders how to use mendacity (the artful use of double-speak) to persuade, embellish, or camouflage their actions to those who are under their leadership. Machiavelli's message is the complete opposite of the biblical concept of servant leadership. Amazingly, he wrote an entire chapter for those who are in leadership in the Church!

Governments are built upon trust. Citizenry is placed under the dominance of a leader, and their vulnerability is subject to his entrusted power.

Unfortunately, very few leaders have the balanced ego and humility to have mastery over themselves. Most succumb to paranoia, believing others are grasping for their rank. Some literally give themselves over to haunting psychoses (characterized by lost contact with reality, as evidenced by delusions, hallucinations, and disorganized speech and behavior). They become liars.

We should expect truth from our leaders. We should demand that liars be held accountable. It should be a criminal offense for a leader to purposefully and manipulatively lie to his followers.

REMEMBER

Expect more from leaders.

READ PROVERBS CHAPTER 17
fivestarman.com/day-107

Day 108: Don't Be Rude

PROVERBS 18:13 (MSG)

Answering before listening is both stupid and rude.

PRINCIPLE

Don't be stupid. Don't be rude.

A ***FivestarMan*** is gallant. *Gallant* is a remarkable word that describes the very core of character within an authentic man. One of the aspects of being gallant is having manners and courtesy.

We're living in a casual culture. "Casual Friday" has turned into casual *every* day. Casual conversation has turned into text-language. In this environment, a man who knows how to conduct himself and represents himself well in conversations will be a real standout.

When we're engaged in conversation, we need to be attentive, make eye contact, listen to others, and respond with appropriateness.

I recently met a man whom I had admired for years. He is a brilliant attorney who has written numerous books. As he and his wife approached a door, I paused to hold it open for them and to introduce myself. I complimented his work and thanked him for his books.

Unfortunately, his response was horribly rude. I have worked very hard to overcome a speech impediment from childhood. Most people would not notice. He not only noticed it, but mocked me. You can imagine the letdown of the high admiration I had for him—so disappointing.

My take away was to conduct an audit on myself and ask, "Have I acted rudely and stupidly toward people?" I want to treat others with the respect we all deserve.

REMEMBER

Don't be rude.

READ PROVERBS CHAPTER 18

fivestarman.com/day-108

Day 109: A Beautiful Wife

PROVERBS 19:14 (NIV)

Houses and wealth are inherited from parents,
but a prudent wife is from the Lord.

PRINCIPLE

The beauty of a wife surpasses all of God's gifts to men.

"So God created man in his own image, in the image of God created he him; male and female created he them" (Genesis 1:27 KJV). When God said, "It is not good for man to be alone," He surgically removed the feminine side of Man to fashion Woman. The male and female have perfect complementary designs.

"For this reason a man will leave his father and mother and shall become united and cleave to his wife, and they shall become one flesh. And the man and his wife were both naked and were not embarrassed or ashamed. . . ." (Genesis 2:24–25 AMP).

God gave many gifts to Man but none surpasses or can be compared to his greatest gift—the gift of a wife. She is Beauty.

Prudent, the Hebrew adjective that our advisor uses to modify the word wife describes the inner beauty that radiates from within her. It means *to have dignity, class, success, intelligence; to be attractive, reserved, understanding,* and *upright.*

"Husbands, in the same way be considerate as you live with your wives, and treat them with respect as the weaker partner and as heirs with you of the gracious gift of life, so that nothing will hinder your prayers" (1 Peter 3:7 NIV).

REMEMBER

A prudent, beautiful wife is from the Lord.

READ PROVERBS CHAPTER 19
fivestarman.com/day-109

Day 110: What Is A FivestarMan?

PROVERBS 20:5 (NIV)

The purposes of a man's heart are deep waters,
but a man of understanding will draw it out.

PRINCIPLE

When a man gains understanding of his purposes, his life becomes a passionate pursuit of authentic manhood.

The Hebrew word, *man,* in this verse is the word, "iysh," meaning *masculine; male, as opposed to a woman.* This word is a reservoir of understanding regarding Man. Words used to describe a man are *husband, manly-minded, valor, citizen, companion, champion, intelligent, nobility, and soldier,* to name a few.

If you'll recall, we categorize the definition of authentic manhood into five distinct purposes every man has within him. He has an adventurous spirit, an entrepreneurial drive, is gallant in relationships, is faithful in character, and is philanthropic in cause. The ***FivestarMan*** draws upon these purposes and expresses them by encouragement daily, engaging with other men weekly, taking excursions monthly, having a spiritual encounter quarterly, and accomplishing great exploits annually.

As we speak to the purposes of men, they cast off things that constrain them. In other words, when a man is engaged in a fight, he doesn't have time for trivial pursuits.

When purpose is unknown, abuse is inevitable. If a man doesn't have the right thing to fight for, he will find the wrong thing to fight against.

Proverbs 20:5 is the foundational scripture for ***FivestarMan***. We are building a movement of authentic manhood.

REMEMBER

Cast off the things that constrain you.

READ PROVERBS CHAPTER 20

fivestarman.com/day-110

Day 111: Be Sharp!

PROVERBS 21:5 (NIV)

The plans of the diligent lead to profit
as surely as haste leads to poverty.

PRINCIPLE

Success is where preparation meets opportunity.

Many men are running wild without restraint. They're scurrying about looking for the next opportunity. Others are in constant preparation mode. Always preparing, schooling, and training, they never seize the opportunity.

Many Israelites had prepared for war against the Philistines, but they didn't seize the opportunity to become heroic and defeat Goliath. David had prepared through his diligence so that when he faced an opportunity, he could take advantage of it. He had fought a lion and a bear so facing a giant warrior was the next step for him to take.

Make no mistake about it. David wasn't hasty. He was a well-calculated man and would only use weapons he had proven. When King Saul offered David his own armor, David refused because they were unfamiliar.

"If the ax is dull and its edge unsharpened, more strength is needed, but skill will bring success" (Ecclesiastes 10:10 NIV).

The word, *skill,* in this verse actually means *dexterity.* It means *able to use the hands gracefully, skillfully, and with precision; able to think quickly and cleverly.* That's what David was able to do with a sling, and when the opportunity came, he was ready.

REMEMBER

Be prepared for your next opportunity. Be sharp!

READ PROVERBS CHAPTER 21

fivestarman.com/day-111

Day 112: A Satisfying Life

PROVERBS 22:4 (MSG)

The payoff for meekness and Fear-of-God
is plenty and honor and a satisfying life.

PRINCIPLE

A satisfying and fulfilled life is the payoff of humility and respect toward God.

Men value profit. Men want to know, what is the payoff in the exchange? David asked the question before taking on the challenge to fight Goliath, "What will be done for the man?"

What does it profit a man who lives contrary to the culture—a man who lives to please God rather than self?

Jesus answered that very question this way, "But seek first his kingdom and his righteousness, and all these things will be given to you as well" (Matthew 6:33 NIV).

This is counter-cultural. The world seeks after material things that can be manufactured. It gathers all the wealth it can, hoping life will be satisfied, full, and secure. People who don't know God and the way He works fuss over *things*.

Our advisor tells us that the payoff for meekness and Fear-of-God is the kind of life everyone is chasing after. But we don't have to chase after it. Everything we need or desire is the byproduct of a lifestyle of believing in Him.

Let me be clear. Seeking God is not about the getting but about the relationship that we have with Him. All the things that satisfy, honor, and supply will come from that relationship.

REMEMBER

A satisfying and fulfilled life is the payoff.

READ PROVERBS CHAPTER 22

fivestarman.com/day-112

Day 113: You Make Me Want To Dance

PROVERBS 23:15–16 (MSG)

Dear child, if you become wise,
I'll be one happy parent.
My heart will dance and sing
to the tuneful truth you'll speak.

PRINCIPLE

The joy of parenting is seeing your children make wise decisions.

Raising children is a huge undertaking. It requires enormous commitment on the parents' part. Schedules are demanding. Energy levels are drained. The financial investment we make for children is equivalent to running a small business. In spite of all of the challenges, I must say that Kay and I enjoyed every stage of our children's lives, but this stage is the best thus far.

We're getting to see God's hand of favor and blessing upon our young adult children. Each of them is experiencing His guidance and intervention on their behalf. We see them making wise decisions regarding their lives.

There is no greater joy than seeing your children make smart decisions. It makes me want to dance and shout. Most of all, it makes me want to bow down and show my gratitude. It humbles me.

I want to encourage you. If you are presently raising children, remember, they will not always be little, demanding, costly, and immature. They will mature into smart, capable, self-sufficient, and wise adults. You're doing an excellent job. Keep it up!

REMEMBER

Your heart will dance, and you will sing over your children.

READ PROVERBS CHAPTER 23
fivestarman.com/day-113

Day 114: Check Your Manhood

PROVERBS 24:10 (MSG)

If you fall to pieces in a crisis,
there wasn't much to you in the first place.

PRINCIPLE

Don't fall to pieces during a crisis. Check your manhood!

"When written in Chinese, the word 'crisis' is composed of two characters. One represents danger, and the other represents opportunity." This quote is often attributed to John F. Kennedy, however, it can also be traced to anonymous journals from missionaries in China. Regardless of the source, the truth remains. When others see danger, men look for the opportunity crisis affords.

During the 70's, in reaction to the U.S. supporting Israel during the Yom Kippur War, OPEC embargoed oil shipments. While others saw the crisis and faltered, rationing supplies and closing stores, Tom Love changed his business model and expanded. Based out of Oklahoma, Love's Country Stores grew a loyalty brand that now exceeds $26 billion in annual revenue. The crisis exposed a great opportunity. Tom took advantage of it.

It takes a strong mental capacity and an even stronger faith to see crisis as opportunity, but that is why men lead. That's why we're given an entrepreneurial drive. We're strong when others falter.

One of the biggest mistakes men make is to wait for a crisis to be conditioned for it. We need to condition ourselves so, when crisis hits, we're prepared.

By the way, don't try to draw your strength from your wife and children. In times of crisis, draw your strength from God. Then turn and strengthen those following you.

REMEMBER

"Be strong and show yourself a man" (1 Kings 2:2 AMP).

READ PROVERBS CHAPTER 24

fivestarman.com/day-114

Day 115: Persistence

PROVERBS 25:15 (MSG)

Patient persistence pierces through indifference;
gentle speech breaks down rigid defenses.

PRINCIPLE

Energy and persistence can't be resisted.

Nothing of great value is ever achieved without facing violent opposition. If you're going to have something in life worth having, it will come at a price of persistence. Persistence is the quality that allows someone to continue doing something or trying to do something, even though it is difficult or opposed by other people.

Champions do daily what the average do occasionally. That's not just our byline. That's a mantra for those who understand persistence. It's the ability to go beyond what causes others to stop. It's the motivation to press through and not give up. It's the second wind of a hard run. It's the extra rep in the workout. It's making another sale before calling it the end of the day.

Persistence gets you through the pain and displeasure of resistance.

REMEMBER

The habit of persistence is the habit of victory.

READ PROVERBS CHAPTER 25
fivestarman.com/day-115

Day 116: The Incorrigible Fool

PROVERBS 26:11 (NIV)

As a dog returns to its vomit,
so fools repeat their folly.

PRINCIPLE

Fools repeat their folly.

Albert Einstein is attributed with coming up with the precise definition of insanity: "doing the same thing over and over again and expecting different results." That certainly applies to the simple-minded man who continues to repeat the same mistakes. A man actually only makes a mistake once because the second time that he does it, it was a conscious decision. As stupid as it might be, he repeats his stupidity.

Proverbs openly ridicules the man who is considered a fool. The Hebrew word for *fool* means *stupid fellow, dullard, simpleton,* and *arrogant one.* A fool is a guy who will not learn the lessons of life or apply wisdom to his decisions.

When I was a boy, I saw a dog eat its vomit. It was so disgusting that I would never forget it. As a teenager, I saw young people making the same mistakes over and over again. When I became an adult, I've seen grown men do the same wrong things repeatedly. And I hate to admit it, but there have been plenty of times that I've played the fool.

Our advisor is not sympathetic to fools. He paints a graphic picture of their folly. We need to learn to be corrected and not repeat stupid mistakes.

Peter refers to this proverb when referencing those who have returned to their life of sin after having tasted the freedom that comes to us in Christ (2 Peter 2:22). It is a disgusting proposition for a person to turn from all of the good that comes to us in the Gospel and go back to dine on the filth of sin.

REMEMBER

Don't be a fool.

READ PROVERBS CHAPTER 26

fivestarman.com/day-116

Day 117: The Kiss Of Betrayal

PROVERBS 27:6 (NIV)

Wounds from a friend can be trusted,
but an enemy multiplies kisses.

PRINCIPLE

Betrayal always comes from someone with enough proximity to kiss you.

It is a description of one of the most insidious moments in Scripture. During the Last Supper, Jesus dipped his bread and handed it to Judas. At that very moment, Satan entered Judas. Many people have been possessed by evil spirits, but very few have been possessed by the actual spirit of Satan. Judas hastily left the room.

When Judas returned to the disciples, they were in the garden. As he approached, Judas kissed Jesus' cheek. Think about that—Satan kissed the cheek of the Son of God!

Unfortunately, all of us have or will experience betrayal. It is always from someone you've trusted—from someone whom you have allowed access into your life—from someone with proximity to you.

REMEMBER

Someone you trust trusts someone you don't.

READ PROVERBS CHAPTER 27
fivestarman.com/day-117

Day 118: To Be Evil-Minded is Nonsense

PROVERBS 28:5 (MSG)

Justice makes no sense to the evil-minded;
those who seek God know it inside and out.

PRINCIPLE

To be evil-minded is nonsense. To seek God is sensible.

Man was created in the image and likeness of God; therefore, within man is a conscience—the seat of appetites, judgment, mind, memory, the seat of emotions, moral character, and the seat of courage. Conscience is the spark of our soul of the divine deposit which governs our actions.

"For that which is known about God is evident to them and made plain in their inner consciousness, because God [Himself] has shown it to them" (Romans 1:19 AMP).

When men consistently refuse the inner voice of their consciences, their hearts become hard and their necks become stiff. For example, during the generation of Noah, "every inclination of the thoughts of the human heart was only evil all the time" (Genesis 6:5 NIV).

That's why there is such a disconnect in our current culture. People are consistently rejecting the inner conscience and are becoming evil-minded. We're living in a time that righteousness doesn't make sense to them. They can't comprehend it.

But, the benefit of seeking God results in a clear and brighter conscience.

REMEMBER

Man is without excuse.

READ PROVERBS CHAPTER 28

fivestarman.com/day-118

Day 119: Directional Intent For Life

PROVERBS 29:18 (AMP)

Where there is no vision [no redemptive revelation of God], the people perish; but he who keeps the law [of God, which includes that of man]—blessed (happy, fortunate, and enviable) is he.

PRINCIPLE

Vision gives directional intent to your life.

Here are Ten Keys to Having Directional Intent:

1. What you keep looking at decides where you will go.
2. You will always move toward the most dominant image in your mind.
3. Proof of desire is pursuit.
4. Champions do daily what the average do occasionally.
5. Habits are the seeds of purpose sown daily.
6. Men decide their futures by the daily disciplines they've adopted.
7. What you do daily decides what you become permanently.
8. Your calendar and your checkbook reveal what you value most in life.
9. Read biographies of great men and adopt their daily disciplines.
10. You can rebound from failure within twenty-four hours simply by adopting a new habit and consistently practicing it for thirty days.

REMEMBER

Great men have great habits.

READ PROVERBS CHAPTER 29
fivestarman.com/day-119

Day 120: Office Politics

PROVERBS 30:10 (NIV)

Do not slander a servant to their master,
or they will curse you, and you will pay for it.

PRINCIPLE

Don't use malicious tactics and scheming against coworkers so that you can get a promotion.

As faithful men, we do not use tactics and scheming to get ahead. Our promotion comes from the practices of integrity, hard work, and getting results. Those who rely upon putting others down so that they look good to the boss end up losing everything, including their jobs.

"Servants, respectfully obey your earthly masters but always with an eye to obeying the real master, Christ. Don't just do what you have to do to get by, but work heartily, as Christ's servants doing what God wants you to do. And work with a smile on your face, always keeping in mind that no matter who happens to be giving the orders, you're really serving God. Good work will get you good pay from the Master. . . ." (Ephesians 6:5-8 MSG)

We don't just serve *under* a boss. We serve *through* the boss to Christ. Our confidence for promotion doesn't hinge on one person. We rely upon God for our promotions.

REMEMBER

When we serve another man's vision faithfully, we qualify ourselves for our own.

READ PROVERBS CHAPTER 30

fivestarman.com/day-120

Day 121: The More You Get, The Less You Are

PROVERBS 1:19 (NLT)

Such is the fate of all who are greedy for money;
it robs them of life.

PRINCIPLE

When you grab all you can get, that's what happens: the more you get, the less you are.

It's paradoxical—the more you get, the less you are. The more you gather and hoard, the less you keep. The more you give away and scatter, the more you will keep, and the more you will become.

The word, *greed,* means *to increase through violence, covetousness, to spoil, to divide.* A covetous person not only wants what another has, but he wants it at the expense of the other person.

One of the most disgusting and embarrassing moments in Scripture is when soldiers (grown men) cast lots to see who would take home the seamless garment Jesus wore. They were pathetic little scavengers—vultures without dignity (John 19:24; Psalm 22:18). That's the picture of those who want increase at the expense of others.

Authentic manhood has two purposes that work in harmony: the entrepreneurial drive gives a man the ability to gather, but the philanthropic cause provides the same man the responsibility to scatter. The entrepreneur uses his drive to meet the needs of his household, grant the desires of his family, and finance his purpose. It's not about what a man gets. It's about his cause.

REMEMBER

The more you crave, the less you are.

READ PROVERBS CHAPTER 1

fivestarman.com/day-121

Day 122: Celebrating Perversity

PROVERBS 2:12 (NIV)

Wisdom will save you from the ways of wicked men,
from men whose words are perverse.

PRINCIPLE

Wisdom will save you from the ways of the wicked.

The moral depreciation of our culture is nothing new. Other generations have experienced decadence and depravity. History is replete with examples of perversion taking over society. The insanity of it all is the repetition of societies that recycle the same old sins.

That's what is happening now.

A clear and distinguishing line is being drawn. There are those who hold to proven principles and lasting values. There are those who not only accept, but also celebrate perversity. They laugh at and mock morality.

Two of the passions of ***FivestarMan***—gallantry and faithfulness—will purposefully protect you from the ways of the wicked. Being gallant will protect your morality and make you courageous in the face of this cultural clash. Being faithful will keep you in the integrity of character and establish you.

Wisdom will establish you and keep you from being entrapped by the deception and perversion of evil.

REMEMBER

Wisdom will save you from the ways of the wicked.

READ PROVERBS CHAPTER 2

fivestarman.com/day-122

Day 123: Strong Mind, Strong Body

PROVERBS 3:8 (AMP)

It shall be health to your nerves and sinews,
and marrow and moistening to your bones.

PRINCIPLE

The Word of God penetrates the very cells of your body.

The Daily Champion is designed to encourage men daily. Remember, a man does not decide his future. He decides his habits which determine his future. We need to have the daily discipline to condition our bodies. We need to be physically fit to fulfill our purposes.

We need stamina to fulfill our purposes. We need to be smart about preparing ourselves for the long term. Seeking God, having a daily discipline of reading the Word of God, and seeking wisdom actually helps nourish our bodies.

"In Him [the Word] was life, and that life was the light of all mankind" (John 1:4 NIV, Author's Note).

The Word of God conditions man—the whole man—body, soul, and spirit. The Word is the seed of life. Therefore, the Word is nourishment.

Add the Word of God to your workout.

REMEMBER

The Word of God gives you a strong mind and a strong body.

READ PROVERBS CHAPTER 3

fivestarman.com/day-123

Day 124: Mentors Or Mistakes

PROVERBS 4:13

Hold on to instruction, do not let it go;
guard it well, for it is your life.

PRINCIPLE

You either gain wisdom through a mentor or by making mistakes.

We're living in unprecedented times. Throughout the history of man, we've never had a time when information has been more accessible than it is right now. We have portals that allow the average guy the ability to penetrate the deepest resources of information, simply from a computer or smartphone.

It wasn't that long ago that only the very wealthy were privileged to access vast amounts of data. The average man was too busy scrapping, working long hours and short nights just to make ends meet.

The real privilege is the amount of time we can save through our technology to gain wisdom and knowledge. We can easily access the greatest minds of history from our smartphones or laptops.

Our advisor tells us to get good advice and to hold on to it tightly. You either gain wisdom through a mentor or by making mistakes. Choose a mentor.

You don't have to know the mentor. You need to listen to what he has said or read what he has written. Let me give you some advice. If you ever have a meeting with your mentor, make sure you've read everything he has written, and don't waste his time by asking a question he has already taken the time to write the answer to. Don't be insulting.

REMEMBER

Choose a mentor.

READ PROVERBS CHAPTER 4

fivestarman.com/day-124

Day 125: God Placed Eternity In The Heart Of Man

PROVERBS 5:11–13 (MSG)

You don't want to end your life full of regrets,
nothing but sin and bones,
Saying, "Oh, why didn't I do what they told me?
Why did I reject a disciplined life?
Why didn't I listen to my mentors,
or take my teachers seriously?"

PRINCIPLE

Don't make decisions with eternal regret.

One of the passions of a ***FivestarMan*** is to leave a legacy with a philanthropic cause. Solomon said God has placed eternity in the heart of man (Ecclesiastes 3:11). We need to live with eternity in mind. We should make decisions based upon eternity. If we don't want to end life full of regrets, we will make decisions with a long-range-lens view.

Some men live with retirement in mind. They think of working fifty years and then finally getting to enjoy some of the fruit of their labor. I've talked with men who spent their entire working lives, striving and laboring to gather enough money so they could finally live a little.

I highly recommend that you shift your thinking. Think eternity. You're not working to live for retirement. Use your entrepreneurial drive to gather resources—enough to meet your needs, enough to grant the desires of your family, and enough to fulfill your purpose.

At the end of your days, you'll conduct an audit of your life. Will you be asking yourself regretful questions?

REMEMBER

As you're going through life, live it eternally minded.

READ PROVERBS CHAPTER 5
fivestarman.com/day-125

Day 126: Living By Principles

PROVERBS 6:22 (MSG)

Wherever you walk, they'll guide you;
whenever you rest, they'll guard you;
when you wake up, they'll tell you what's next.

PRINCIPLE

Principles are timeless.

One of the things I love about the book of Proverbs is how practical it is for everyday living. However, there is a helpful process that assures we have practical application in reading Proverbs daily.

Precepts are established foundational truths that are unchangeable, irrevocable, and eternal. When we read the Word of God, we need to interpret the principle that a precept has established. A principle gives us a clear understanding of the universal nature of the precept. Then, we can apply the principle and put it into practice.

The advice we receive is able to give us guidance. It will also protect us and give us a forecast and directional intent. Living by principles is wisdom.

REMEMBER

Living by principles is wisdom.

READ PROVERBS CHAPTER 6

fivestarman.com/day-126

Day 127: Dead Meat

PROVERBS 7:22–24 (NIV)

All at once he followed her
like an ox going to the slaughter,
like a deer stepping into a noose
till an arrow pierces his liver,
like a bird darting into a snare,
little knowing it will cost him his life.

PRINCIPLE

The Adulteress is a skilled hunter, and men are her game.

When will men understand that the Adulteress is not a friend, but a foe? She is a ruthless and skilled hunter who knows how to stalk her prey. She is patient. She is cunning. She knows how to set the trap.

The best defense is to understand the tactics of the hunter. It's important to keep our distance. Adultery is primarily an issue with proximity. We can avoid most of the issues and threats of adultery by keeping a safe zone.

Keys To Keep From Becoming Dead Meat:

- When a woman enters a room, bounce your eyes away from her. Don't gaze at her.
- Keep a respectful distance from women—at least two or three arms' lengths.
- If you're approached by a woman, take a step back to reinforce your distance.
- Most adulteresses will not approach a man who seems focused and busy.
- Never engage in flirtatious conversation.
- Don't even play with the idea that it's harmless to flirt. (I had a friend who lost everything—his wife, his job, the respect of his children, his reputation, etc.—because he allowed an email flirtation to develop into an affair.)

REMEMBER

Don't become a trophy on the wall of the adulteress.

READ PROVERBS CHAPTER 7

fivestarman.com/day-127

Day 128: Strong Men

PROVERBS 8:13 (AMP)

The reverent fear and worshipful awe of the Lord includes the hatred of evil;
Pride, arrogance, the evil way, and perverted and twisted speech I hate.

PRINCIPLE

You know a man by who his friends are, as well as, who his enemies are.

Have you noticed most people have a distorted concept of Christians? I'm referring to the idea that Christian men are some sort of milquetoast, weak-minded, soft-spoken people.

Promoting the idea that you can be a strong man and a Christian at the same time is one of the goals of ***FivestarMan***. We need to be bold enough to speak up and face the foe of our times—a perverted, twisted, arrogant evil that mocks Christ and all who follow Him.

It's a cowardly generation who will not fight the foe who will one day enslave their children. So, how do we do that?

We must be strong in the weapons of our warfare—strong enough to tear down strongholds.

"We demolish arguments and every pretension that sets itself up against the knowledge of God…" (2 Corinthians 10:5 NIV).

We need to know the Word of God. We need to be well versed in it, prepared to speak articulately when necessary. Stand up, put your shoulders back, and confront the culture with authentic manhood.

REMEMBER

Refuse to live beneath the dignity of the One who gave you life.

READ PROVERBS CHAPTER 8

fivestarman.com/day-128

Day 129: Mock Life And Life Will Mock You

PROVERBS 9:12 (AMP)

If you are wise, you are wise for yourself;
if you scorn, you alone will bear it and pay the penalty.

PRINCIPLE

Live wisely and wisdom will permeate your life. Mock life and life will mock you.

When you make wise decisions, you're the beneficiary of them. Wisdom is the ability to discern a matter, judge it by looking at the different angles, foreseeing the possibilities of a decision, and the application of that decision.

You also receive a payback if you're scornful. The word *scorn* means *to act with impudence, foolishly, or as a mocker.*

Let me explain. There are a lot of men who make decisions without thinking. They're flippant about life.

The good news or the bad news is that, either way, the person receives the payback from their decisions—the reward of either a life of wisdom or a life of foolishness.

REMEMBER

Don't mock yourself into ruin.

READ PROVERBS CHAPTER 9
fivestarman.com/day-129

Day 130: Words Matter

PROVERBS 10:11 (AMP)

The mouth of the righteous is a fountain of life,
but the mouth of the wicked conceals violence and evil.

PRINCIPLE

Words matter.

Have you noticed how important words are? Not too long ago someone released a recording of a private conversation of the billionaire owner of the NBA Clippers basketball team. He was suspended by the league because of the racially toxic words that he said. Ironically, the same week, he was to receive a lifetime achievement award from the NAACP. He opened his mouth and revealed a dark cave of abuse.

"A good man brings good things out of the good stored up in his heart, and an evil man brings evil things out of the evil stored up in his heart. For the mouth speaks what the heart is full of" (Luke 6:45 NIV).

The mouth exposes the heart of man. Literally, he is what he speaks. His character is the compilation of his thoughts. Those thoughts are expressed through his words.

REMEMBER

If any of your words matter, than all of your words matter.

READ PROVERBS CHAPTER 10

fivestarman.com/day-130

Day 131: Good Work Is A Virtue

PROVERBS 11:18 (MSG)

Bad work gets paid with a bad check;
good work gets solid pay.

PRINCIPLE

Good work is a virtue. It is the representation of a man.

God gave man a job before He gave man a wife. We have a purpose in business. A ***FivestarMan*** is entrepreneurial, which means God placed within a man the desire to meet his needs, grant the desires of his family, and to finance his purpose.

Our advisor encourages us not just to work to get by, but to do our work with excellence. You know what to expect from the average guy, but a champion exceeds all expectations.

"Work with a smile on your face, always keeping in mind that no matter who happens to be giving the orders, you're really serving God. Good work will get you good pay from the Master…" (Ephesians 6:7 MSG).

What kind of attitude and skill would we work with if we considered that we were working directly for the Master? That's how we should approach our work, regardless of whether we are working for ourselves or for someone else.

REMEMBER

Let's be honorable men and do a great job!

READ PROVERBS CHAPTER 11
fivestarman.com/day-131

Day 132: Chasing Fantasies

PROVERBS 12:11 (NLT)

A hard worker has plenty of food,
but a person who chases fantasies has no sense.

PRINCIPLE

A man who follows worthless pursuits is lacking in sense. He is without understanding.

God has given men an incredible gift—the ability to imagine, to have dreams, and to have visions. This gift is incredibly powerful when used for shaping and inspiring an idea. However, if this gift isn't connected to the purpose of authentic manhood, a man could easily begin chasing fantasies.

The current culture of young men is obsessed in playing fantasy games. Many of them have given up the field of contest for the comfort of the couch. They've degraded their adventurous spirit into a make-believe world. Their characters on screen are conditioned, swift, skilled, and agile; however, their reality is anything but the hero on screen.

God has bigger plans for you than sitting on the couch playing fantasy games. He is calling you to step out onto the field of contest.

REMEMBER

A man who is engaged in a fight doesn't have time for trivial pursuits.

READ PROVERBS CHAPTER 12

fivestarman.com/day-132

Day 133: Holy Frustration

PROVERBS 13:12 (NLT)

Hope deferred makes the heart sick,
but a dream fulfilled is a tree of life.

PRINCIPLE

What you've hoped for will come to pass and fulfill your dream.

The prophet Daniel was troubled in spirit, and the visions that flickered in his mind became disturbing. During a season of prayer, the angel Gabriel came to him in response to three weeks of fasting and prayer. Interestingly, Gabriel revealed insight to things that happen during our prayer time. For the three weeks Daniel had been praying, the prince of Persia (referring to a demonic principality) delayed Gabriel's coming and answering Daniel's prayer. (See Daniel 10:12-14.)

The Apostle Paul describes a "frustration" in our prayer time, when we don't know the answer to something we need to know. In such cases, the Holy Spirit helps us in our weakness and actually prays through us! (See Romans 8:26.)

I am reminded of this when at times I have been praying and expressing my faith yet have failed to receive an answer in a timely manner. This can be extremely frustrating, but it's also a time to remember that nothing of great value is ever achieved without facing violent opposition.

The word *deferred* means *to prolong, to drag,* or *to draw out.* Don't give up on what you've expressed your faith in and set your hope upon.

REMEMBER

Don't become weary in well doing.

READ PROVERBS CHAPTER 13

fivestarman.com/day-133

Day 134: Life Isn't Simple

PROVERBS 14:15 (NIV)

The simple believe anything,
but the prudent give thought to their steps.

PRINCIPLE

Life isn't simple. It takes careful thought and planning to live.

There's never been a time for more information to be at our fingertips (literally). However, unless you sift through the information, you're going to be duped into believing anything. There are people with an agenda that promotes false information, misinformation, and outright lies.

When I was young and naïve I trusted. Now that I'm older and wiser, I test.

We should be cautious when considering what we're willing to believe. We need to be prudent, sensible, skillful, and wise when considering information.

One day a salesman wanted to recruit me into a marketing strategy that promised financial independence and elaborate company rewards. To close the deal, he spoke disparagingly about a competitor, even saying that they have an alliance with Satan. He pointed to a picture of a mark on his competitor's product. Knowing that I am a Christian, he assumed I would take up the cause against this evil corporation.

I thanked him for sharing the opportunity and told him I would get back to him soon. After he left, I called his competitor and asked for their public relations department. I inquired about the emblem on their products and asked for the history behind it. After explaining the mark, I knew that the salesman had fed me misinformation and lies. Obviously, I declined the invitation to be involved with his marketing strategy.

REMEMBER

You cannot rise above your belief system.

READ PROVERBS CHAPTER 14

fivestarman.com/day-134

Day 135: Do Not Despise Discipline

PROVERBS 15:10 (MSG)

It's the school of hard knocks for those who leave God's path,
a dead-end street for those who hate God's rules.

PRINCIPLE

Discipline reveals legitimacy.

As one son said, "When I was eighteen years old, I thought my dad was an idiot. Now, that I'm twenty-five years old, it's amazing how much he has learned in the last seven years."

Discipline never seems pleasant when it's being delivered, but after, it produces good results and the person becomes grateful for it. Discipline also does something amazing. It gives a child a sense of belonging and legitimacy.

Let me add, the discipline I'm referring to is whole training and education (relating to the cultivation of the mind and moral values, and draws upon the purpose).

The very act of reading ***The Daily Champion*** demonstrates that you do not despise discipline. You're not satisfied with the school of hard knocks. You're not going down a dead-end street of life. You've yielded your will and desire to be brought up as a legitimate son of God!

REMEMBER

God is treating you as a true son.

READ PROVERBS CHAPTER 15

fivestarman.com/day-135

Day 136: The Lord Determines Our Steps

PROVERBS 16:9 (NLT)

We can make our plans,
but the Lord determines our steps.

PRINCIPLE

Man plans the way he wants to live, but God makes him able to live it.

Man is blessed with the capacity to think, plan, esteem, calculate, invent, judge, compute, count, and imagine. We can close our eyes and design a yard with our imaginations or construct a home and fill it with furnishings. After we create it in our minds, we can calculate the cost and judge whether or not we can afford it.

As good as it is to make plans, it's better when we align those plans with God's directional intent for His purposes.

"God's wisdom is something mysterious that goes into the interior of his purposes. You don't find it lying around on the surface.... The Spirit... dives into the depths of God and brings out what God planned all along" (1 Corinthians 2:7, 10 MSG).

God doesn't keep secrets *from* us, but He hides them *for* us. He holds them close so we will seek Him to find out those deep purposes.

Most of the secrets I've learned from God come in the night. Dreams and visions seem to be the language of the Spirit. So, don't waste another night just sleeping.

"I will praise the Lord, who counsels me; even at night my heart instructs me" (Psalm 16:7 NIV).

REMEMBER

Go to sleep with an expectancy to learn from the Spirit of God.

READ PROVERBS CHAPTER 16

fivestarman.com/day-136

Day 137: Take No Offense

PROVERBS 17:9 (MSG)

Overlook an offense and bond a friendship;
fasten on to a slight and—good-bye, friend!

PRINCIPLE

Repeating or harping on a matter separates even close friends.

Everyone has an opportunity to be offended. What should we do when someone offends us? The word picture for the Hebrew word *offense* is when someone places an obstacle in another's path to cause him or her to stumble or lose footing and fall. There are times when people purposefully maneuver and manipulate obstacles into our paths—in business, family matters, or even in spiritual matters.

When someone throws stones your way, turn them into building blocks for your next promotion!

Don't take offense. Overlook it and go on. Keep stepping up and moving forward in your purpose, and nothing will stop you.

"The stone which the builders rejected has become the cornerstone" (Mark 12:10 NKJV).

Jesus didn't take offense when others were picking up stones to throw at Him. He just kept walking toward His goal. He turned rejection into the cornerstone of His purpose. Imagine, some of the very ones who picked up stones to throw at Jesus became converts of His when He went to the cross. By His overlooking their offense, they became His friends.

You never know. Some who seem to hate you or have worked against you may someday become your friends.

REMEMBER

Take the stones and make them steps toward your next level.

READ PROVERBS CHAPTER 17

fivestarman.com/day-137

Day 138: Your Gift Makes Room For You

PROVERBS 18:16 (AMP)

A man's gift makes room for him and brings him before great men.

PRINCIPLE

You have a gift.

The entrepreneurial drive in a ***FivestarMan*** is a stream of purpose that must be drawn upon. It is a deep sense of financial purpose. There is no better way to fulfill this purpose than to draw upon the gift that is on deposit within you.

God placed within you a divine deposit that will enable you to meet the needs of your life, to supply the desires of your family, and to finance your purpose.

However, most men go their entire lives without truly discovering, sharpening, and exercising their gifts. I've noticed that men often discredit their gifts because they seem common or ordinary. They think because something is so easy for them, it must be common. They assume this without noticing most people can't do what they find so easy.

If you dig deep and draw upon the divine deposit, you will soon discover that the gift itself distinguishes you from your peers and begins to open doors, enlarge your influence, provide opportunities, and ushers you out of obscurity. The gift makes room for you.

REMEMBER

The gift makes room for you.

READ PROVERBS CHAPTER 18

fivestarman.com/day-138

Day 139: Lazy Bones

PROVERBS 19:15 (NIV)

Laziness brings on deep sleep,
and the shiftless go hungry.

PRINCIPLE

Laziness leads to purposelessness.

If you read the Bible, you will soon discover a disdain toward laziness. Our physical bodies are not designed for prolonged leisure.

My grandfather was a very strong man—a man's man. His strength didn't come from the gym, but from hard work at the glass factory. As a boy, I had him show me his biceps. They were huge! After he retired, I saw that very strong man sit down. He sat down in his LazyBoy recliner (one of the worst inventions every made) and grew increasingly tired and large. He hated what he morphed into in the last few years of his life. His weight gain caused his knees tremendous pain. He struggled to get out of his chair.

A few years ago, I saw a successful man take early retirement. He had enough money to live comfortably and leave an inheritance for his children. However, after he retired, he began to wander aimlessly. He became a busybody, meddling in other people's affairs.

We should live our lives in perpetual motion toward fulfilling our purpose. That's not to say that we shouldn't take days off. God ordered a day for rest, reflection, and recharging. But that's very different than shifting our energy down to a crawl and becoming lazy.

REMEMBER

Don't retire from your purpose.

READ PROVERBS CHAPTER 19

fivestarman.com/day-139

Day 140: Representing God To Our Children

PROVERBS 20:7 (MSG)

God-loyal people, living honest lives,
make it much easier for their children.

PRINCIPLE

Live in such a way that your children receive the byproduct of your life.

Recently a man approached me after I spoke on the topic of how God's blessings have generational impact. The man took exception to the idea that God is a good enough god for us to be blessed in the first place.

Attempting to make his case, misquoting Scripture and taking it out of context, completely misinformed on sound doctrine, I asked him questions regarding his understanding of God. Unfortunately, he did not know the character and nature of God. He simply had a couple of ideas that he was determined to drive home. When he saw I wasn't persuaded, he postured himself as if to hit me. My host pastor and an usher intervened. The pastor told me the man had caused issues in other churches before attending there.

I can't tell you how disappointing it was to see this man's anger and inappropriate behavior on full display in front of his wife and child. Sadly, his child will be influenced by his irrational behavior and bad theology.

The daily decisions we make—our understanding of God, and how we communicate His character—not only affects us, but also it affects the lives of our children.

REMEMBER

Make it easier for your children, represent God properly .

READ PROVERBS CHAPTER 20

fivestarman.com/day-140

Day 141: The Quarrelsome Wife

PROVERBS 21:9 (NIV)

Better to live on a corner of the roof
than share a house with a quarrelsome wife.

PRINCIPLE

A marriage is designed for completion, not for competition.

There are some marriage relationships that are more adversarial than they are adaptable. If a husband-wife relationship is quarrelsome, contentious, or filled with strife, that relationship is teetering on the brink of collapse.

The Bible speaks of a notorious woman who serves as the symbol of the worst kind of wife. Her name was Jezebel. She was an unchaste, tarnished, tacky woman. The name *Jezebel* means, *without cohabitation.* Even though she was married to Ahab, Jezebel remained single in her mind. She was a worthless whore who did evil in the eyes of God.

Unfortunately, there are men who find themselves in this kind of an adversarial relationship. These men are committed to Christ and are pursuing the deep purposes of a ***FivestarMan***; however, their wives are hindering everything they're working toward. They are unevenly yoked, carrying the entire load while their wives drag their feet. Their wives won't take their husbands' lead. In fact, they're striving against their husbands and want to lead them.

Our advisor sums it up perfectly. It is better to have a small corner on the deck of the home than to be inside the house, hearing a wife railing against everything.

REMEMBER

Some marriages lack cohabitation.

READ PROVERBS CHAPTER 21

fivestarman.com/day-141

Day 142: Directional Intent For Children

PROVERBS 22:6 (AMP)

Train up a child in the way he should go [teaching him to seek God's wisdom and will for his abilities and talents],
Even when he is old he will not depart from it.

PRINCIPLE

Give your children directional intent. As they mature, they'll know where to go.

When it was time for my first child to learn to drive, I became grateful for the infrastructure of curbs. Curbs are important. They narrow the road and keep you out of the ditch.

For every mile of road there are two miles of ditch.

It's important that children have curbs in their life. They need to know their boundaries. Many times children will venture off from you and look back as if to say, "Do you see me?" As they keep creating distance, they also keep looking back to see if you're still watching over them. They're waiting to see if you will snap your fingers and pull them back into proximity.

If a parent never establishes boundaries, children will keep going until they are outside of their parent's voice and watchful eye.

Parenting gives children a narrow road to travel. It gives directional intent. As children mature into young adults, those established roads will keep them on track so that they won't get lost.

REMEMBER

Give your children directional intent.

READ PROVERBS CHAPTER 22

fivestarman.com/day-142

Day 143: Don't Get Flush With Envy

PROVERBS 23:17 (NIV)

Do not let your heart envy sinners,
but always be zealous for the fear of the Lord.
There is surely a future hope for you,
and your hope will not be cut off.

PRINCIPLE

You always move toward what you're focused upon.

Sometimes it appears that sinners are living it up and enjoying life. If we're not careful we'll see a small portion of a person's life and think that things are really working for them. At times, it can be difficult not to envy those guys.

A picture of the word *envy* is the flush redness in the face after your emotions have boiled up. It's when you've seen someone with the things you want, and you become jealous and burn with zeal about it.

At the core of envy is a measure of unbelief. A person begins to judge others and wonder why God hasn't blessed them with the same measure of life and substance.

Our advisor tells us to stop looking at sinners and turn our emotional energy and desire toward the things of God. That's where our hope and future is. When you put your confidence in God, you won't find yourself worrying about what others have or how they got it.

Bounce your eyes away from others and focus on your hope of the future.

REMEMBER

You move in the direction of your focus.

READ PROVERBS CHAPTER 23
fivestarman.com/day-143

Day 144: Men Matter!

PROVERBS 24:11 (NIV)

Rescue those being led away to death;
hold back those staggering toward slaughter.

PRINCIPLE

Men matter!

On my way to catch a flight, a working man's truck passed me. Shortly after, a sheriff's car came speeding by and pulled behind the truck. Another police officer sped by to catch them. Then another. A few miles later, the truck came to a stop on the interstate. The police pulled strategically around the truck. I pulled far to the right to pass and turned to see the man stand outside his truck. He pulled up a pistol. The police fired from three angles.

That was the first time I had witnessed the killing of a man. It was haunting enough as a passerby. I can't imagine what the police officers experienced.

The news reports that evening told the back story. The man was facing tremendous financial pressure and succumbed to the temptation to rob a bank. An ill-conceived and hasty decision turned into the permanence of death.

Our advisor tells us to rescue those who are being led away to death. ***FivestarMan*** is more than a program. It's more than a cute little message and logo. We're a movement to raise the voice of authentic manhood. Why? Because men's lives are worth rescuing!

My emotions are responding to this purpose, even as I write this. Men matter! It's time that we stop playing silly little games. It's time to stand up, put our shoulders back, and speak to this culture!

REMEMBER

Men matter!

READ PROVERBS CHAPTER 24

fivestarman.com/day-144

Day 145: Respect Brings Intimacy

PROVERBS 25:17 (NIV)

Seldom set foot in your neighbor's house—
too much of you, and they will hate you.

PRINCIPLE

Every relationship is governed by a line between respect and familiarity.

Familiarity breeds contempt. Every relationship is governed by a line between respect and familiarity. If that line is crossed the relationship becomes contemptuous.

It can happen to the best of relationships—between family members, with dear friends, in marriages, and even in our relationship with God. When one person becomes familiar with another, they begin to treat each another as common, with disdain, or even fully venting anger or hatred.

A raised voice or derogatory comments are signs of familiarity. Put downs or dismissive gestures are also disrespectful.

You attract what you respect, and you repel what you disrespect. If you want to lose a relationship, allow yourself to become too familiar with another person.

What is interesting about this principle is the more respectful you are, the more intimate the relationship actually becomes. For example, as we show God the respect He deserves, we draw closer to Him. However, if we treat Him as common, He withdraws from us.

REMEMBER

The only remedy for familiarity is respectful distance.

READ PROVERBS CHAPTER 25
fivestarman.com/day-145

Day 146: Don't Be A Foolish Know-It-All

PROVERBS 26:12 (AMP)

Do you see a man wise in his own eyes and conceit? There is more hope for a [self-confident] fool than for him.

PRINCIPLE

The only one worse off than a fool is a know-it-all.

We're surrounded by the most narcissistic of all generations, those who look down their elitist noses and want to dictate their foolishness to everyone but themselves. They teach theories in our universities. They pass laws on the populace but exempt themselves. They've prophesied their apocalyptic doomsday scenarios. "It's the end of the world as we know it." That is unless, of course, we submit our freedoms and lifestyles to satisfy their demands.

"Although they claimed to be wise, they became fools" (Romans 1:22 NIV).

The problem for the know-it-alls is that they don't know what they don't know. They're worse than fools because they aren't just ignorant and simple-minded, their minds are perverted, warped, and delusional.

The funny thing about these so-called "smart" people is that they're playing right into the hand of God. Their wisdom is foolishness. Don't worry about these kinds of people. They will suffer from their own stupidity. Their perverted minds will turn on them.

REMEMBER

Don't be a foolish know-it-all.

READ PROVERBS CHAPTER 26

fivestarman.com/day-146

Day 147: The Seat Of Appetites

PROVERBS 27:7 (NLT)

A person who is full refuses honey,
but even bitter food tastes sweet to the hungry.

PRINCIPLE

You can't conquer the world without first denying your own appetite.

Isaac had twin sons: Esau who was born first and Jacob who grasped the heel of his brother. Esau was a man's man—an adventurer, hunter, athletic, rugged. The scent of the wild rested upon him. Most men would relate to Esau more than they would his younger brother Jacob—a tent dweller, domestic—a momma's boy. Esau was named, "Red." Jacob was named, "Deceiver."

Red was a strong man, but he had a weak will. He didn't consider longevity and legacy. Jacob bartered a cup of pottage for Red's birthright—the Patriarchal Blessing. Red couldn't see past the next meal. His appetite controlled him. Red's stomach became his god.

"Their destiny is destruction, their god is their stomach, and their glory is in their shame. Their mind is set on earthly things" (Philippians 3:19 NIV).

Within the heart of man is the "seat of appetites"—the core of what motivates him, moves his decisions, and decides his emotions.

Jesus revealed His mastery after fasting for forty days and nights in the wilderness, and Satan tempted him with a grand bargain. "Turn the rocks into loaves of bread." (See Matthew 4:1–4).

Jesus' response is classic, "Man shall not live on bread alone."

REMEMBER

You can't conquer the world without first denying your own appetite.

READ PROVERBS CHAPTER 27

fivestarman.com/day-147

Day 148: Who's In Charge?

PROVERBS 28:12 (MSG)

When good people are promoted, everything is great,
but when the bad are in charge, watch out!

PRINCIPLE

Unless you're faithful with what's another man's, you don't qualify for your own.

Sometimes the right people are promoted and put in positions of leadership that directly affect us, and we benefit greatly. However, there are other times when the wrong person is put in charge, and the consequences are horrible. What do you do when you're placed underneath a hostile leader?

David is an example of someone who served faithfully under a man like that. David's king was manic-depressive. Saul wasn't just unhealthy. He was demonically harassed and vented paranoia, trying multiple times to kill David.

David had opportunities to take his revenge on his king; however, he yielded to the instruction, "Do not touch my anointed ones; do my prophets no harm" (1 Chronicles 16:22, Psalm 105:15).

Interestingly, there is a principle for promotion that comes with serving faithfully under harsh leadership. When you show proper respect, not only to those who are kind, considerate, and reasonable, but also to those who are difficult, overbearing, unjust, and crooked, God will see the mistreatment and will bring promotion into your life.

How can you justify serving this kind of person and expect a promotion? Because you serve *through* leadership and not *around* it. As you serve through a hostile leader, you're serving the Lord Himself, and He will bring promotion into your life.

REMEMBER

Faithfulness rewards you.

READ PROVERBS CHAPTER 28

fivestarman.com/day-148

Day 149: Don't Make Flippant Vows

PROVERBS 29:20 (NIV)

Do you see someone who speaks in haste?
There is more hope for a fool than for them.

PRINCIPLE

Some men lack a boundary between their minds and tongues.

The Bible tells the story of Jephthah. He was a man's man—a mighty warrior. He was conditioned by the field of contest.

As Jephthah was preparing for a battle, he spoke in haste saying, "...Whatever comes out of the door of my house to meet me when I return in triumph from the Ammonites will be the Lord's and I will sacrifice it as a burnt offering" (Judges 11:31 NIV).

This was a flippant vow made from the adrenaline of preparing for battle. If he would have stopped to think, he certainly would have realized that anything coming out of the door of his house would be a family member. His daughter was the first one to come out of his home!

God was not pleased with this act of foolishness. God is not asking for child sacrifice. The only time God asked for this was with Abraham, concerning Isaac. Yet, Abraham declared God would be the provider of the sacrifice. God did give the sacrifice—His only begotten son, Jesus.

But God didn't make the promise in haste. The Bible says that before the foundation of the Earth the Lamb was slain (Revelation 13:8).

We need to be careful with our words.

REMEMBER

Never make a flippant vow while you are filled with spiritual excitement.

READ PROVERBS CHAPTER 29

fivestarman.com/day-149

Day 150: The First Command With A Promise

PROVERBS 30:11 (MSG)

Don't curse your father
or fail to bless your mother.

PRINCIPLE

The first command that comes with a corresponding promise is the honorable relationship of children with fathers and mothers.

The King James Version translates today's verse this way, "There is a generation that curseth their father, and doth not bless their mother." It speaks specifically to a generation that curses their parents. We're certainly living in a day that fulfills this—a generation that has disobeyed the first command with a promise.

"Honor your father and your mother, so that you may live long in the land the Lord your God is giving you" (Exodus 20:12 NIV).

What has caused this generation to turn in such dishonor toward their parents? It's revealed in the warning from the prophet Malachi, "See, I will send you the prophet Elijah before that great and dreadful day of the Lord comes. He will turn the hearts of the fathers to their children, and the hearts of the children to their fathers; or else I will come and strike the land with a curse" (Malachi 4:5 Author's Paraphrase).

Because fathers have abandoned their rightful place of honor, their children have responded with their own rejection. Their hearts have turned away. It's a protocol of honor. Unless the disastrous epidemic of dishonor is corrected, the land will be struck with a curse. The responsibility to correct this problem primarily relies upon fathers.

If fathers turn back toward their children, their children will respond appropriately.

REMEMBER

Fathers have a responsibility to lead in the protocol of honor.

READ PROVERBS CHAPTER 30

fivestarman.com/day-150

Day 151: Drunkenness Is Not For Kings!

PROVERBS 31:4–5 (NIV)

It is not for kings, Lemuel—
it is not for kings to drink wine,
not for rulers to crave beer,
lest they drink and forget what has been decreed,
and deprive all the oppressed of their rights.

PRINCIPLE

Drunkenness is not for kings.

The pet name Bathsheba gave her son Solomon was, *Lemuel,* which means *for God.* Her motherly teachings are now passed on to us, teachings that are designed for a king who is living for God.

These teaching are good for us as we press toward the mark of a higher calling of authentic manhood. We're not satisfied to remain average guys. We want to excel—to live to the ideal of authentic manhood—to be true ***FivestarMen***.

Today's instruction is for us to establish the boundary of our appetite concerning drinking wine and beer. We are to keep our wits about us and remain sober-minded as leaders. We have too many responsibilities to be exposed to drunkenness. Too many people are counting on us for us to lose our heads.

She goes on to say that wine and beer are best used as sedatives to dull the pains of life's despair and terminal condition. That's not us! We're leaders. We're men who are pursuing life at a higher level. We're authentic men.

REMEMBER

Keep your wits about you.

READ PROVERBS CHAPTER 31

fivestarman.com/day-151

Day 152: When Wisdom Calls, Answer the Phone

PROVERBS 1:24 (NLT)

I called you so often, but you wouldn't come.
I reached out to you, but you paid no attention.

PRINCIPLE

Wisdom is trying to reach you.

Some men have self-defeating habits of not responding to phone calls or emails. They're lazy when it comes to taking a moment and promptly responding to those who are attempting to connect with them. It is a demonstration of incredible arrogance. I believe it is breaking a fundamental principle based upon, "Love others as well as you love yourself" (Mark 12:31 MSG).

The manner in which you respond to those who call upon you is the manner in which God responds when you call upon Him.

When someone has reached out to us in any way, we should make it a priority to show respect by answering or returning their call as soon as possible. My goal is to respond within a few minutes or, at the latest, a few hours, even if my response is that a more detailed response may follow.

The Bible teaches that many have entertained angels without knowing it (Hebrews 13:2). Imagine—people called upon God in prayer, seeking His help, only to fail to show hospitality to the angels who were sent to deliver the answer to their prayers.

Wisdom is wanting to connect with you! The answer to all you need and desire in life is found in answering her call.

REMEMBER

Wisdom is trying to reach you. Answer the phone.

READ PROVERBS CHAPTER 1

fivestarman.com/day-152

Day 153: Romancing Spirits

PROVERBS 2:18 (NIV)

Surely her house leads down to death
and her paths to the spirits of the dead.

PRINCIPLE

The seductress is a spirit and she leads to death.

As you read ***The Daily Champion*** and the corresponding chapter in Proverbs, you find a few subjects become repetitious. It seems that adultery is one subject Solomon can't emphasize enough. It may be because he knew the story of his parents. The affair of David and Bathsheba continues to be an example of betrayal and serves as a warning of the collateral damage adultery causes.

It would be easy to write the story off as a bored man being attracted to a bathing woman. Most people just chalk up adultery to a demonstration of flesh overcoming morality. However, there's more. There's always something working behind the scenes instigating the affair.

There is a filthy spirit behind this temptation. It whispers in the ear, "You can have her. You want to gaze into her seductive eyes. You want to taste the honey upon her lips. You want to caress the softness of her skin. She is desire."

It's an insidious plot. It is demonic. A fallen spirit entices men into adultery. It's a romancing spirit. The seductress is a spirit, and it is evil. When a man is taking this path, he is romancing the spirits of death.

REMEMBER

Don't go to bed with filthy spirits.

READ PROVERBS CHAPTER 2
fivestarman.com/day-153

Day 154: Safe And Sound

PROVERBS 3:21-26 (MSG)

Dear friend, guard Clear Thinking and Common Sense with your life;
don't for a minute lose sight of them.
They'll keep your soul alive and well,
they'll keep you fit and attractive.
You'll travel safely,
you'll neither tire nor trip.
You'll take afternoon naps without a worry,
you'll enjoy a good night's sleep.
No need to panic over alarms or surprises,
or predictions that doomsday's just around the corner,
Because God will be right there with you;
he'll keep you safe and sound.

PRINCIPLE

God is with you, and you'll be safe and sound.

Have you ever watched videos of people doing the craziest things possible? Things that are certain to cause them pain? Stupid tricks turn out disastrous for them. Watching these people can cause your jaw to drop and your head to shake, as you exhale, "What were they thinking?" Actually, they weren't thinking clearly and don't practice common sense.

Clear thinking is vital to a good life. Common sense keeps us safe and sound. It gives us a base of knowledge and wisdom for living.

Look at the benefits of common sense. It will keep you alive and well, fit and attractive. You'll travel safely, have energy, take power naps, and at night you'll sleep soundly. If alarms go off, you won't panic. Doomsday scenarios won't cause you to dig a hole and hide. That's why it's important to keep reading Proverbs and becoming a champion.

REMEMBER

Sleep tight.

READ PROVERBS CHAPTER 3

fivestarman.com/day-154

Day 155: The Bread And Wine Of Violence

PROVERBS 4:16-17 (NIV)

For they cannot rest until they do evil;
they are robbed of sleep till they make someone stumble.
They eat the bread of wickedness
and drink the wine of violence.

PRINCIPLE

Some men have taken the communion elements of violence.

Jesus made an astonishing statement. "As were the days of Noah, so will be the coming of the Son of Man" (Matthew 24:37 AMP). How were the days of Noah?

There are many comparisons of the generation of Noah and this present generation. Most notably is the violence of mankind. Every inclination of the thoughts of men's hearts conceived wickedness.

In our culture, we're seeing the hearts of men turn toward wicked imaginations. Some men have purposed themselves to do evil. We have made violence a type of entertainment. Immature minds don't distinguish between the real and the imagined. They feed on the spilling of blood and become thirsty for flesh—the bread and wine of violence.

As fathers, we need to make sure our sons have a moral code of good versus evil. We should be certain they're not feeding upon the elements of violence such as video games that use role playing and fantasy arts that replace sound minds with delusions. Don't allow your son to become obsessed with gaming.

REMEMBER

God has bigger plans for your son than sitting on the couch playing fantasy games.

READ PROVERBS CHAPTER 4
fivestarman.com/day-155

Day 156: Don't Expose Yourself

PROVERBS 5:15-17 (NIV)

Drink water from your own cistern,
running water from your own well.
Should your springs overflow in the streets,
your streams of water in the public squares?
Let them be yours alone,
never to be shared with strangers.

PRINCIPLE

Don't expose yourselves to public disgrace.

This is an incredible use of a double entendre—saying one thing with the intention of being understood to convey a message that would be socially awkward, or even offensive, to state directly.

Solomon argues about the indignity and shame of what is meant to be a private matter that is exposed to publicly display. The indecent exposure referenced is concerning the life-seed of man flowing in the streets, not just water from a cistern. His suggestive advice is to not allow your stream to be shared with strangers.

This culture has lost all refinement regarding their private affairs—sexting, indecent photography, sexual suggestions, etc. They are exposing themselves to public disgrace.

Men, we're not dogs! We're not homeless animals roaming the streets looking for a hydrant to relieve ourselves. Don't expose yourself.

REMEMBER

Drink water from your own cistern.

READ PROVERBS CHAPTER 5

fivestarman.com/day-156

Day 157: Light Overcomes Darkness

PROVERBS 6:23 (NIV)

For this command is a lamp, this teaching is a light, and correction and instruction are the way to life.

PRINCIPLE

Darkness does not have the power to overcome light!

Historically, darkness is representative of the force of evil. It is tempting to conclude that darkness is an all-consuming force—that it is impossible to resist, but that isn't true. In fact, it is the opposite. Light overcomes darkness every time.

God demonstrated the power over darkness when He said, "Let there be light!" and there was light (Genesis 1:3 NIV). When He released His Word, Light overwhelmed dark matter. Jesus demonstrated that He was the Light that overcomes darkness when He came to the Earth as a man. "The light shines in the darkness, and the darkness has not overcome it" (John 1:5 NIV).

When we read the Word of God, we are shining a light into the dark matter of wrong thinking—doubt, fear, unbelief—and bringing correction to our way of life. Just as light penetrates darkness, the Word of God exposes the forces of evil.

As you're reading the Bible, receiving the instruction, correction, and reproving of the Word of God, you drive out the dark matter of evil and expose it for what it is.

REMEMBER

Light overcomes darkness.

READ PROVERBS CHAPTER 6

fivestarman.com/day-157

Day 158: Hell—The Chambers Of Death

PROVERBS 7:27 (NKJV)

Her house is the way to hell,
descending to the chambers of death.

PRINCIPLE

Hell is real. Don't go there.

Remember Albert Einstein's famous quote: "Insanity is doing the same thing over and over again and expecting different results." That pretty much sums up what Proverbs says about adultery. Men and women do it again and again, but they keep expecting different results.

Adultery is not something to trifle with. It is a damnable experience. We are so culturally callused by cheating that it hardly registers in our consciences as a moral deficiency. Unfortunately, our society is no longer repulsed by it. In fact, it has become our entertainment.

As I write this, I am aware that many men reading ***The Daily Champion*** have committed adultery. My intent is not to condemn but to challenge you to live up to the standard of authentic manhood. Frankly, I don't want you to experience the hellishness that you will go through committing adultery. Make no mistake about it. Adultery destroys authentic manhood.

You're better than that! I know you want the best in life, and you value your family and your relationship with God too much to be flippant with fooling around.

Solomon's life experience taught him the collateral damage of adultery. He knew that the path of adultery leads to the chambers of death and Hell.

REMEMBER

Don't go there!

READ PROVERBS CHAPTER 7

fivestarman.com/day-158

Day 159: Proof Of Desire Is Pursuit

PROVERBS 8:14 (AMP)

Counsel is mine, and sound wisdom:
I am understanding, power and strength are mine.

PRINCIPLE

You do not have the right to anything in your life that you are unwilling to pursue.

Solomon paid a heavy price for wisdom. He offered a thousand burnt offerings unto the Lord. The Lord offered to grant the desires of Solomon's heart. Because Solomon asked for wisdom, God granted everything else Solomon could have wanted.

Proverbs is the collection of wisdom Solomon passed on to us. Solomon spoke three thousand proverbs. He wrote one thousand and five songs. He mastered botany, ethology, zoology, and architectural design. He mastered finances and behavioral sciences. Here's how he summed everything up.

Four Steps into a Successful Life:

1. **Begin with counsel.** Counsel is the faculty of forming plans, an instrument to execute a purpose. It ensures success.
2. **Listen for sound wisdom.** As you listen to counselors, you must discern sound advice. Sound wisdom is described as *erecting* or *raising up*. Wisdom is edifying, and it builds you up.
3. **Gain understanding.** Understanding is the art of learning. It is a specialty skill and intellect comparable to comprehending a language others don't know and hearing and knowing the interpretation.
4. **Demonstrate strength in your decision.** Begin with gathering counsel. Gain wisdom and pull out what is sound and agreeable. Develop a specialty in the matter. Then you are strengthened to succeed.

REMEMBER

Wisdom is the principal thing.

READ PROVERBS CHAPTER 8

fivestarman.com/day-159

Day 160: Bad Wife—Bad Marriage

PROVERBS 9:13 (MSG)

Then there's this other woman, Madame Whore—
brazen, empty-headed, frivolous.

PRINCIPLE

Not every woman is representative of godliness.

Our objective at ***FivestarMan*** is to empower men who are so focused upon the original purposes of manhood that we earn respect and have an influential voice. The passions of manhood are so ordered that a wife should be the beneficiary of her relationship with a ***FivestarMan***.

Unfortunately, not every man is married to a woman who desires biblical manhood. Some wives are like Jezebel, who was a married woman without cohabitation. This kind of wife is foolish, a murmurer, and brazen. She is always in an uproar.

If you're married to this kind of woman, I am sorry. *(Know that I have prayed for you while writing this.)* I believe if you dedicate yourself to becoming the man God has purposed for you to be, you may redeem your marriage, but it will take time to sow the seeds of your words to produce a harvest that will be pleasing.

The Apostle Paul tells us the Church and Christ are similar to a marriage. At times the Church doesn't reflect well on the Groom; however, Jesus continues to sanctify us through His Word. It can be very frustrating to see the Church not acting in the way we should, but we are not without hope. Your marriage is not without hope, either.

REMEMBER

Be encouraged.

READ PROVERBS CHAPTER 9

fivestarman.com/day-160

Day 161: Quick-Draw Forgiveness

PROVERBS 10:12 (AMP)

Hatred stirs up contentions,
but love covers all transgressions.

PRINCIPLE

We are most like Christ when we cover sins.

When Jesus was being beaten, ridiculed, and crucified, He remained in control. While antipathy rallied against Him, He made this request, "Father, forgive them for they don't know what they do" (Luke 23:34).

An early follower of Jesus, Stephen, was persuasive in speech and demonstrated signs and wonders. Jealous leaders stirred up contention, and, during his hasty trial, haters began throwing stones. As he was being martyred, Stephen said, "Lord, do not hold this sin against them" (Acts 7:60).

Interestingly, a young man named Saul (who became Paul) was there. With his forgiveness, Stephen released this murderer (the most influential Apostle in Christianity) from his record.

This is the pinnacle of covering transgressions, yet we're often much quicker on the draw to lash out against anyone who shows us dislike. If anyone trespasses upon our rights, we want to straighten them out.

I will admit, I have been quick to let people know where they stand with me. I've never been accused of being patient. Sometimes my Oklahoma nature is to fight first, then ask questions.

But I've seen the wisdom of covering transgressions. Both Jesus and Stephen were in control of themselves during their deaths. When hatred moved people to kill them, they responded with forgiveness. They proved better than their adversaries.

REMEMBER

The one who forgives is in control.

➔ READ PROVERBS CHAPTER 10

fivestarman.com/day-161

Day 162: Pivotal Decisions

PROVERBS 11:19 (NLT)

Godly people find life;
evil people find death.

PRINCIPLE

It is in your moments of decision that your destiny is shaped.

It's a decision that you make. It almost sounds too simple. Choose life or choose death. "See, I have set before you today life and good, death and evil" (Deuteronomy 30:15 NKJV).

Most men don't plan to destroy their lives. They make destructive decisions at pivotal times that have severe consequences. I've found that the worst time to make destiny decisions is when you're tired. Tired eyes rarely have good focus. When you are tired, your decision-making ability is very limited and is often hasty.

Nine Reasons Not To Make Decisions When You're Tired:

1. Obstacles appear bigger than they really are.
2. Disappointments seem much heavier than they really are.
3. Your goals seem unattainable.
4. Your dreams seem to be fantasies.
5. Your relationships seem shallow.
6. Your words become careless and rash.
7. You're more sensitive to offense.
8. Your mind becomes cluttered with mistakes.
9. You can't distinguish the immediate from the distance.

REMEMBER

Don't allow others to force you into decisions when you're tired.

READ PROVERBS CHAPTER 11

fivestarman.com/day-162

Day 163: Man Is A Developer

PROVERBS 12:14 (NIV)

From the fruit of their lips people are filled with good things,
and the work of their hands brings them reward.

PRINCIPLE

Man is a developer and a cultivator by God's design.

God allowed the seeds of Eden to remain dormant until He created Adam to cultivate them (Genesis 2:5.) Only after He created Adam did God release the seed, shrubs, and plants to spring up. That tells us a lot about God's intention in man's design.

God gave man the employment of working the garden of Eden. Even before Adam had a wife, he had a job. The word translated as *work* in Genesis 2:15 is a Hebrew word that means *to labor* or *to dress.* The word translated as *take care of* means *to guard, preserve, protect,* and *celebrate.*

By God's design, man is a developer and cultivator. Deep within the desire of man is the appetite to improve whatever he touches.

A man cultivates his wife with his words. His words work just as seed works. A man sows a seed for a determined harvest. A man speaks words that will come to flourish in his wife.

The idea of cultivating your wife has amazing benefits in your life. You are not trying to make her something she is not. You are simply growing the deep seeds of greatness within her.

REMEMBER

It's a fantasy to expect a future marriage you haven't sown a seed to harvest.

READ PROVERBS CHAPTER 12
fivestarman.com/day-163

Day 164: Authority Speaks Through Leadership

PROVERBS 13:17 (NLT)

An unreliable messenger stumbles into trouble,
but a reliable messenger brings healing.

PRINCIPLE

Authority flows through leadership, not around it.

FivestarMan honors the protocol of authority. We call this "The Centurion Principle." It is foundational to understand how God speaks through leadership. It empowers men to understand their important position within the protocol. God places us *under* authority so that we can manage what He has placed us *over*.

When the centurion approached Jesus, he made a bold request on the behalf of a servant who was very sick. What caused Jesus to marvel at this man's faith was his keen understanding that the spoken words of Jesus carried the same authority that His physical presence would offer. This amazing insight distinguished the centurion above all others in Israel.

There is another lesson here to consider: It was vitally important for the messenger to reliably deliver the message.

The centurion said, "For I also am a man under authority, having soldiers under me. And I say to this one, 'Go' and he goes; and to another, 'Come,' and he comes; and to my servant, 'Do this,' and he does it" (Matthew 8:9 NKJV).

The Lord said to Jeremiah, "I am [actively] watching over my word to fulfill it" (Jeremiah 1:12 AMP).

Let's be faithful messengers and deliver God's Word with integrity.

REMEMBER

God places you *under* authority so you can manage what you are placed *over*.

READ PROVERBS CHAPTER 13

fivestarman.com/day-164

Day 165: Be Alert And Sober-Minded

PROVERBS 14:16 (MSG)

The wise watch their steps and avoid evil;
fools are headstrong and reckless.

PRINCIPLE

Men should be vigilant and sober-minded at all times.

Not long ago, I was in the airport in Santiago, Chile, preparing to board the plane for an all-night commute back to the States. Suddenly, the Earth was shaking under our feet. We were experiencing a 7.2-richter-scale earthquake. Interestingly, I surveyed my surroundings and found an open space near the exit door. It appeared to be a good place with nothing large overhead that could fall upon me. I moved toward that area and remained alert. Soon the excitement was over.

Have you noticed that there are a lot of men who seem to be going through the motions? They're meandering through life. Some men are acting as if life is a permanent vacation—that is until something begins to shake things up.

Wise men are very careful to observe their surroundings at all times. When they walk into a room, they scan the room, looking for the exits, calculating the risks within the room. The wise man who is driving is constantly scoping out the roads, looking for hazards, and carefully observing other drivers.

As men, we need to be alert. We need to be fully present in our surroundings. We should carefully study the options of whatever a situation may demand.

REMEMBER

Be alert and sober minded.

READ PROVERBS CHAPTER 14
fivestarman.com/day-165

Day 166: Hell Holds No Secrets

PROVERBS 15:11 (MSG)

Even hell holds no secrets from God—
do you think he can't read human hearts?

PRINCIPLE

God is omniscient, knowing all and seeing all. He knows the heart of man.

God, our Creator, is omniscient. He is all-knowing and infinite in knowledge. There are no secrets that can be held from Him. Our advisor says that even Sheol and Abaddon (Hell) are completely exposed to God. God has the ability to know the thoughts that lie within the hearts of all men.

The heart of man is the seat of his appetites and the seat of his purposes. The character of a man lies within his heart. God knows it all: your appetites, passions, and character. God examines your ways. It's "The Closet Principle." What you do in secret is what moves you in public. The secrets of your heart will be revealed.

God also knows the evil inclinations of men's hearts. He examined the hearts of men during the generation of Noah and found that they were inclined to evil. So much evil (and this is an astonishing statement) that God actually grieved and felt emotional pain for creating man.

As God surveyed the hearts of men, He discovered the inner thoughts and intents of Noah, and Noah found His favor.

God knows the depths and secrets of your heart, and, yet, He still loves you! He still believes in you.

REMEMBER

There are no secrets.

READ PROVERBS CHAPTER 15

fivestarman.com/day-166

Day 167: Legitimate Leaders Do Not Exploit

PROVERBS 16:10 (MSG)

A good leader motivates,
doesn't mislead, doesn't exploit.

PRINCIPLE

Legitimate authority does not exploit followers.

Jesus' call to action was, "Follow me and I will make you…" (Mark 1:17 NKJV). As a great leader of men, Jesus practiced "The Law of Mutual Benefit." When men left everything they had, surrendering their lives and futures for the cause of Christ, they did so without knowing or forecasting exactly what they would receive out of it. However, Jesus would not exploit those who followed Him.

In fact, you see this played out in a young, wealthy man who desired to follow Jesus, but became unwilling to do so when Jesus challenged him. This young man assumed he would be exploited if he followed Jesus. Upon his rejection and departure, the other disciples responded, "Jesus, we left everything to follow you."

Jesus' response to this statement is vital to understand His leadership, "I assure you that everyone who has given up house or brothers or sisters or mother or father or children or property, for my sake and for the Good News, will receive now in return a hundred times as many houses, brothers, sisters, mothers, children, and property…" (Mark 10:29–30 NLT).

Jesus will not exploit you when you choose to follow Him. A legitimate authority does not exploit followers.

REMEMBER

Good leaders do not exploit followers.

READ PROVERBS CHAPTER 16

fivestarman.com/day-167

Day 168: Friends And Mentors

PROVERBS 17:10 (NLT)

A single rebuke does more for a person of understanding
than a hundred lashes on the back of a fool.

PRINCIPLE

If you want sympathy, go to a friend. If you want solutions, go to a mentor.

As difficult as it can be, receiving a reprimand can be a gift of tremendous value. The word *rebuke* means *to restrain* or *resist*. The word picture for a rebuke is that of a barrier restraining the sea from its advances out of its boundaries.

As adventurous and entrepreneurial men, we must have people in our lives who are willing and able to rebuke our advances and help protect our boundaries. Men who can teach us restraint.

The challenge for us is to receive a rebuke correctly and from the right person. This kind of rebuke is more accurately given by a father, a seasoned mentor, or from the Word of God. Very few peers have the ability, knowledge, or wisdom to censure us correctly.

There is an idea in men's ministry circles that suggests, "We need people who will hold us accountable." I understand what they're saying; however, I also know that every man who ever asked me to hold him accountable stopped talking to me.

Your accountability should be established in the proper protocol of authority ("The Centurion Principle"). Enlisting a friend to hold you accountable will soon cause a rift in your friendship.

REMEMBER

Friends are for sympathy. Mentors are for solutions.

READ PROVERBS CHAPTER 17

fivestarman.com/day-168

Day 169: The Naïve Trust. The Wise Test.

PROVERBS 18:17 (NIV)

In a lawsuit the first to speak seems right,
until someone comes forward and cross-examines.

PRINCIPLE

When I was young and naïve, I trusted people; when I matured and gained wisdom, I tested them.

There's an old show from the 1960's called, ***Perry Mason***. A defense attorney, Perry Mason, used his skills as a cross-examiner to turn the tables on witnesses during trials. Mason was so skillful that the witness would usually confess his guilt openly in court.

When we hear a story, we should be very careful and not jump to conclusions until we test the account with other factors.

Not long ago an acquaintance approached me privately. He looked me in the eyes and confessed, "I made a horrible mistake by prejudging you. Someone said something and painted a picture about you that I believed. They did so for their own advantage. I was wrong. Please forgive me."

I knew the situation that he was confessing. Interestingly enough, the lie he believed didn't affect me as much as it affected him. He was the one who suffered loss in the situation.

A few years ago, a man I had admired and worked for was told an untruth about me. He jumped to a conclusion without asking me about it. He believed a lie that severed our relationship.

Believing a lie is a dangerous thing. Once you believe a lie, other lies become easier to accept, and your thinking becomes darkened.

REMEMBER

Be wise and cross-examine a story to discover the truth.

READ PROVERBS CHAPTER 18

fivestarman.com/day-169

Day 170: Don't Reward Temper Tantrums

PROVERBS 19:19 (MSG)

Let angry people endure the backlash of their own anger;
if you try to make it better, you'll only make it worse.

PRINCIPLE

If you reward temper tantrums, you will have to do it repeatedly.

We've all seen the emotional outburst of a child in the checkout line, screaming and kicking about, only to see the embarrassed parent appease the brattish behavior with a toy or candy. That child knows exactly how to behave to get his way.

Unfortunately, those children grow into adults who continue to throw temper tantrums to get their way in life. In a marriage, a wife pouts to manipulate her husband. When he gives in to her manipulation, she will use it again and again. On the job, the young and immature boss throws tantrums to get his way, always on the edge, on the tipping point of embarrassingly childish behavior. Rather than instruction and inspiration, this kind of immaturity uses intimidating tactics.

My wife and I had an agreement when it came to this in our children, and it was simple: We did not reward emotional outbursts of immaturity or bad behavior.

My goal was to teach my children that it is much better to live under my blessing than to live outside of it.

REMEMBER

Don't be manipulated into rewarding temper tantrums.

READ PROVERBS CHAPTER 19

fivestarman.com/day-170

Day 171: The Enemy Called Average

PROVERBS 20:8 (MSG)

Leaders who know their business and care
keep a sharp eye out for the shoddy and cheap.

PRINCIPLE

Nothing destroys a business faster than being average.

My friend John Mason wrote a bestseller called, ***The Enemy Called Average.*** Average is an enemy that is often underestimated because of its creeping ability. When people or businesses allow average to become their standard, they may not notice it at first, but they will soon see its eroding effect.

Not long ago, I stood in the checkout line of Walmart. The cashier was working like a robot. She never made eye contact, never greeted me, didn't ask if I needed anything. She simply ran my purchases over the scanner and waited for me to swipe my card to move on. I stood there awaiting her discovery of me. When she finally realized I hadn't paid for my purchases, she looked at me to find my half smile awaiting a proper greeting.

She gave me a half-hearted apology. I asked her, "Have you ever read the book ***Made in America*** by Sam Walton?"

Amazingly, she said, "No, never heard of it."

I've met executives at Walmart. I know that they would be appalled at my experience. Walmart is a true "American Dream" story. They have revolutionized the retail and merchandising industry. However, if they do not get a handle on their associates' acceptance of average, even Walmart will crumble into cultural oblivion.

REMEMBER

You're better than average. Make sure you represent your business above the norm.

READ PROVERBS CHAPTER 20
fivestarman.com/day-171

Day 172: Unanswered Prayers

PROVERBS 21:13 (MSG)

If you stop your ears to the cries of the poor,
your cries will go unheard, unanswered.

PRINCIPLE

The manner in which you respond when someone is in need determines how God responds when you are in need.

As I was driving, my prayers were spontaneously being spoken out loud. The church I pastored at the time was facing a substantial financial need. As soon as my prayer was offered, I looked ahead at the intersection to see a man with a sign that read, "Out of work. Family needs food. God bless."

At that moment, I felt prompted within my spirit to give to that man in need. As I looked in my billfold, I only had a $100 bill. I have to admit that I was hesitant. I considered the amount. It was large to my estimation. The light had changed, and I only had a moment to decide. I immediately grabbed the hundred, rolled down the window, and offered it to the man.

Within minutes, I received a phone call telling me that a large offering had been made that met the church's need. As I meditated on the circumstances, I felt confident that these two situations were, in fact, connected.

Anytime I've asked God to meet a need in my life, God has shown me someone for whom I had the resources to meet a need in their life.

REMEMBER

Don't ignore the cries of the poor.

READ PROVERBS CHAPTER 21

fivestarman.com/day-172

Day 173: The Burden Of Debt

PROVERBS 22:7 (NIV)

The rich rule over the poor,
and the borrower is slave to the lender.

PRINCIPLE

Debt brings a staggering burden of responsibility upon the borrower.

After their father died, two men faced enslavement until the prophet Elisha told their mother to acquire as many pots as she could. He told her to take the jar of oil she had and start pouring it into the pots. After she had filled every vessel, the prophet instructed her, "Go, sell the oil and pay your debts. You and your sons can live on what is left." (See 2 Kings 4:1-7.)

I understand that this was a miracle, but there are principles we can draw from as it relates to becoming debt free.

- The key to your debt freedom is within your reach. Something you presently have can become a miracle product.
- She involved her sons. When a family faces a crisis, everyone should face the challenge together.
- He told her to borrow pots for her new industry. Connections with friends or family can help you with a miracle.
- He told her not to ask for "just a few." Lack can make you small minded.
- She closed the door. You may have to isolate yourself to get work done.
- When you have a miracle of supply, get busy and sell.
- "The Law of Exchange" takes what you have that others need so you can have what you need.
- Pay off your debts first before you live it up.

REMEMBER

When you're debt free, you are a master not a slave.

READ PROVERBS CHAPTER 22

fivestarman.com/day-173

Day 174: Protect Your Legacy

PROVERBS 23:20–21 (NIV)

Do not join those who drink too much wine
or gorge themselves on meat,
for drunkards and gluttons become poor,
and drowsiness clothes them in rags

PRINCIPLE

A man who cannot control his desire will never leave a legacy.

It is an amazingly blunt statement. "But Esau I have hated, and I have turned his hill country into a wasteland and left his inheritance to the desert jackals" (Malachi 1:3 NIV).

What was the object of God's wrath toward Esau? Esau couldn't control his appetite. Esau didn't value the blessing his father would give him. He didn't think beyond his next meal; therefore, his heritage became a wasteland.

Another example of a man who forfeited his legacy was Samson. Samson was an incredibly strong man with an equally destructive appetite. He was given an unusual assignment at birth. God instructed his parents to raise him as a Nazarite—a man in covenant with God that required obedience by not touching anything dead, not drinking wine, and not allowing a razor to cut his hair. Samson was flippant toward his covenant. He withdrew a honeycomb from within a lion's carcass; thus, breaking his promise. Being weak-minded toward his covenant also caused Samson to be weak-willed toward women.

If we're going to leave a legacy, we must protect it from our own weaknesses and appetites. You will never protect your legacy, if you can't control your appetite.

REMEMBER

Don't allow temporary hunger to cost you a lifelong legacy.

READ PROVERBS CHAPTER 23
fivestarman.com/day-174

Day 175: Get Your Fight Back!

PROVERBS 24:16 (AMP)

For a righteous man falls seven times and rises again,
but the wicked are overthrown by calamity.

PRINCIPLE

You can't keep a good man down.

In the movie, ***Rocky***, the underdog boxer was given a cursory fight with the champion, Apollo Creed. Rocky was poor, clumsy, and simple—but there was something within him that craved more. The fight would give him more than a different lifestyle. It would give him a different life.

During the fight, the champ was going to allow the upstart to take a fall after a few rounds to make a good show. Rocky had something else in mind. Every time Apollo Creed knocked him down, Rocky struggled to his feet. Both men were bruised and battered by the end of the fight, but Rocky never took the fall.

That's the kind of drive we should have. "OK, you're going to get a few licks in, but I'm going to keep coming back until you are so tired you can't hit me anymore. Then, I'm going to beat you."

Job was an incredible man. He was so distinguished that Satan took note of him to accuse him and attack everything he held dear. Job was attacked multiple times, yet kept his integrity. "He shall deliver you from six troubles. Yes, in seven no evil shall touch you" (Job 5:19 NKJV).

You may have been facing some tough times lately. You've been knocked down a few times. Get your fight back!

REMEMBER

You're not down for the count.

READ PROVERBS CHAPTER 24

fivestarman.com/day-175

Day 176: Unreliable People

PROVERBS 25:19 (NLT)

Putting confidence in an unreliable person in times of trouble
is like chewing with a broken tooth or walking on a lame foot.

PRINCIPLE

In times of stress, you need confidence.

A while ago I injured my foot during a CrossFit routine. As much as I wanted to keep going and continue my workout, I couldn't. It took months to heal. My steps became unstable due to the pain that shot up my leg.

When you're facing the challenges of life, you need to have stability. You want to be sure-footed. You want to know that your footing will give you the support you need to resist the challenge.

Our advisor likens us putting our confidence in irresponsible people to walking on a lame foot. That's a great analogy.

Several years ago, I went through a very difficult time. I was amazed at how people I had helped, supported, even some I employed, scattered at the first sign of trouble. I weathered the storm and came through it with my integrity intact; however, I also made a list of people who proved to be unreliable during times of crisis.

Since then, I have had several friends face challenges. I have made it a point to step up my help for them, making phone calls, writing notes, and even sending money. I want to prove myself reliable.

REMEMBER

Don't put your confidence in unreliable people.

READ PROVERBS CHAPTER 25

fivestarman.com/day-176

Day 177: Adventure Vs. Monotony

PROVERBS 26:13 (NLT)

The lazy person claims, "There's a lion on the road!
Yes, I'm sure there's a lion out there!"

PRINCIPLE

Adventure may hurt, but monotony will kill you.

The greatest temptation in a man's life is comfort.

My grandfather was a strong man. His strength came from the factory not the gym. He was hardened. But I watched my grandfather morph into a bored, apathetic man in retirement. His hardened body became soft and flabby.

Recently I had a conversation with a young entrepreneur who was discussing plans for the future. He was considering leaving an employment because his boss wasn't engaged in the business anymore. He seemed to have checked out. He became bored. I suggested to the young man that he never make plans for the future with someone who doesn't have plans.

King David won every battle he fought on the field of contest. In one particular battle, he was almost killed. Counselors advised David never to enter the field again. They said he was much too valuable to engage in a fight. I would suggest that King David was much too valuable to *not* have engaged on the field of contest.

The only battle King David lost was on the balcony of boredom.

Don't allow yourself to become bored—not on the job—not in marriage—not in your walk with God. Boredom kills.

REMEMBER

Take the risk. Get back out on the field of contest.

READ PROVERBS CHAPTER 26

fivestarman.com/day-177

Day 178: A Man Who Strays

PROVERBS 27:8 (AMP)

Like a bird that wanders from her nest,
so is a man who strays from his home.

PRINCIPLE

You will never hold onto what you're ungrateful for.

A good friend of mine seemed to have it all—his dream job, a beautiful wife, healthy and growing kids who admired him greatly, and, yet, he lost it all by straying from his home. It made me wonder, "Why would he give it all up?"

Men, we have to understand what we're doing here on Earth. We have purposes to live out. We're designed by God to take care of our families. It's our responsibility and part of being an authentic man.

I believe one of the reasons men stray from their homes is that they're not grateful for what they have. They take it all for granted and fail to give thanks. It's easy to compare ourselves with those who have more, rather than to show humility by recognizing all who have less.

Did you know that if you make $33,000 per year, you are in the top one percent of income earners globally? That's right. Ninety-nine percent of the world makes less than you do. Check out how rich you are at the Global Rich List (globalrichlist.com).

We're afforded so much opportunity. We need to take advantage of our potential to meet our household needs, grant the desires of our families, and finance our purposes. A little humility and gratitude for this privileged position in life will help keep you at home.

REMEMBER

Look around your home, and show a little gratitude.

READ PROVERBS CHAPTER 27

fivestarman.com/day-178

Day 179: Leadership Abuse

PROVERBS 28:16 (MSG)

Among leaders who lack insight, abuse abound,
but for one who hates corruption, the future is bright.

PRINCIPLE

Never underestimate the destructive power of ignorant leaders.

Where are the leaders? We're facing a real crisis of leadership in politics, business, church, communities, and in the home. Greed, timidity, aimlessness, narcissism, and corruption are rampant among the current collection of leaders.

"Where the purpose is unknown, abuse is inevitable." —Myles Munroe

If a man doesn't understand his purpose as a leader, those under his responsibility will suffer abuse.

For many years, I consulted churches, non-profits, and businesses on leadership and principles for increase. I can't tell you how many scenarios I found where the leadership simply didn't know their purpose. The collateral damage of these men was horrendous.

Unfortunately, we have too many leaders who have their own agendas and ideologies, rather than doing what is best for the people they're responsible for leading. However, for those leaders who know how to lead and hate the corruption of their purpose, the future is bright.

We have a responsibility as authentic men to be leaders who know our purpose as leaders so that we do not abuse those under our responsibility.

REMEMBER

Know what a leader is and does.

READ PROVERBS CHAPTER 28
fivestarman.com/day-179

Day 180: Testing Before Honor

PROVERBS 29:21 (AMP)

He who pampers his servant from childhood will have him expecting the rights of a son afterward.

PRINCIPLE

Mature leaders test before they promote.

I've been in the position of a leader for many years, and one of the mistakes that I've habitually made is to treat my employees too generously before they deserved it. My mistake wasn't that I was too kind, but that I elevated them beyond their proven faithfulness. I often would speak highly of them to others. Interestingly, we have a warning about this in a letter from Paul to his young protégé, Timothy.

"He must not be a recent convert, or he may become conceited and fall under the same judgment as the devil" (1 Timothy 3:6 NIV).

Paul warns that this kind of conceit will lead to the same sin as the devil. That's a frightening scenario.

Unfortunately, I have seen this repeatedly. Young men have been elevated beyond their proven ability.

I've learned that in my naïveté, I actually hurt my protégés by puffing them up, promoting them before their time. I shouldn't have done it. It was poor leadership on my part.

We need to be very careful not to pamper those who serve us, and prepare them for greater promotion in their life.

REMEMBER

Test before you promote.

READ PROVERBS CHAPTER 29

fivestarman.com/day-180

Day 181: Be Gallant

PROVERBS 30:12 (MSG)

Don't imagine yourself to be quite presentable
when you haven't had a bath in weeks.

PRINCIPLE

Don't be haughty and arrogant in your self-estimation.

A ***FivestarMan*** is gallant. To be gallant means being fashionably groomed and appropriate for every occasion. That means that we are to be presentable. We should make an effort to be appropriately dressed.

To be appropriately dressed means that we do not dress to be a distraction at an occasion and to draw attention to ourselves. We're simply appropriate. As authentic men, we should dress to demonstrate some dignity to represent our manhood well.

As I travel to speak to men each week, I must work ahead to determine what the appropriate attire is. For example, if I am speaking at a church, I have to check to see what they're wearing. In some churches the men wear suits and ties, while in others, jeans and untucked shirts are the norm. If I get it wrong, I'm inappropriate for the service and will actually cause a distraction. It would be just as inappropriate to overdress as it would be to underdress.

Another area where we need to be observant is in our grooming. Old style barbershops are making a resurgence. There is nothing that compares with a good shave and trim from a real craftsman.

Let's step up our game in our dress and personal hygiene.

REMEMBER

Represent yourself and manhood with class.

READ PROVERBS CHAPTER 30

fivestarman.com/day-181

Day 182: The Laugh Is On You

PROVERBS 1:26 (MSG)

Since you laugh at my counsel
and make a joke of my advice,
How can I take you seriously?
I'll turn the tables and joke about your troubles!

PRINCIPLE

The tables are turned when you laugh at Wisdom.

Have you ever heard someone laugh at the most inappropriate time?

It's a shocking turnaround when trouble strikes us because of our total disregard for Wisdom's warnings, and the laugh is on us.

Some men are completely oblivious to the precepts and principles of Scripture. They disregard sound advice. They don't accept rebukes. They thumb their noses against Wisdom's warnings.

When a man mocks (mimics in derision) and laughs at these warnings, Wisdom turns the tables around and allows their mockery to boomerang upon them.

When you're in trouble, life takes on a serious tone. You don't want people to be jovial around you. It's like laughing at a funeral. It's inappropriate. So it is with being trivial when Wisdom is speaking to you.

REMEMBER

The precepts and principles of Wisdom are no laughing matter.

READ PROVERBS CHAPTER 1

fivestarman.com/day-182

Day 183: Good Company

PROVERBS 2:20 (MSG)

So—join the company of good men and women,
keep your feet on the tried-and-true paths.

PRINCIPLE

If our steps are ordered of the Lord, so are our relationships.

Relationships have residue. In other words, the people with whom we associate rub off on us. You've heard the saying that some people are guilty by association.

We know that this is true when we observe the company with whom our children want to hang out. How many teenagers have gotten into irreparable harm simply by being with the wrong people at the wrong time? How many prisoners would trace their illegal activities to the "friends" that they had early in life?

The same is true for us. The people you do life with will rub off on you. They will have an effect on you. You will affect them.

There are some people who can't stay in step with you. I've learned that there are relationships that have an expiration date. They were seasonal. Not every relationship is lifelong. This really takes discernment to know and govern in your life because we want to stay connected with people.

If our steps are ordered of the Lord, so are our relationships. Some relationships are for this part of your journey, while others have the ability to keep on the same track with you through life.

REMEMBER

Join a good company of people.

READ PROVERBS CHAPTER 2
fivestarman.com/day-183

Day 184: Your Hand Is God's Hand

PROVERBS 3:27 (MSG)

Never walk away from someone who deserves help;
your hand is God's hand for that person.
Don't tell your neighbor "Maybe some other time" or "Try me tomorrow"
when the money's right there in your pocket..

PRINCIPLE

When you do good for someone, your hand becomes God's hand.

I've had a lot of men say to me, "I want to be used by God." I believe they deeply desire to do something significant and meaningful.

It's easy to be used by God. Simply find a need someone has and meet it. Your hand is God's hand to that person. God used you.

For any spirit to accomplish something upon the Earth requires a person who yields to that spirit, whether good or bad. Even God's Spirit requires a person—a living, breathing, active person—to work in the Earth.

God wanted a man to lead His people out of the bondage of slavery in Egypt so He recruited a man. Moses became God's hand. Man needed to be redeemed so God sent His only Son. The Word of God became flesh and took on human form. Jesus became God's hand on the Earth.

You don't have to be Moses or Jesus to be used significantly by God. Your significance is found when you do not withhold good from people. You can meet the need of someone today.

REMEMBER

Don't ask God to meet the need of someone if you have the power to meet it.

READ PROVERBS CHAPTER 3

fivestarman.com/day-184

Day 185: A Lifestyle Of Right Living

PROVERBS 4:18 (NIV)

The path of the righteous is like the morning sun,
shining ever brighter till the full light of day.

PRINCIPLE

A lifestyle of right living makes maturity a brilliant example to see.

Most people when they grow old bend, slow down, and take on a darkness with their age. Have you seen the scarring of sin and the age spots of wickedness? It doesn't have to be that way. We can live in such a way that as we mature we become a brighter example of godliness.

A professor in college stood out in the most remarkable way. She was the most beautiful older woman I've ever seen. Her eyes were bright. Her posture was elegant. The words she spoke were not slurred but were clear and articulate. She knew the Word of God like the back of her hand. She had three earned doctorates. A brilliant professor, I marveled at her example of godliness.

One day she said, "I am working on my old-age face, and I want it to be a happy face—bright and cheerful."

Moses is a biblical example of this brilliance of right living. When he died at the full age of one hundred and twenty years, his eyes were not weak, nor his strength diminished (Deuteronomy 34:7).

REMEMBER

As we mature, we can become a brighter example of right living.

READ PROVERBS CHAPTER 4
fivestarman.com/day-185

Day 186: Enjoy The Wife Of Your Youth

PROVERBS 5:18 (NIV)

May your fountain be blessed,
and may you rejoice in the wife of your youth.

PRINCIPLE

Enjoy the wife you married as a young man!

We live in a crass culture. Men have little restraint in speaking about what otherwise would be inappropriate. The challenge is to address the issues of modern culture without stooping to its level.

When speaking to men, I often use artful language to speak on matters that might otherwise be considered off limits. So many men are living in a rough-and-tumble world. We need to be able to address issues and deal with them truthfully.

Our advisor has an artful way of describing something that otherwise could be an awkward statement. He often uses double entendre to speak about these things.

In today's proverb, the reference to a *fountain* is speaking of the eruption of the male's stream being blessed. That's not something you would often hear, but it references a real issue of our day—a lack of vitality.

Recent studies have discovered a direct link between overstimulation of the eyes to a lack of stimulation, or vitality, of a male. This is a real challenge of our culture. The more a man gazes upon women, the less alive he is with his spouse.

You'll never flourish in your relationship with your wife if your eyes are not devoted to her. If you devote yourself to love the wife of your youth, your relationship will flourish in every way.

REMEMBER

May your fountain be blessed!

READ PROVERBS CHAPTER 5

fivestarman.com/day-186

Day 187: A Smooth-Talking Woman

PROVERBS 6:24 (NIV)

Keeping you from your neighbor's wife,
from the smooth talk of a wayward woman.

PRINCIPLE

Don't listen to flattery.

There are two types of speakers who aren't worth listening to: those who are cynical critics and those who use flattery. Neither speaks with honesty.

Our advisor in the book of Proverbs warns men to avoid the smooth talk or flattery of the neighbor's wife. This woman is dangerous because of proximity. She is too close. She's familiar. She thinks that because she shares a neighborhood she has access to you.

Be very proactive to guard yourself against a woman like this. Don't allow yourself to get close enough for her smooth talk to be heard by you only. Don't have a private conversation with her. Don't allow her to tickle your ear with her words.

Never allow another woman to get close enough to whisper in your ear. Keep your distance.

REMEMBER

All sin involves proximity.

READ PROVERBS CHAPTER 6

fivestarman.com/day-187

Day 188: There's No Free Lunch

PROVERBS 7:1–2 (MSG)

Dear friend, do what I tell you;
treasure my careful instructions.
Do what I say and you'll live well.

PRINCIPLE

Love learning.

What are you willing to pay for a good life?

Each year, eBay is used to auction off a nice lunch at the New York City steakhouse Smith & Wollensky. In 2014, Andy Chua won the auction with a bid of $2.2 million. Chua and seven guests enjoyed a meal with famed investor, "the Oracle of Omaha," Warren Buffett. I'm sure the meal was fine and the conversation was enjoyable, but why would anyone pay so much for a lunch?

Mr. Chua's generosity went to a good charity, but this luncheon was about something more than philanthropy. It was about connecting with a contemporary that is, and will be, a historical legend. Mr. Buffett's homespun wisdom is studied at investment schools and seminars worldwide. He is the oracle of investing.

We need to make the most of the opportunity we have with the book of Proverbs. It is a man writing oracles of wisdom to his son. "Life's little instruction book" is the greatest compilation of wisdom ever gathered, and it's ours for the taking.

Shockingly, I meet men every week who don't have an appetite for learning. I'm amazed at their foolishness. In this life, there's no free lunch.

REMEMBER

There's no free lunch.

READ PROVERBS CHAPTER 7

fivestarman.com/day-188

Day 189: How To Recognize Legitimate Authority

PROVERBS 8:15–16 (MSG)

With my help, leaders rule, and lawmakers legislate fairly;
With my help, governors govern, along with all in legitimate authority.

PRINCIPLE

Wisdom is the prerequisite for leaders.

Four Recognizable Traits of Legitimate Authority.

1. **The Benefit of Power**—One Greek synonym for *authority* is "energeia," which means *superhuman power.* Authority above you should give you power you do not possess on your own. Jesus received all authority and transferred it to His followers (Matthew 28:18-19).
2. **The Benefit of Protection**—Another synonym is "exousia," meaning *to rule* and *cover with protection.* Legitimate authority shelters and protects. The people of Israel had established leadership, but their leaders did not have authority. The crowds were amazed at Jesus because "He taught them as one having authority" (Matthew 7:28-29 NKJV).
3. **The Benefit of Provision**—The synonym for *authority,* "dunamis," means *power and influence which belongs to riches and wealth.* 1 Corinthians 9:7 asks, "Who serves as a soldier at this own expense?" (NIV) Men under authority, should draw provision.
4. **The Benefit of Promotion**—"Ishus" is a synonym which means *ability* or *force.* The natural process of following great leaders should result in becoming better by default. Jesus said, "Follow Me, and I will make you ..." (Matthew 4:19 NKJV).

Authorities should not use manipulation or control. You should have no sense of intimidation or insecurity while serving a leader. You should have a sense of confidence, respect, and motivation, when you're submitted to legitimate authority.

REMEMBER

Legitimate authority has benefits.

READ PROVERBS CHAPTER 8

fivestarman.com/day-189

Day 190: Street Wise And Safe

PROVERBS 9:4 (MSG)

Are you confused about life, don't know what's going on?

PRINCIPLE

Men need to be street wise and protect themselves.

Have you ever been in an unfamiliar city and found yourself in a blighted area? You look around, and the seedy area of town is crawling with sinful opportunity. Not long ago, my wife and I were in Los Angeles, and we found ourselves in one of those areas. She was quick to suggest that we look for a new neighborhood.

As men, we have a tendency to be aware of our surroundings and to be prepared for whatever could put us in danger. When I walk into new surroundings, I am constantly surveying the room. I want to know the exit plan. I want to know where I can go to protect my family.

This is something that we need to be proactive in teaching our sons. They need to be focused, alert, sober-minded, and wise regarding their surroundings.

Be alert and of sober mind. Your enemy the devil prowls around like a roaring lion looking for someone to devour (1 Peter 5:8).

REMEMBER

We need to be street wise and safe.

READ PROVERBS CHAPTER 9

fivestarman.com/day-190

Day 191: Family I.D.

PROVERBS 10:13 (MSG)

You'll find wisdom on the lips of a person of insight,
but the shortsighted needs a slap in the face.

PRINCIPLE

A real man of faith believes for things that will require longer than his lifetime to come to pass.

A ***FivestarMan*** lives to leave a legacy. In other words, our daily decisions and personal appetites are determined by a long-range view.

These kinds of people are described in Hebrews 11—men who lived and thought beyond themselves.

How did they do it? They saw it way off in the distance, waved their greeting, and accepted the fact that they were transients in this world. People who live this way make it plain that they are looking for their true home (Hebrews 11:16).

A man of faith believes for things that will require longer than his own lifetime to come to pass. We need to think long term. I have a friend who mentors fathers to think in terms of two hundred years for their family. This kind of thinking gives them directional intent. It empowers them to not make hasty decisions. It dictates wisdom in decision making.

Think this way in terms of being a steward of your family I.D. (Intentional Direction). This will cause you to consider the consequences of your decisions.

REMEMBER

In light of your family I.D., how does this decision measure up?

READ PROVERBS CHAPTER 10

fivestarman.com/day-191

Day 192: Man Of Integrity

PROVERBS 11:20 (MSG)

God can't stand deceivers,
but oh how he relishes integrity.

PRINCIPLE

A *FivestarMan* has integrity.

Remember, there are five purposes that define authentic manhood (a ***FivestarMan***). They are: an adventurous spirit, an entrepreneurial drive, gallantry in relationships, faithfulness in character, and a philanthropic cause.

A ***FivestarMan*** is faithful. He is a man of integrity. Integrity is true to God's original intent. *Integrity* is defined as *a firm adherence to a code, especially moral or artistic values.* It is being *whole.* Integrity is being *true to form; incorruptible.*

When we believe in our hearts that Jesus is Lord and we confess with our mouths that belief, we experience a new birth in the Spirit. That confession is the consummation of the incorruptible Seed of God's Word! We are reborn with integrity—wholeness, true to form, incorruptible.

We can't have authentic manhood without this spiritual experience. We can't fulfill the original intent of authentic manhood without having integrity.

This changes everything.

REMEMBER

You are born of incorruptible Seed.

READ PROVERBS CHAPTER 11

fivestarman.com/day-192

Day 193: Don't Blow Up

PROVERBS 12:16 (MSG)

Fools have short fuses and explode all too quickly;
the prudent quietly shrug off insults.

PRINCIPLE

When you know the source of insults is a fool, it's easy to shrug it off.

I grew up under my mother's second husband. He was a hot-head. He would explode in anger. He used his anger to manipulate and control my mother. He would throw his juvenile tantrums, slam his fist against the wall, lash out with curses.

Even as a child and especially as a teenager, I had a unique way of responding to his foolishness. I quietly shrugged off his temper as amusement. I knew this was not a stable, rational, or a smart man. I developed a strong sense of security in my own right. Although his verbal assaults came daily, I brushed them off.

When you know the source of insults is a fool, it's easy to shrug it off.

Unfortunately, I've seen leaders use these same tactics on the job. Using this kind of sophomoric behavior is beneath authentic manhood.

Let's lead by inspiration, not intimidation. Let's master the skills to communicate and draw upon the gift of a person. We will accomplish greater things by using wisdom rather than exploding in violent rhetoric.

REMEMBER

Don't blow up.

READ PROVERBS CHAPTER 12

fivestarman.com/day-193

Day 194: Walk With The Wise

PROVERBS 13:20 (NIV)

Walk with the wise and become wise,
for a companion of fools suffers harm.

PRINCIPLE

You gain wisdom either through pain or through mentors. Choose mentors.

About twenty-five years ago I started playing golf with a gentleman who was about fifteen years older than me. He was a successful professional and enjoyed the comforts of a prosperous career. His children were entering their teenage years. I was able to see him navigate their experiences with wisdom and, at times, under very difficult circumstances. Not only did he teach me the basics of golf—a game I really enjoy—he mentored me in many other ways. I learned from his experience.

That's the beauty of walking with someone who has experience in life that you haven't had yet. You prosper at their expense.

Now, I'm at the other end of the spectrum, helping younger men navigate the challenges of life, hoping to help them avoid some of the pains that come from bad experiences.

REMEMBER

Choose a mentor. Gain some wisdom. Walk with the wise.

READ PROVERBS CHAPTER 13

fivestarman.com/day-194

Day 195: Illusive Dreams

PROVERBS 14:18 (MSG)

Foolish dreamers live in a world of illusion;
wise realists plant their feet on the ground.

PRINCIPLE

Imagination can be one of man's greatest assets or one of his worst liabilities.

There is an amazing opportunity that lies ahead for the man who can dream great dreams and awaken to the hard work to fulfill them. I've known men who were idealists but were never practical—those who seemed to have no limits to their imagination but could never put their hands to work and get things done.

There must be a practical application to your imagination.

No doubt you've had ideas God has deposited within you; however, it takes your cooperation to awaken to those ideas and implement a plan to bring them into reality—otherwise, your idea will become someone else's invention.

But it's not solely about the work. There's a danger in not giving yourself to the dream process. Some men have given up on their ability to dream dreams. Don't become so practical that you can't imagine possibilities. The Bible says young men will see visions and old men will dream dreams (Acts 2:17). The Spirit of God will help any man to dream again.

REMEMBER

Take action steps toward your dreams.

READ PROVERBS CHAPTER 14

fivestarman.com/day-195

Day 196: Mockers Avoid Wisdom

PROVERBS 15:12 (NIV)

Mockers resent correction,
so they avoid the wise.

PRINCIPLE

Mockers use juvenile tactics to avoid the truth and wisdom.

The Bible is clear. One of the signs of the Last Days is that people will become childish regarding the promises of God. They will mock and ridicule God. Mockers use this tactic to avoid the truth God's Word brings. Mimicry and making fun of the characteristics and mannerisms of people who are passionate about the truth is childish behavior.

The Bible warns: "First of all, know [without any doubt] that mockers will come in the last days with their mocking, following after their own human desires" (2 Peter 3:3 AMP).

We need to be alert to this kind of rhetoric because its subtle humor can catch us off guard. We can find ourselves agreeing with people when they haven't really made a reasonable argument.

Without being political, we need to be vigilant to not allow our politicians to use this tactic to sway public opinion. We are facing serious matters, and we need to handle them with serious thought and wisdom.

REMEMBER

Don't laugh with the mockers.

READ PROVERBS CHAPTER 15

fivestarman.com/day-196

Day 197: Involve God In Your Work

PROVERBS 16:11 (MSG)

God cares about honesty in the workplace;
your business is his business.

PRINCIPLE

Our business is God's business.

A ***FivestarMan*** is entrepreneurial. He brings to market his ability to produce. Everything he touches prospers. He involves God in his work.

There are some men who try to segregate their work from their faith. They justify their dishonesty as "business." That's not how God sees it. Our business is His business. There's no separation.

Joseph is a man who was blessed in all his business affairs. Potiphar recognized his household was successful because of Joseph's integrity. "The Lord was with Joseph so that he prospered, and he lived in the house of his Egyptian master" (Genesis 39:2 NIV).

Even while Joseph was a slave, he prospered. The common misunderstanding of prosperity would cause us to stumble over this statement. The word, *prosper* means *to advance, make progress, succeed, be profitable.* Joseph prospered even while he was a slave. He performed his master's business with excellence and integrity.

My work should reflect my faith. I don't want to embarrass the cause of Christ because my work isn't a good example of Him.

"And work with a smile on your face, always keeping in mind that no matter who happens to be giving the orders, you're really serving God" (Ephesians 6:7 MSG).

REMEMBER

Involve God in your work.

READ PROVERBS CHAPTER 16

fivestarman.com/day-197

Day 198: The Messenger Of Death

PROVERBS 17:11 (MSG)

Criminals out looking for nothing but trouble won't have to wait long—
they'll meet it coming and going!

PRINCIPLE

Those who rebel against God and do evil will face the Messenger of Death.

Have you ever watched a television show featuring dumb criminals? It's pretty amazing when you see the stupidity of some people. You wonder, *What were they thinking?* (They *weren't* thinking—at least not rationally.)

We live in a time when those who are bent on destruction will do whatever they can to destroy and be destroyed. We can examine the seeds of evil that were sown into the lives of the wicked. We can analyze their parents, their education, and their home life, but the reality is, some people just have dark minds. Many people think with evil intentions.

For those who do evil and rebel against God, the seeds of their destruction will arise against them. They will reap what they've sown. The unfortunate consequence is the collateral damage of their destructive ways on those around them.

REMEMBER

The Messenger of Death will be sent against the wicked.

➲ READ PROVERBS CHAPTER 17
fivestarman.com/day-198

Day 199: A Brother's Offense

PROVERBS 18:19 (NKJV)

A brother offended is harder to win than a strong city,
And contentions are like the bars of a castle.

PRINCIPLE

When a brother turns away from you, don't underestimate their offense.

Every time I read the story of Cain and Abel, I am stunned at the hatred that sprung from jealousy and antipathy within Cain's soul. What could have caused such animus within him?

Amazingly, it was an offering. The first murder ever committed was a fratricide—a brother murdering a brother.

Cain's jealousy arose out of comparison. Cain gave a token offering to the Lord. It was just something left over, an afterthought. Abel gave the firstborn of his flock. It was his best, his most-prized possession. It was the first of all his labor. It represented so much. It represented everything else that would follow.

God looked with favor upon Abel, but Cain's offering didn't receive God's favor. Why should it? It wasn't right. It wasn't special. It was an offensive gesture. Rather than correcting his own character flaws of ingratitude, stinginess, and arrogance, Cain's anger exploded in premeditated murder.

REMEMBER

Cowards see a brother's pursuit of excellence as an offense. Champions see it as a goal.

READ PROVERBS CHAPTER 18
fivestarman.com/day-199

Day 200: Align Your Plans With God's Purposes

PROVERBS 19:21 (AMP)

Many plans are in a man's mind,
But it is the Lord's purpose for him that will stand (be carried out).

PRINCIPLE

The plans within your mind should be in harmony with the purposes of God.

One thing I've learned about men is that they certainly have a lot of plans. It seems that everyone has a plan. Yet, very few actually understand if their plan fits within the purposes of God.

Jesus told a story about a man who had an exceptional increase in his harvest. The man lamented about his overflowing barns. "Then he said, 'Here's what I'll do: I'll tear down my barns and build bigger ones. Then I'll gather in all my grain and goods, and I'll say to myself, Self, you've done well! You've got it made and can now retire. Take it easy and have the time of your life!'" (Luke 12:16-19 MSG).

This wealthy man certainly was being entrepreneurial (a purpose of authentic manhood); however, he wasn't faithful (another purpose of authentic manhood). Although he was wealthy, he didn't align his plans with God's purposes.

That's what a lot of men do. They use the deep purposes within them only for themselves. The five purposes of authentic manhood work in agreement with each other. They align in harmony to bring about God's plans.

REMEMBER

Check with God before you boast about your plans.

READ PROVERBS CHAPTER 19

fivestarman.com/day-200

Day 201: I Am Clean

PROVERBS 20:9 (NIV)

Who can say, "I have kept my heart pure;
I am clean and without sin"?

PRINCIPLE

Perfection isn't the goal—excellence is.

Let's face it. We've all blown it. No one is perfect. As we strive toward authentic manhood, there are times we're going to blow it, but perfection isn't the goal—excellence is.

To excel means *to exceed in a fixed measure, to abound, to overflow*. To be a ***FivestarMan*** is to be a man in the passionate pursuit of authentic manhood. In other words, as we gain an understanding of the five purposes in us, we're getting better and better at them. Remember: Champions do daily what the average do occasionally. So, let's push ourselves to be ever improving.

"We all, who with unveiled faces contemplate the Lord's glory, are being transformed into his image with ever-increasing glory, which comes from the Lord, who is the Spirit" (2 Corinthians 3:18 NIV).

We're works in progress as we're being transformed into the image of perfected manhood—the image of Jesus.

REMEMBER

Your real competition is the man you were yesterday. Will you beat him today?

READ PROVERBS CHAPTER 20
fivestarman.com/day-201

Day 202: Justice Triumphs

PROVERBS 21:15 (MSG)

Good people celebrate when justice triumphs,
but for the workers of evil it's a bad day.

PRINCIPLE

Authentic manhood celebrates justice.

The word *justice* in our verse today means *one who has a just cause.* As authentic men, each of us are born with a fight. I know that crosses the sensitivities of some people, but we are fighters.

If we do not have a worthy cause to fight for, we'll find the wrong thing to fight against.

It is part of our philanthropic and gallant purposes: philanthropic, because we have a genuine care and concern for our fellow man; gallant, because we act in a chivalrous manner to defend the weak.

Those who only fight for themselves will always find an enemy who is stronger. Those who fight for justice will triumph against evil with God on their side.

REMEMBER

You have a worthy cause to fight for.

READ PROVERBS CHAPTER 21

fivestarman.com/day-202

Day 203: Generosity Is A Character Trait

PROVERBS 22:9 (NIV)

The generous will themselves be blessed,
for they share their food with the poor.

PRINCIPLE

When a man's character reflects generosity, he is most like his Heavenly Father.

The idea of generosity is a natural reflection of the character of a ***FivestarMan***. We are philanthropic, which means God has placed a deep purpose within us to reflect His nature.

Think about it. No one is more generous than our Father God. He has given us everything. All things were made by Him, and nothing was made except by Him (John 1:3). God, the Father gave us His only begotten Son (John 3:16).

Being generous is natural and spontaneous. We give quickly by the prompting in our hearts. A deep river of purpose moves us with compassion.

You may be just developing this expression of being a ***FivestarMan***. As you draw upon it, you'll discover a satisfaction and joy that comes from this purpose like none other.

REMEMBER

God was generous even before we deserved it.

READ PROVERBS CHAPTER 22

fivestarman.com/day-203

Day 204: Respect Your Father

PROVERBS 23:22 (MSG)

Listen with respect to the father who raised you,
and when your mother grows old, don't neglect her.

PRINCIPLE

A son has a responsibility to respect his father and keep a loving relationship with his mother.

The last words of the Old Testament give a startling warning, "See, I will send the prophet Elijah to you before that great and dreadful day of the Lord comes. He will turn the hearts of the fathers to their children, and the hearts of the children to their fathers; or else I will come and strike the land with total destruction" (Malachi 4:5 NIV).

This warning is directed to fathers. If they do not return, even repent, toward their children, the land will suffer total destruction. There is a kinetic relationship between men and the Earth. The relationship is a result of sin. It began with Adam. When he embezzled from God's property (the Tree of the Knowledge of Good and Evil), the land was thrust into poverty.

Paul said the Earth is trembling in the pains of childbirth awaiting the revelation of the sons of God (Romans 8:20-21).

Today's proverb is speaking to sons. The onus is placed upon sons to be respectful to their fathers and keep a loving relationship with their mothers.

REMEMBER

Listen respectfully to your father and continue to love your mother.

READ PROVERBS CHAPTER 23

fivestarman.com/day-204

Day 205: Good Sportsmanship

PROVERBS 24:17 (NIV)

Do not gloat when your enemy falls;
when they stumble, do not let your heart rejoice,
Or the Lord will see and disapprove
and turn his wrath away from them.

PRINCIPLE

Don't spike the ball when you've scored. Be a good sport.

David's rebellious son Absalom orchestrated a treasonous insurrection against his father, and Absalom died in a tree of rebellion. Two messengers heralded the news to David. Ahimaaz gave the good news of the victory in battle but avoided telling David the bad news about his son. The Cushite messenger flippantly spoke of Absalom's death, "May the enemies of my Lord the king and all who rise up to harm you be like that young man" (2 Samuel 18:32 NIV). This displeased the king.

This is a lesson to not gloat over the downfall of those who oppose you. It's contrary to most people's response when seeing the destruction of their enemies, but it is God's way. We're not to be cheerful and joyful when anyone suffers.

As this applies to good sportsmanship, I'm a fan, but I'm not going to be obnoxious when my team wins. It's just not that important. We should show good sportsmanship.

REMEMBER

Be a good sport.

READ PROVERBS CHAPTER 24
fivestarman.com/day-205

Day 206: Salt On Wounds

PROVERBS 25:20 (NIV)

Like one who takes away a garment on a cold day,
or like vinegar poured on a wound,
is one who sings songs to a heavy heart.

PRINCIPLE

Showing respect when others are facing sadness and tragedy is polite behavior.

A ***FivestarMan*** is gallant. A gallant man conducts himself appropriately on every occasion. We need to have a good understanding of decorum. Having good taste in conduct and appearance is important. Showing respect when others are facing sadness and tragedy is polite behavior.

Unfortunately, our society has lost its politeness. Recently, a tragedy hit the world scene. Hundreds were killed, but those in leadership showed no sympathy. Even though the tragedy involved another country, our leaders failed to show decorum. They barely mentioned it, focusing their attention on the trivial matters of their own political agendas. Their social media posts were trite and flippant. It was as if juveniles were in positions that require seasoned experts.

You may not know what good manners are. You may not be aware of the protocols of decorum, but that's no excuse to be disrespectful. Take the time to learn some manners and how to conduct yourself politely in society.

Some men may brush this off as unimportant, but being polite is part of being gallant.

REMEMBER

Don't pour salt on wounds.

READ PROVERBS CHAPTER 25

fivestarman.com/day-206

Day 207: Laziness

PROVERBS 26:14–15 (MSG)

Just as a door turns on its hinges,
so a lazybones turns back over in bed.
A shiftless sluggard puts his fork in the pie,
but is too lazy to lift it to his mouth.

PRINCIPLE

Laziness is the habit of resting before you get tired.

The writer of Proverbs isn't sympathetic to a lazy man. He mocks his inaction and questions his purpose of existence. He compares the turning of the slothful man to a door on hinges. He ridicules the lazy person's inability to lift a fork for the satisfaction of a good taste of life.

An authentic man is very active and even aggressive to get things done. Action is a prerequisite of success. You've heard it said, "It's easier to steer a moving car." The same is true for us. It is easier to go in the right direction when we're already taking action.

"I'd be more frightened by not using whatever abilities I'd been given. I'd be more frightened by procrastination and laziness." —Denzel Washington

God has greater plans for you than you just sitting in comfort on your couch.

REMEMBER

The greatest temptation for a man is comfort.

READ PROVERBS CHAPTER 26

fivestarman.com/day-207

Day 208: Pleasant Fragrance

PROVERBS 27:9 (NIV)

Perfume and incense bring joy to the heart,
and the pleasantness of a friend
springs from their heartfelt advice.

PRINCIPLE

Good advice from honest friends is like a fragrance lingering in the air and reminding us of them.

I have a hypersensitivity to smells. As I travel, it is incredibly difficult to stay in a hotel room that has not been thoroughly cleaned. I notice the residue of the presence of others. I try not to be obsessive about it, but it makes me keenly aware of the impression that lingers long after our presence has departed.

That's the sense I get when reading today's proverb. The memory that good advice leaves on a person is equated to a pleasant fragrance that lingers long after they are gone.

The Apostle Paul said Christ giving Himself for us was like a fragrant offering. The lingering aroma of His sacrifice reminds our Heavenly Father of the acceptable sacrifice that was pleasing to God (Ephesians 5:2).

Paul also exhorts us that financial gifts leave a fragrance. They, too, are a sacrifice that is pleasing and acceptable to God.

REMEMBER

Who you are and what you do lingers in your aftermath.

READ PROVERBS CHAPTER 27
fivestarman.com/day-208

Day 209: The Back Of The Dragon

PROVERBS 28:18 (MSG)

Walk straight—live well and be saved;
a devious life is a doomed life.

PRINCIPLE

The best path is the straight path.

It almost seems too elementary, but is this principle is true: *Walk straight. Live well.*

God has given all of mankind the free gift of salvation. He has provided an easy path—a straight path—to living well and being saved. Jesus said, "I am the way and the truth and the life. No one comes to the Father except through me" (John 14:6 NIV).

But many choose a devious life, even though it is a doomed life. The word *devious* means *perverted, twisted,* or *crooked.*

Not long ago, I had the opportunity to ride a Harley on "The Back of the Dragon," VA Route 16, the two-lane ribbon over the three mountains between Tazewell and Marion, Virginia. The ride was amazing; however, for unseasoned riders or riders who lose focus, it could be dangerous.

You're going to have to navigate some dangerous circumstances in life. If you're devious, you're doomed. If you ride the back of the dragon (speaking of the devious path of Satan), you will find life to be very difficult and dangerous.

REMEMBER

Keep your eyes on the road. Don't get distracted by the scenery around you.

READ PROVERBS CHAPTER 28
fivestarman.com/day-209

Day 210: Don't Be Displaced By Anger

PROVERBS 29:22 (MSG)

Angry people stir up a lot of discord;
the intemperate stir up trouble.

PRINCIPLE

You may not be punished *for* your anger, but you'll be punished *by* it.

Anger has caused more issues in men's lives than can be calculated. Seriously, we must understand how susceptible we are to the volatility of anger. Don't get me wrong. There are circumstances and causes worthy of our anger; however, we must choose anger wisely.

Anger without a cause brings discord and trouble.

Also, we must be selective about whom we associate with, especially if they are angry people. Angry people cause collateral damage. Discord is the seed of defection and rebellion. If you give it place, it will displace you.

REMEMBER

If you give anger a place, it will displace you.

READ PROVERBS CHAPTER 29

fivestarman.com/day-210

Day 211: Don't Be Stuck Up

PROVERBS 30:13 (MSG)

Don't be stuck-up and think you're better than everyone else.

PRINCIPLE

We're not better than other men—but we're not less, either.

Do you have a healthy ego? Do you think more highly of yourself than you should? Or do you struggle with not having any self-assurance?

The old saying is true. "For every mile of road, there are two miles of ditch."

You can border on narcissism, or you can be completely insecure. Neither is healthy.

The Apostle Paul demonstrated a balance in his ego. "I do not think I am in the least inferior to those 'super-apostles'" (2 Corinthians 11:5 NIV). Paul's confidence was not in himself. It was in his identity in Christ. "May I never boast except in the cross of our Lord Jesus Christ, through which the world has been crucified to me, and I to the world" (Galatians 6:14 NIV).

As we are passionately pursuing authentic manhood, it's important that we stand tall and strong, knowing who we are as men, as living examples of the dignity of manhood. We must be men who know our strength is in Christ.

REMEMBER

We're not better or less than other men.

READ PROVERBS CHAPTER 30

fivestarman.com/day-211

Day 212: Speak Up!

PROVERBS 31:8 (NIV)

Speak up for those who cannot speak for themselves,
for the rights of all who are destitute.
Speak up and judge fairly;
defend the rights of the poor and needy.

PRINCIPLE

In every man's life, there's a moment when he either steps up to be a man, or he shrinks back into obscurity.

Giving voice to those who have no voice is the noble duty of authentic manhood.

"Injustice anywhere is a threat to justice everywhere." —Martin Luther King

A ***FivestarMan*** is philanthropic. He loves humanity. He has a deep purpose to better humanity with his life. Philanthropy is heroic, sacrificial, and the giving of oneself so others may be benefited by one's efforts.

We are most like God the Father when we who have a voice speak up for those who do not; when we who have strength use it to lift up; when we who have means share with those who do not; when we stand toe-to-toe against the adversary of those who cannot defend themselves.

As men, we should not presume the title of hero, but we certainly should act as one for those who are weak.

In every man's life, there is a moment when he either steps up to be a man, or he shrinks back into obscurity.

REMEMBER

Step up, and speak up.

READ PROVERBS CHAPTER 31

fivestarman.com/day-212

Day 213: Don't Curse God When Tragedy Strikes

PROVERBS 1:27–28 (AMP)

When your panic comes as a storm and desolation and your calamity comes on as a whirlwind, when distress and anguish come upon you.

Then will they call upon me [Wisdom] but I will not answer; they will seek me early and diligently but they will not find me.

PRINCIPLE

***ALL* tragedy is a result of the fallen world.**

How should we respond to tragedy? Jesus' response can serve as a lesson. "Those eighteen who died when the tower in Siloam fell on them—do you think they were more guilty than all the others living in Jerusalem? I tell you, no! But unless you repent, you too will all perish" (Luke 13:4-5 NIV).

Jesus said we may think tragedy is a judgment of sin; however, ALL tragedy is a result of the fallen world.

In the face of tragedy, here are comments you should *NOT* make:

- They deserved it, and God is teaching them something.
- All things work together for good. *(This is taking a scripture completely out of context and applying all acts as good.)*
- They lacked faith.
- I am just glad it didn't happen to us.
- God did this. *(Don't sin with your lips by accusing God of causing tragedy.)*

These are responses we *SHOULD* have:

- What can I do to help?
- Who is responding, and how can I help them?
- How can I pray?

REMEMBER

Don't curse God when trouble strikes.

READ PROVERBS CHAPTER 1

fivestarman.com/day-213

Day 214: Men Of Integrity

PROVERBS 2:21 (AMP)

For the upright shall dwell in the land, and the men of integrity, blameless and complete [in God's sight], shall remain in it.

PRINCIPLE

Integrity is a personal strength. It is impregnable.

A ***FivestarMan*** is faithful. He's a man of authenticity, honor, and integrity. Being a man of integrity is foundational to authentic manhood. *Integrity* means *completeness, wholeness,* or *being undivided.*

"The foundation stones for a balanced success are honesty, character, integrity, faith, love, and loyalty." —Zig Ziglar

James warns us about a man who acts with duplicity. "He is a double-minded man, unstable in all his ways" (James 1:8 NKJV).

A man who lacks integrity wavers, much like a man on a ship without a rudder. He lacks directional intent and commitment. He is tossed by the waves and overwhelmed by the wind. However, if he has a rudder, he has the ability to use the wind to his advantage and overcome the waves that resist him.

Integrity is a personal strength. It is impregnable.

When Job faced the challenges of his life, his wife mocked him. His "friends" spoke harsh words, but his reply was, "Let God weigh me on the scales of justice, for he knows my integrity" (Job 31:6 NLT).

REMEMBER

When you go through a tough time, hang onto your integrity. You'll get through it.

READ PROVERBS CHAPTER 2

fivestarman.com/day-214

Day 215: It's Overdue

PROVERBS 3:28 (NIV)

Do not say to your neighbor,
"Come back tomorrow and I'll give it to you"—
when you already have it with you.

PRINCIPLE

How you respond when someone calls on you is the way God responds when you call on Him.

Years ago, I was frustrated. People delayed paying me money that was owed to me. I would do work quickly but had difficulty getting paid on time. It was discouraging.

One day, as I was reading this verse, I felt prompted to look deeper into this text. I found the answer to my problem. I had a habit of delaying paying invoices until the last day they were due, even when I had the money to pay days earlier. It wasn't stinginess, but my fear of lack caused me to hesitate.

I saw very quickly I was operating in the Biblical principle of sowing and reaping. As I delayed paying bills, others delayed what was due to me.

I changed my habits and started paying bills as soon as I had an invoice, and I saw the change almost immediately. Those with whom I did business began paying me for my services on time.

REMEMBER

How you respond when someone calls on you is the way God responds when you call on Him.

READ PROVERBS CHAPTER 3
fivestarman.com/day-215

Day 216: Distracted Driving

PROVERBS 4:19 (NLT)

But the way of the wicked is like total darkness.
They have no idea what they are stumbling over.

PRINCIPLE

The light shines in the darkness, and the darkness does not comprehend it.

Distracted driving has become epidemic. People are barreling down the road, one hand on the wheel while the other hand is texting. Is the message they're sending important? No, it's trivial. Yet, they're willing to gamble on death and disregard the collateral damage they could cause. Their eyes dart back and forth. They fixate on the text—then, *BAM!*

Texting and driving is a symptom of a deeper issue in our culture. It's an expression of foolish people who flippantly move through life distracted by the trivial. Suddenly, and without warning, they cause a crash.

A few days ago, I saw a news website. Right next to a story about hundreds of people who were tragically killed was a story about the breakup of a Hollywood couple who haven't contributed one ounce of purpose to this planet. It was alarmingly disgusting to me. Hundreds of people were killed, yet their deaths rated equal billing with the ridiculous distraction of fools.

Some people are oblivious to the dangers around them and blind to what is going on in the world. Too many are obsessed with the worthless, inconsequential matters of life.

REMEMBER

The light shines in the darkness, and the darkness does not comprehend it.

READ PROVERBS CHAPTER 4

fivestarman.com/day-216

Day 217: Cheap Thrills

PROVERBS 5:20 (MSG)

Why would you trade enduring intimacies for cheap thrills with a whore?
for dalliance with a promiscuous stranger?

PRINCIPLE

Cheap thrills can't replace a faithful wife.

To be honest, it just doesn't make sense to me when I see men trade the loyalty of love for a tryst with a tramp. The intimacy that a husband and wife celebrate with one another can't, and shouldn't be compared to a cheap thrill with a whore.

Authentic man understands a marriage bond to faithfulness can't be beaten. It is truly a celebration of two who have become one.

This culture promotes the promiscuous lifestyle as if that's where the fun is, but let's judge the fruit. You don't see people bouncing around from one sexual relationship to another celebrating joyfully in life. They're depressed, drunk, or drugged out of rational thinking.

Be a ***FivestarMan***. Be the kind of man who stands taller with integrity. Be the husband who sets the standard. Prove yourself faithful to your wife.

REMEMBER

A whore should never displace a faithful wife.

READ PROVERBS CHAPTER 5
fivestarman.com/day-217

Day 218: Fire Walker

PROVERBS 6:28 (MSG)

Can you walk barefoot on hot coals and not get blisters?

PRINCIPLE

Don't play with fire.

A motivational guru selling high-energy tapes on infomercials also pitches high-end seminars where people get pumped up and take their turn walking on hot coals. There's a trick to be able to walk on coals without getting burned.

The coals must be positioned just right and held at the perfect temperature for the seminarians to succeed. The goal of this fire walking is to get people to step out of their comfort zone and do something they would consider impossible.

Unfortunately, two dozen people were seriously burned at a San Diego conference.

It doesn't take fire walking to realize you can get burned. One of the deep passions of authentic manhood is exercising the adventurous spirit. We challenge men to move off the comfort of the couch and get back on the field of contest. We encourage men to take excursions: to golf, hunt, ride bikes, fish, etc.—to do something that fulfills the adventurous spirit.

However, don't do things stupidly. Be rational about it. Be wise in making risky decisions.

REMEMBER

Play with fire, and you'll get burned.

READ PROVERBS CHAPTER 6

fivestarman.com/day-218

Day 219: Are You Home?

PROVERBS 7:19–20 (MSG)

My husband's not home; he's away on business,
and he won't be back for a month.

PRINCIPLE

Stay connected to your wife, regardless of where you are.

Solomon looked out the window to see a married woman scour the neighborhood for her next victim to seduce. She found a naïve young man who quickly became her prey and stepped into her halfway house to Hell.

When I read this passage each month, I wonder, *Where is the husband?* We know he is away on business, but why does his wife feel such freedom to wander the streets?

I am aware there are unfaithful and dishonorable women in marriages; however, ***The Daily Champion*** is written to encourage men so I want to address the husband's role.

As husbands, we should be present in our marriages and aware of our relationships, whether we're away or at home.

I've traveled for years, and I always made it a point to stay connected to my family, no matter where I was. I stayed in close contact with my wife. When I returned home, I spent extra time with my children and took my wife out on dates. I wanted my return to be a celebration and not to allow a bitter root to cause them to despise my travels.

Now my wife travels with me most of the time. We get to enjoy our times together and celebrate a lifetime of faithfulness to one another.

REMEMBER

Be present.

READ PROVERBS CHAPTER 7
fivestarman.com/day-219

Day 220: Four Benefits Of Wisdom

PROVERBS 8:18 (NIV)

With me are riches and honor, enduring wealth and prosperity.

PRINCIPLE

A relationship with Wisdom brings benefits into our lives.

As we've been reading Proverbs every day, we quickly see that Wisdom is personified, meaning, it's not a mystical abstract. We can have a viable relationship with Wisdom. Look at the side benefits of having a relationship with Wisdom: riches and honor, enduring wealth and prosperity.

There is confusion about these terms because some have miscommunicated their purposes, even preaching Christ for personal gain; nevertheless, it's important for us to understand them and their Biblical meaning from the original language in which they were penned.

Riches—"osher" in Hebrew means *to be happy, to accumulate what is of value, to build up, to erect.* This means that you have abundant possessions.

Honor—"kabowd" means *dignity, reputation, splendor.* It means you have a weight or *gravitas* about you. Your presence commands attention.

Enduring wealth—"atheq" and "hown" mean your riches will endure the test of time. They will advance and enlarge over your lifetime. This is a tremendous benefit for leaving a legacy.

Prosperity—"tsĕdaqah" in Hebrew actually means *righteousness.* This benefit refers to the virtue, justice, and right standing we have. Prosperity isn't referring to the material, but the spirit and soul of man. It means your journey will go well.

REMEMBER

As we gain Wisdom, we will also have the byproduct of these four benefits in our lives.

READ PROVERBS CHAPTER 8

fivestarman.com/day-220

Day 221: Use Good Judgment

PROVERBS 9:6 (NIV)

Leave your simple ways and you will live;
walk in the way of insight.

PRINCIPLE

Don't pass on to your children the simple ways of your past.

As you pursue authentic manhood, you're going to discover there are a lot of things—habits, attitudes, belief systems—that are better left in the past. You do not want these to be passed onto your children.

One of the real challenges that we face at times is the feeling of disloyalty to our parents or grandparents for changing. It may surprise you, but some people who complained about the weak appetites of their parents are now addicted to the same things their parents were—alcohol, drugs, adultery, etc.

Don't leave this for your children to deal with. YOU need to be the man. YOU must step up and change the simple ways and begin to live.

Learn to use good judgment.

REMEMBER

Don't carry the past into the future.

READ PROVERBS CHAPTER 9
fivestarman.com/day-221

Day 222: Payday Someday

PROVERBS 10:16 (MSG)

The wage of a good person is exuberant life;
an evil person ends up with nothing but sin.

PRINCIPLE

There's a payday for all men—whether good or evil.

It seems elementary doesn't it? If a man is bent toward evil and his life's motivation is clocking in every day to do the deeds of darkness, the payoff is death. That's it.

"For the wages of sin is death, but the free gift of God is eternal life through Christ Jesus our Lord" (Romans 6:23 NLT).

Equally as simple is the reward of the man who has made it his vocation to do good. If his life's work is to sharpen his character and to excel in good, his life has an incredible day of reckoning—the exuberant life!

"The thief's purpose is to steal and kill and destroy. My purpose is to give them a rich and satisfying life" (John 10:10 NLT).

When a man invests his life into evil, the thief comes to collect the debt. But Jesus' purpose is to pay you a handsome wage for living righteously.

REMEMBER

There's always a payday.

READ PROVERBS CHAPTER 10

fivestarman.com/day-222

Day 223: Enlarge Your World

PROVERBS 11:24 (MSG)

The world of the generous gets larger and larger;
the world of the stingy gets smaller and smaller.

PRINCIPLE

When we give to enhance the cause of mankind, we enlarge our world.

A ***FivestarMan*** is philanthropic. The word *philanthropic* means *with a love for humanity*. It is a deep purpose for authentic manhood to enhance the condition of humanity; thus, this word best represents what it means to be like Christ. Who has raised the standard of humanity more than Christ?

When we gather resources with the entrepreneurial drive, we balance that purpose by scattering a portion of our resources with a philanthropic cause. Our lives are more than the accumulation of cars, clothes, and cottages. We live for a cause.

The amazing thing is that as we show our generosity, our world expands! It grows larger and larger. However, if we horde and hide—if we are stingy and greedy, our world shrinks. We become small men.

Let's make our world huge! Let's be generous on every occasion. Our generosity, as we distribute it, will cause people to lift up their hands and thank God.

REMEMBER

Enlarge your world.

READ PROVERBS CHAPTER 11

fivestarman.com/day-223

Day 224: Cutting Words

PROVERBS 12:18 (NLT)

Some people make cutting remarks,
but the words of the wise bring healing.

PRINCIPLE

Words can cut like a knife. Some words have the ability to do surgery.

Very few men realize the incredible potential of harm or health their words have. We can be flippant when it comes to our speech. If we speak rashly, the harm may be irreparable, but if we speak with precision, our words can bring healing.

"For the word of God is alive and powerful. It is sharper than the sharpest two-edged sword, cutting between soul and spirit, between joint and marrow. It exposes our innermost thoughts and desires" (Hebrews 4:12 NLT).

The writer of Hebrews pinpoints the precision of God's Word. It has the ability to divide between soul and spirit and joints and marrow. It is able to reveal the inner thoughts and desires of a person.

To be transparent, I have matured in my use of words. I used to take pride in my ability to cut people with my words if they displayed a meanness or arrogance toward me or someone I loved. I've worked hard to use more wisdom with my words. I want people to be encouraged and strengthened by what I have to say.

REMEMBER

Be careful with sharp words. They can be dangerous.

READ PROVERBS CHAPTER 12

fivestarman.com/day-224

Day 225: The Company Of The Wise

PROVERBS 13:20 (NLT)

Walk with the wise and become wise;
associate with fools and get in trouble.

PRINCIPLE

If you're the smartest guy in the room, you need a new crowd.

I've seen this principle played out countless times. When young men have the opportunity to be around seasoned and mature men, they grow right before your eyes.

As a young man, I had the opportunity to be around some very wise men. I never left their presence without having nuggets of wisdom to digest. As I've matured, I've worked diligently to continue my quest to gain wisdom. I've also worked hard to pass on what I've learned to younger men. In fact, that is the goal of ***The Daily Champion***. It's my attempt to be a conduit to pass on whatever wisdom I've gained to you.

On the other side of the coin, if you associate with fools, you'll see your life fall to pieces. Making alliances with fools will cost you.

What do you do if you're stuck? I recommend you open as many books as you possibly can, and start reading. We're so blessed to have access to so many great books full of wisdom from great men.

REMEMBER

Look around for wise men, and keep their company.

READ PROVERBS CHAPTER 13

fivestarman.com/day-225

Day 226: Work Brings Profit

PROVERBS 14:23 (NLT)

Work brings profit,
but mere talk leads to poverty!

PRINCIPLE

Profit is excellence.

The Hebrew word for *profit,* "mowthar," means *excellence.* It represents the margin over the cost of something. So, excellence should be expected. It is abundance. It is the increase.

Work brings profit.

I've noticed a trend of late that causes me concern for some men. It seems many men are all talk and no action. Solomon warns that talk alone isn't enough. Confession without corresponding action is meaningless and will only lead to poverty.

There are men who are described as "clouds without rain." In other words, they make a lot of promises but never deliver. I've known men who can talk really big, but, when it comes to deliverables, they never show up.

REMEMBER

Confession without discipline is a delusion.

READ PROVERBS CHAPTER 14

fivestarman.com/day-226

Day 227: Depression

PROVERBS 15:13 (MSG)

A cheerful heart brings a smile to your face;
a sad heart makes it hard to get through the day.

PRINCIPLE

Not everyone who laughs is happy.

The news of Robin Williams' death years ago was a shock. How could a comedy genius succumb to so much sadness that he would take his own life? Many whispered in their own souls, *If he was so depressed that he took his own life, where is my hope?*

I grew up watching Williams. He was funny and, without a doubt a genius; however, I wondered about the darkness of his humor. It seemed as if something was boiling underneath his smile. You could see sadness in his eyes.

Not everyone who laughs is happy.

I fought depression as a young man. I had it all—a beautiful wife, three wonderful children, a home, a successful career. Life was good, but there was a despair that I fought. My victory over the haunting cloud of depression came when I began to show gratitude for all God had favored in my life—gratitude for Him, for my family, for everything. Gratitude broke through, and the darkness gave way.

That's been more than twenty years ago. Even though I've had challenging times since then, I've never faced the spirit of depression since.

REMEMBER

Laughter is good medicine. Laugh out loud in gratitude for your life.

READ PROVERBS CHAPTER 15

fivestarman.com/day-227

Day 228: Moral Leadership

PROVERBS 16:12 (MSG)

Good leaders abhor wrongdoing of all kinds;
sound leadership has a moral foundation.

PRINCIPLE

Leadership must meet the moral challenge of the day.

There has always been a deficit of moral leadership. It's not new to our day; however, we must be courageous enough to recognize, even demand, that our leaders have morality at their foundation.

It is not our position at ***FivestarMan*** to be political, but I want to use an example that demonstrates the need for moral clarity. During the Clinton scandal, the argument for his defense became that the inappropriate relationship he had with an intern was a "personal" matter. That argument would never fly in the private sector. A CEO would be escorted out immediately.

Unfortunately, the collateral damage of excusing this abhorrent behavior had repercussions on the entire nation. As a pastor, I saw the definition of "sexual relationship" become merely "friends with benefits." Unfortunately, the foundation stone of morality was redefined in our society.

REMEMBER

Sound leadership must honor a moral foundation and abhor wrongdoing of all kinds.

READ PROVERBS CHAPTER 16

fivestarman.com/day-228

Day 229: Simple-Minded Men

PROVERBS 17:12 (MSG)

Better to meet a grizzly robbed of her cubs
than a fool hellbent on folly.

PRINCIPLE

Never underestimate the destructive power of a simple-minded man.

For the last couple of years, I've had the incredible opportunity to speak at conferences in Alaska. It's been especially enjoyable to hear the adventurous stories that the men have of the last great wilderness. One thing I've picked up is that these men have tremendous respect for bears. They don't fool around with them.

As wild and dangerous as the wilderness can be, it's a walk in the park compared to the destructive power of a fool hellbent on folly. Never underestimate the destructive power of a simple-minded man.

When I was young and naïve, I couldn't comprehend this principle. Now that I have some experience in dealing with people, I can't emphasize it enough. Don't mess with a fool. Keep your distance. Don't let them get too close to you or your business.

REMEMBER

I'd rather fight a grizzly than tangle with a fool.

READ PROVERBS CHAPTER 17

fivestarman.com/day-229

Day 230: The Good Wife

PROVERBS 18:22 (NLT)

The man who finds a wife finds a treasure,
and he receives favor from the Lord.

PRINCIPLE

A good wife is proof God favors you.

It's a regular occurrence at conferences and church services for men to come to me with a huge sigh and complain, "I want a good marriage, but I don't know how to start."

I recommend you start with yourself. Don't try to change your wife. Change yourself and allow her to see a change. In most cases, your wife will be so moved by your change that she'll want to get on board.

Recently, at a church, a lady came up to me to thank me for one of my books. She exclaimed, "We've been married for 18 years. After ***FivestarMan,*** my husband changed things subtly, but those changes made a profound difference in our marriage."

I must also say there are some women who will not get on board with their husbands. It is incredibly sad and disappointing. Some women have a Jezebel spirit. Jezebel personified a woman with evil intentions. The name actually means, "without cohabitation." In other words, she was a married woman not joined in partnership with her husband. She had no intention of being united. She was independently minded and would not follow the lead of her husband.

REMEMBER

If you have a good wife, you're favored of God.

READ PROVERBS CHAPTER 18

fivestarman.com/day-230

Day 231: Loyalty Is Attractive

PROVERBS 19:22 (NLT)

Loyalty makes a person attractive.
It is better to be poor than dishonest.

PRINCIPLE

A loyal person is attractive and draws the attention of leaders.

My experience has placed me in positions that required me to lead anywhere from a few workers up to two hundred and fifty employees. I can tell you this proverb can't be over emphasized. A loyal employee is attractive. There is nothing more repulsive than giving someone employment only to see them prove to be unfaithful and disloyal.

Unfortunately, disloyal people usually have an uncanny ability to demonstrate their destructive power at the most-crucial times.

To be perfectly transparent, I hate disloyalty. I hate it with a passion. It is the spirit of Lucifer himself and is disgusting! *(Was that honest enough?)*

The idea that as you're paying someone a salary—the paycheck that is feeding their families—and they turn with ingratitude to work against you is a pathetic act of cowardice. How do you respond to the dishonest person?

Look at the words of Jesus. "I watched Satan fall from heaven like a lightning [flash] ..." (Luke 10:18 AMP).

I recommend you terminate a disloyal person as quickly as possible without hesitation.

REMEMBER

Disloyalty isn't just a bad decision. It's a character flaw.

READ PROVERBS CHAPTER 19
fivestarman.com/day-231

Day 232: I Want To Be A Man

PROVERBS 20:11 (NLT)

Even children are known by the way they act,
whether their conduct is pure, and whether it is right.

PRINCIPLE

Within the heart of a boy is a man wanting to express himself.

We received this email at ***FivestarMan*** from a young woman:

My dad is always bringing me books to read. I couldn't understand why he gave me a book entitled, ***The Resurrection of Authentic Manhood.*** *I hadn't noticed the book had gone missing from my dresser, but then my son started asking me strange questions. "Did you know Pastor Sawyer's dad was in the war?" "Did you know his dad went to Heaven?" And then he said, "Pastor Sawyer respected his father because he didn't do bad things, and he loved him.*

Later, I went into my eight-year-old son's room to see him asleep with his arm cuddling the book. After he awakened, I asked him, "Why are you reading such a hard book? This is written for adults."

He looked at me and said, "Momma, I want to be a man!"

This fatherless boy will face many obstacles in his journey toward authentic manhood. That's one of the reasons ***FivestarMan*** exists. We want to help boys to become men.

REMEMBER

Every man has a boy looking at them. The question becomes, "Do they want to be a man like you?"

READ PROVERBS CHAPTER 20

fivestarman.com/day-232

Day 233: Nothing Is Hidden

PROVERBS 21:12 (NLT)

The Righteous One knows what is going on in the homes of the wicked;
he will bring disaster on them.

PRINCIPLE

Men will give an account for the evil they do.

The stories are horrific, stories of abuse within the home and insidious evil. It's hard to comprehend why people treat their families with such evil.

As a pastor, I was made aware of things I can't even describe, and I would not even allow myself to speak of the evil that was done. If we're not careful, we can become calloused by the evil men do.

Let me be very clear: Men will give an account for the evil they do!

If a man raises his hand to strike a woman, he has forfeited his manhood and is a poor excuse for man. If a father perverts the hand designed to bless his children and molests them, God has mercy on his soul, but he will face a fitting judgment for his evil.

Make no mistake about it: the Righteous One knows what is going on in the homes of the wicked, and His wrath will be poured out upon them.

This isn't a word of encouragement for perpetrators of evil, but it is encouraging for those who have seen their evil deeds. It is refreshing to know that the wicked will not get away with it.

REMEMBER

Nothing is hidden.

READ PROVERBS CHAPTER 21
fivestarman.com/day-233

Day 234: Drive Out The Mocker

PROVERBS 22:10 (NLT)

Throw out the mocker, and fighting goes, too.
Quarrels and insults will disappear.

PRINCIPLE

Strife is the manifested presence of evil.

I grew up in a quarrelsome home. My mother's second husband used intimidation tactics to control her. He treated her with horrible disrespect. He ranted and raged to get his way. He was a little man with a huge ego, a tyrant in the home.

My wife and I made a pact early in our marriage that we would have a peaceful home. We determined the atmosphere would be an inviting place of refuge. As our children were growing up, their friends wanted to hang out at our home, largely because of the peace that could be felt in it.

Kay and I never yelled at each other. I know that sounds hard to believe, but it's true. It was never an option for us to raise our voices to get our way. We were selective about whom we invited into our home and of the shows we watched to protect the atmosphere. We refused to let strife be our guest.

Some people want the drama. They enjoy a soap-opera lifestyle and thrive on emotional roller coasters. But they also get the results of that lifestyle—insults, quarrels, fighting, and mocking—they reap a whirlwind of torn relationships.

REMEMBER

Drive out the mocking, fighting, insults, and strife.

READ PROVERBS CHAPTER 22

fivestarman.com/day-234

Day 235: Invest Wisdom In Your Children

PROVERBS 23:24 (NLT)

The father of godly children has cause for joy.
What a pleasure to have children who are wise.

PRINCIPLE

The reward of fathering is witnessing children make wise decisions.

It is impossible to measure the joy and pleasure that comes from seeing your children make wise decisions.

Recently, one of my daughters made a life-changing decision. When I was asked about it, I responded that I had invested a couple of decades raising my daughter for this occasion. I'd seen her previously make wise decisions that were contrary to her feelings. That proved to me she could carefully weigh her choices.

How do you raise a child to make wise decisions? I believe you teach them to forecast the benefits or consequences of their choices. Let them play out the scenarios with you without your personal judgment while they're talking it out. Then ask a question or two to help them navigate things with discernment.

It's good to draw an example or two from the Word of God and show the consequences that resulted in bad decisions. Contrast that with a personal example of how you navigated a decision and the benefits that came from it.

REMEMBER

Invest wisdom in your children.

READ PROVERBS CHAPTER 23

fivestarman.com/day-235

Day 236: Favoritism

PROVERBS 24:23 (NLT)

It is wrong to show favoritism when passing judgment.

PRINCIPLE

Some people want to hold you to laws from which they have exempted themselves.

This is an important principle when you're leading people. Have you noticed there are some people whom you just like? There is something magnetic about them that draws people into favoring them above others.

There are others who are disguised. They seem to be likable and may have an attractive appearance, but if you get to know them, they lack integrity, use manipulative strategies, or even have evil intent.

Jesus dealt with these kinds of people and called them out. "What sorrow awaits you teachers of religious law and you Pharisees. Hypocrites! For you are so careful to clean the outside of the cup and the dish, but inside you are filthy—full of greed and self-indulgence!" (Matthew 23:25 NLT)

The religious leaders worked very hard to use God's Holy Word to control people rather than to draw them closer into a relationship with God. Jesus pulled no punches in rebuking them. He wasn't impressed with their cover ups. Their disguises didn't work. They were showing themselves favoritism over principle.

REMEMBER

Don't show favoritism when passing judgment.

READ PROVERBS CHAPTER 24

fivestarman.com/day-236

Day 237: Kindness To Your Enemy

PROVERBS 25:21 (NLT)

If your enemies are hungry, give them food to eat.
If they are thirsty, give them water to drink.

PRINCIPLE

When we show kindness to our enemies, we act in a Christ-like manner.

This one is tough. In fact, I'm pretty confident some men will read today's verse and just skip it. For those who will consider and begin to apply this principle, they could see a dramatic change. This proverb stretches us to adopt the mind of Christ.

When Man sinned against God, the relationship was severed. Men became hostile and developed antipathy against God. Yet, even while we were sinners—haters and hostile—God loved us. He showed His love by giving us the Bread of Life and the Water of His Spirit.

Jesus demonstrated this kindness to a Samaritan woman who came to a well. Jews did not associate with Samaritans. When Jesus asked the woman for water, her reply was revealing, "You are a Jew and I am a Samaritan woman. How can you ask me for a drink?"

Then Jesus offered her an answer, "If you only knew the gift God has for you and who you are speaking to, you would ask me, and I would give you living water" (John 4:9-10 NLT).

Following the example of Jesus, we should look for opportunities to help those with whom there is hostility.

REMEMBER

It's not easy, but there is a reward system attached to acting out this incredible principle.

READ PROVERBS CHAPTER 25

fivestarman.com/day-237

Day 238: Lazy Smart Aleck

PROVERBS 26:16 (NLT)

Lazy people consider themselves smarter than seven wise counselors.

PRINCIPLE

You can't tell a lazy man anything. He's too smart to listen to you.

I've been around a few men like this, gluttonous lazy men who act as if they're the smartest men in the room. These kinds of guys are amazingly arrogant, boastful, and demanding. They're lazy smart alecks.

I am not trying to be cruel, but Proverbs rebukes slothfulness. Men are created for action, not for comfort. I believe the worst invention for men is the LazyBoy chair.

Get up and keep moving!

REMEMBER

God has a higher plan for you than making you comfortable.

READ PROVERBS CHAPTER 26

fivestarman.com/day-238

Day 239: Nag, Nag, Nag

PROVERBS 27:15–16 (MSG)

A nagging spouse is like
the drip, drip, drip of a leaky faucet;
You can't turn it off,
and you can't get away from it.

PRINCIPLE

The tactic of nagging is a tenacity to get what you want.

Believe it or not, the nagging of a woman is actually a pretty smart tactic for her to get her way. In fact, Jesus used the example of a nag to demonstrate the tenacity of prayer that is often required.

A widow went to the man who had authority to protect her, namely the judge, and pleaded with him constantly, "Give me justice in this dispute with my enemy."

The judge ignored her for a while, but finally he said to himself, "I don't fear God or care about people, but this woman is driving me crazy. I'm going to see that she gets justice, because she is wearing me out with her constant requests!" (Luke 18:3-5 NLT)

Here's the lesson for men. We're in the position of authority. A nagging wife is making her request known to get her petition answered. We can gripe about it, but there is often truth in her constant badgering.

I'm pretty confident you're not going to share this ***Daily Champion*** with your wife, but take some time to consider it!

REMEMBER

The quickest way to stop your wife from nagging is to do what she asks of you.

READ PROVERBS CHAPTER 27

fivestarman.com/day-239

Day 240: The Law Of Seed

PROVERBS 28:19 (NIV)

Those who work their land will have abundant food,
but those who chase fantasies will have their fill of poverty.

PRINCIPLE

It's fantasy to expect a harvest when you haven't sown a seed.

In my estimation, the greatest principle is "The Law of Seed." It's the principle that governs the Earth. It is the currency of the world. All currencies work within this law. God established the food supply of the Earth to work by it. God even established this principle within the genetic code of mankind.

No one living can escape this. "God is not mocked; for whatever a man sows, that he will also reap" (Galatians 6:7 NKJV). Jesus said if you can comprehend this one principle, you will understand the secret of the kingdom of God. (See Luke 8:9-15.)

Don't write this off as "prosperity teaching." Don't be robbed of this truth because you have a biased belief system. This is about much more than money (although the Apostle Paul used this principle to explain financial sowing and reaping in 2 Corinthians 9:8).

God established this law and used it to sow His Son, the Word of God in the flesh, into the Earth as the incorruptible Seed of God's Word by which we are saved! Praise God!

REMEMBER

This is the greatest principle. Meditate on it, and it will change your life.

READ PROVERBS CHAPTER 28

fivestarman.com/day-240

Day 241: The Opinions Of Men

PROVERBS 29:25 (MSG)

The fear of human opinion disables;
trusting in God protects you from that.

PRINCIPLE

If you have the approval of God in the morning, the opinions of men do not matter during the day.

"Jesus knew their thoughts and said to them: 'Any kingdom divided against itself will be ruined, and a house divided against itself will fall'" (Luke 11:17 NIV).

Because Jesus understood the instability of men's opinions, He didn't base His personal assurance and confidence upon them. He clearly sought the approval of His Father above all others.

"And a voice from heaven said, 'This is my Son, whom I love; with him I am well pleased'" (Matthew 3:17 NIV).

The approval of God empowered Jesus to walk independently of men's opinions.

I want to encourage you to seek the approval of God. Confirm your position in Christ and be confident of that relationship. If you do, you won't care what others think.

This is something I established very early in my walk with God. When I made a decision to follow Christ, I was alienated from almost every single "friend" that I previously had. This developed a tenacity in my character which has served me well to help me do what God directed me to do.

REMEMBER

The opinions of men are shallow and temporal.

READ PROVERBS CHAPTER 29

fivestarman.com/day-241

Day 242: It's Not Your Business

PROVERBS 30:10 (NLT)

Never slander a worker to the employer,
or the person may curse you, and you will pay for it.

PRINCIPLE

Don't attempt to correct someone who influences millions when you have the influence of a gnat.

Social-media platforms have many positive benefits, but they can also expose some very bad behaviors. Slander is one of them. Some people have used these platforms to call out people they don't like or with whom they disagree. Often the person posting the opposition has a very small following and attempts to correct someone who has a voice to speak to thousands or even tens of thousands.

Not only is this an unwise tactic to attempt to gain influence, it can be slanderous.

A friend of mine recently felt very passionate about writing an "open letter" to a minister who literally influences millions of people. My friend wrote a scathing attack against what he perceived was a flaw in this minister's character. My friend asked me what I thought about his post, expecting me to jump on his band-wagon. My response surprised him.

I told my friend that he should delete his "open letter" and apologize for posting it. It was slanderous. He was attempting to correct someone whom he did not know, have a relationship with, or have any authority to correct. I suggested that it was not right to complain to God about someone who works for Him. That's not anyone else's business. It's like attempting to correct a worker at a company where you're not employed.

REMEMBER

If it's not your business, it's not yours to correct.

READ PROVERBS CHAPTER 30

fivestarman.com/day-242

Day 243: The Priceless Value Of A Good Wife

PROVERBS 31:10–11 (NLT)

Who can find a virtuous and capable wife?
She is more precious than rubies.
Her husband can trust her,
and she will greatly enrich his life.

PRINCIPLE

The value of a good wife can't be measured.

Many attempts have been made to calculate the replacement cost of a wife. Some estimate the annual cost would be $125,000. However, as Oscar Wilde suggested, a cynic (or an economist, in this case) "knows the price of everything but the value of nothing."

Value is determined by market demand. Since wives are not traded on the open market, we can't put a price on their value. What we do know is that after seeing Man alone, God concluded Man needed a helpmate.

"So God created man in His own image… male and female He created them" (Genesis 1:27 NKJV). At this stage, Adam had both genders within him. God surgically extracted the feminine side, and, now, the only feminine side of a man should be his wife. She is a perfect complement.

Single guys, I recommend you make discerning decisions regarding whom you date. Never date a girl who is not a candidate for a proposal.

Married guys, I encourage you to show how much you value your wife. If she isn't all you thought she would be, spend quality time, effort, and money to cultivate what attracted you to her in the first place. Don't sow negative words expecting positive results.

REMEMBER

The male and female have perfect complementary designs.

READ PROVERBS CHAPTER 31
fivestarman.com/day-243

Day 244: Choking On Bitter Fruit

PROVERBS 1:31 (NLT)

Therefore, they must eat the bitter fruit of living their own way,
choking on their own schemes.

PRINCIPLE

If a man devises his own schemes, he will suffer from his own stupidity.

We've previously talked about "The Law of Seed." In this case, the fruit is bitter because the seeds were destruction. I'm amazed at the repetitive stupidity of some men. They come up with their own devices, plans, schemes, and principles, and they expect to escape destruction as if they're going to beat the odds. It doesn't work that way.

When men come up with their own schemes and principles, they will have to live with them and try to swallow their bitterness, which usually chokes them.

Proverbs is written so we can live by the wisdom of God. Apply His principles and plans for your life.

REMEMBER

Let's be smart about our living.

READ PROVERBS CHAPTER 1

fivestarman.com/day-244

Day 245: Panning For Gold

PROVERBS 2:3–5 (MSG)

That's right—if you make Insight your priority,
and won't take no for an answer,
Searching for it like a prospector panning for gold,
like an adventurer on a treasure hunt,
Believe me, before you know it Fear-of-God will be yours;
you'll have come upon the Knowledge of God.

PRINCIPLE

The most valuable commodity on Earth is wisdom.

They're called the "forty-niners," approximately 300,000 adventurers who were seeking gold in California. They overcame substantial hardship to get there. Amazingly, the first to arrive simply picked up the gold off the ground. Then they had to start working the streams and panning. As more and more harvested the commodity, new sophisticated technology advanced, resulting in enormous new wealth.

Solomon, our advisor, was an extremely wealthy man. It would be almost impossible to compare with his wealth. He was arguably the richest man who ever lived.

He attributes the amassing of his wealth to one thing: wisdom. Wisdom is the principal thing.

Very similar to panning for gold, we must sift through the worthless to pick out the valuable. But if we discover it, our lives are changed forever. Wisdom is the greatest commodity.

REMEMBER

Wisdom is the greatest commodity.

READ PROVERBS CHAPTER 2
fivestarman.com/day-245

Day 246: Spoiling For A Fight

PROVERBS 3:30 (MSG)

Don't walk around with a chip on your shoulder,
always spoiling for a fight.

PRINCIPLE

A strong man doesn't strut his strength looking for a fight.

The *Long Island Telegraph* reported on 20 May, 1830, "When two churlish boys were determined to fight, a chip would be placed on the shoulder of one, and the other demanded to knock it off at his peril." This is similar to drawing a line in the sand and daring your opponent to step over the line.

When circumstances are volatile and a fight is about to break out, the best thing to do is either walk away or get to it. Posturing doesn't show strength. It's just annoying.

Growing up in Oklahoma, I was in a few fights. Even though I tried to never start one, I was determined to either put up or shut up.

There's a perception in Christianity that we must take abuse, no matter what the circumstances. My theology allows me to defend my family and myself. I have no hesitation to do so, but I will not put a chip on my shoulder, waiting for the next tough guy to knock it off. I do all that I can to avoid those kinds of circumstances.

REMEMBER

Don't be spoiling for a fight.

READ PROVERBS CHAPTER 3
fivestarman.com/day-246

Day 247: The Father's Voice

PROVERBS 4:20 (NLT)

My child, pay attention to what I say.
Listen carefully to my words.

PRINCIPLE

A father's voice is irreplaceable.

The statistics are overwhelming. The evidence is indisputable. The absence of a father's directional intent in his children's lives causes irreparable harm to them and collateral damage to society.

Malachi warned that we must have a prophetic voice call to the deep purposes of fathers to return to their children (Malachi 4:5-6).

Make no mistake about it. A father's voice is irreplaceable for children.

I can't fathom how fathers walk away from their children's lives. It is mind-boggling to me that a man will cower to the whims of his ex-wife or just abandon his children altogether. You may have an ex-wife, but you don't have ex-children. They need your voice.

I've encouraged men never to give up their rights and responsibilities to parent their children.

REMEMBER

Dad, your voice is irreplaceable.

READ PROVERBS CHAPTER 4

fivestarman.com/day-247

Day 248: Do Not Dishonor Authentic Manhood

PROVERBS 5:9 (NLT)

If you do, you will lose your honor
and will lose to merciless people all you have achieved.

PRINCIPLE

Do not dishonor authentic manhood and forfeit all of your earnings.

Our advisor pulls no punches when it comes to the warnings about the adulteress. He had seen it as an adult male. He knew the circumstances of his father and mother's adulterous affair that wreaked havoc upon the house of David. Solomon also observed the fallout of adultery from his unique position of leading a nation.

His father, David, was the most honorable man—a king of impeccable character who risked his own life multiple times for the sake of honor; yet, the night of boredom that led to his affair changed all of that. David's reputation was plunged into scandal.

Men, you're the gate of authority. The gate you open is the gate the enemy will use to access your home to destroy it. David lost four children: the infant child from Bathsheba, the defilement of Tamar, the murder of Amnon, and the rebellion and death of Absalom. Adultery is deadly.

REMEMBER

Refuse to live beneath the dignity of authentic manhood.

READ PROVERBS CHAPTER 5
fivestarman.com/day-248

Day 249: The Spirit Of Jealousy

PROVERBS 6:34 (MSG)

For jealousy detonates rage in a cheated husband;
wild for revenge, he won't make allowances.

PRINCIPLE

Husbands have an internal warning sign. Jealousy is a holy discernment.

Most people think of jealousy as a negative trait, but in reality, it is a signal that can arise when the one we're committed to strays. In fact, a husband actually has this internal warning within his spirit.

The Law of Moses addresses how to handle when a wife, while under her husband's authority, goes astray and defiles herself, or when the spirit of jealousy comes upon a man, and he becomes jealous of his wife. (See Numbers 5:30.)

A husband has positional authority to provide, protect, promote, and empower his wife. Husbandry is the practice and art of cultivation. A husband's words are seeds sown that produce a determined harvest.

Just as a farmer knows his field and cares for it, drawing out the best that it has to offer, so a husband cares for, nurtures, and draws out the best in his wife. A farmer is also keenly aware of trespassers who try to come onto his property, as a husband should be concerning his marriage.

I want to be clear: This isn't something to play with. It is a spiritual sense that must be carefully confirmed. Don't jump to rash conclusions or allow delusional thoughts to lead you astray. This is a matter of serious spiritual discernment.

REMEMBER

Jealousy isn't something to trifle with.

READ PROVERBS CHAPTER 6

fivestarman.com/day-249

Day 250: Seduced By Smooth Talk

PROVERBS 7:21 (NIV)

With persuasive words she led him astray;
she seduced him with her smooth talk.

PRINCIPLE

Don't give an adulteress proximity to speak seductively to you.

The adulteress uses the art of persuasion to captivate her victims. She is smooth in her language and flirtatious in the rhythm of her speech. Don't underestimate her tactics. She is a seasoned schemer.

What's the best way to keep from being led astray by her? It's as simple as proximity.

You can't sin with an adulteress without yielding the proximity to accept her persuasive words into your ears. You may think this is oversimplifying things, but it's really that simple.

Knowing the pitfalls many of my friends have fallen into and seeing men's sloppy behavior regarding flirtation with women, I established and have lived by rules to keep my distance from other women. This limits the ability for an adulteress to speak to me.

REMEMBER

Keep your distance.

READ PROVERBS CHAPTER 7

fivestarman.com/day-250

Day 251: Begin With Wisdom

PROVERBS 8:22 (NLT)

The Lord formed me from the beginning,
before he created anything else.

PRINCIPLE

God began with wisdom.

The more we dig into the science behind Creation, the order of things, and the laws which govern the universe, the more we see the remarkable qualities of wisdom.

There are simply too many governing laws in place here for our universe to be an accident. Order and natural laws show the wisdom of God.

Just as the Lord founded everything upon wisdom, we should establish everything upon wisdom, as well. We must have order in our lives and govern them with the principles of wisdom. We're creationists, not evolutionists. We don't rely upon random occurrences. We're not waiting on something to happen for us. We make things happen in our lives by applying the principles of wisdom.

Reading a chapter of Proverbs each day gives us the wisdom we need to establish a rhythm and structure for our lives. As you read, apply the wisdom you receive, and bring your life into order.

REMEMBER

Begin with wisdom.

READ PROVERBS CHAPTER 8

fivestarman.com/day-251

Day 252: Don't Waste Your Time

PROVERBS 9:8 (MSG)

So don't waste your time on a scoffer;
all you'll get for your pains is abuse.

PRINCIPLE

Don't waste your time on the minutia of mockers.

In my line of work, I'm exposed to different types of people. I've learned the hard way that you can't reason with some people, especially those who are cynical and arrogant. In more than a few instances I've made statements that set people off on rants of wrath. I used to try to reason with them, state my case, support my conclusions with scriptures, and try to convince them of my point of view. But a lot of people simply won't accept correction.

If for some reason I misspoke or didn't communicate clearly, I try to reword my statement; however, if someone is just scoffing at me and getting personal in their attack, I don't waste my time. I have too much to do than to be sidetracked by their babble.

Mockers don't argue from principle. They transform into caricatures and attack personally rather than substantially. They use straw-man arguments, aligning you in their imaginations as an opponent. This is a shallow form of debate, but that's all they have.

Go on and reason with those who are wise and they will be even wiser. Spend your energy on hearers not mockers.

REMEMBER

Don't get dragged down into the minutia of arguments.

READ PROVERBS CHAPTER 9

fivestarman.com/day-252

Day 253: The Disciplined Life

PROVERBS 10:17 (MSG)

The road to life is a disciplined life;
ignore correction and you're lost for good.

PRINCIPLE

The disciplined life is really living.

Most of us feel a little twinge when we hear the word *discipline*. It doesn't bring us fond memories; however, discipline is an extremely positive attribute when we learn to accept it. In fact, if you want to live life to the fullest, you need to embrace discipline. It's for your good.

Discipline is the ability to hear instruction and adjust your mind, will, and emotions to submit to its teaching and wisdom.

For an example, when you implement the discipline to read Proverbs every day, your mind begins to think thoughts with godly wisdom. You're renewing your mind. After a few months of discipline, this process will become a passion—a habitual exercise you can't imagine going without in your life.

Take a look around and survey your life. Are you living slothfully or disorderly? Are there areas of your life where you need discipline? Are there appetites you can't control? When you're reading Proverbs, are there instructional statements you're avoiding? Or even skipping altogether?

You're a man. It's your life and your choice. You can decide not to have discipline, but the person you're hurting most is yourself.

REMEMBER

Live it up! Be disciplined.

READ PROVERBS CHAPTER 10

fivestarman.com/day-253

Day 254: The Storms Of Life

PROVERBS 10:25 (NLT)

When the storms of life come, the wicked are whirled away,
but the godly have a lasting foundation.

PRINCIPLE

You can have confidence when facing storms.

As long as we live in this world, we'll all face the challenges that come with a frustrated Creation.

"For the creation was subjected to frustration, not by its own choice, but by the will of the one who subjected it, in hope that the creation itself will be liberated from its bondage to decay and brought into the freedom and glory of the children of God" (Romans 8:20–21 NIV).

The false notion that believers are immune from storms causes some to question their faith. We're not immune, but we can certainly face storms with confidence. Jesus demonstrated His confidence when He faced a storm.

"The disciples went and woke him up, shouting, 'Master, Master, we're going to drown!' When Jesus woke up, he rebuked the wind and the raging waves. Suddenly the storm stopped and all was calm" (Luke 8:24 NLT).

Obviously, Jesus knew this storm wasn't orchestrated by His Father. How did Jesus handle it? He rebuked it.

When you're facing a storm in life, don't assume God is putting you through it. Have the confidence to rebuke it, and you'll find yourself on a solid foundation when the storm is over.

REMEMBER

Storms roll through, but the righteous have a firm foundation.

READ PROVERBS CHAPTER 11

fivestarman.com/day-254

Day 255: Plans Or Schemes

PROVERBS 12:20 (MSG)

Evil scheming distorts the schemer;
peace-planning brings joy to the planner.

PRINCIPLE

If a man gives himself over to evil scheming his mind becomes distorted.

Men have a remarkable ability to use their imagination to engineer, create, draw, design, write, visualize, and plan. Our thoughts can work through troubles and crisis. We can strategize and see possible futures. It's fascinating that God has given us such a gift of unlimited ability.

However, if we misuse our imaginations, we can darken our thoughts and move toward evil. Plotting and scheming evil brings a distortion into our minds. That's one of the real possibilities of gazing upon pornography. The man who gives himself to lustful fantasies darkens his mind. His thinking becomes distorted and perverted.

"We demolish arguments and every pretension that sets itself up against the knowledge of God, and we take captive every thought to make it obedient to Christ" (2 Corinthians 10:5 NIV).

We can control our thoughts. We can take captive any thought that does not align with God's Word. This will make us planners, not schemers. In the end, our plans will bring joy into our lives.

REMEMBER

Don't waste your thinking.

READ PROVERBS CHAPTER 12
fivestarman.com/day-255

Day 256: Leave A Legacy

PROVERBS 13:22 (MSG)

A good life gets passed on to the grandchildren....

PRINCIPLE

A good man leaves an inheritance for his children's children.

One of the passions of authentic manhood is to leave a legacy. Men have a deep desire to be remembered. Solomon said God placed eternity within the heart of man, so we desire to leave our mark—to be significant (Ecclesiastes 3:11).

I live with the desire to receive one compliment in my life. This desire helps me make decisions. It motivates me to focus on my purpose. It helps me cast off the things that could restrain me. The single compliment I desire is to hear my children tell their children is that they serve the God of their father.

My motivation in life is pretty simple. I want to leave a legacy.

REMEMBER

Live your life with the end in mind.

READ PROVERBS CHAPTER 13

fivestarman.com/day-256

Day 257: Secure Your World

PROVERBS 14:26 (MSG)

The Fear-of-God builds up confidence,
and makes a world safe for your children.

PRINCIPLE

Those who do not fear God will face paranoia and insecurity. Those who fear God will build a secure fortress for their children.

The world is volatile and dangerous—seemingly always on the verge of implosion. Haven't you noticed how insecure the economic, governmental, and social systems are?

As insecure as the world is, your world—the part that you control (your house, finances, properties, and family) can be secure if you fear God.

The word, *fear* isn't referring to paranoia or terror but *reverential awe* and *respect* toward God. It's interesting that those who don't fear God face the threat of terror, but those who do fear Him are secure.

REMEMBER

Secure your world.

READ PROVERBS CHAPTER 14

fivestarman.com/day-257

Day 258: Junk-Food Mind

PROVERBS 15:14 (NLT)

A wise person is hungry for knowledge,
while the fool feeds on trash.

PRINCIPLE

Gain understanding of your purposes, and you'll control your appetites.

The Hebrew word for *heart,* "lāv," means *seat of appetites or seat of purposes.* The laborer's appetite drives him. It drives him to work. Take away a man's appetite, and you rob him of a purpose.

Each week when I speak to men, one of my goals is to stir up a hunger pain for a purpose within them. The challenge is the apathy that comes with what I call a "junk-food mind." Some men have been feeding on garbage. Their minds are cluttered with rotting thoughts.

It's interesting what happens when men hear the five purposes that reside deep within them (an adventurous spirit, an entrepreneurial drive, gallant relationships, faithfulness in character, and a philanthropic cause). They lean forward as if they're getting into a ready stance. They become motivated!

Stop feeding on the junk that doesn't matter in your world. Stop stuffing your face with the minutia of mindless waste.

REMEMBER

Get hungry for knowledge.

READ PROVERBS CHAPTER 15

fivestarman.com/day-258

Day 259: Good Leader Vs. Bad Leader

PROVERBS 16:14–15 (MSG)

An intemperate leader wreaks havoc in lives;
you're smart to stay clear of someone like that.
Good-tempered leaders invigorate lives;
they're like spring rain and sunshine.

PRINCIPLE

Leaders can wreak havoc or invigorate your life.

Have you ever worked for someone who flew off the handle at the smallest of things? Intemperate leaders are emotional extremists. They lack control of themselves and take it out on anyone and everyone who is near them.

Serving under this kind of leadership can be incredibly discouraging. As you're wanting to improve your lot in life and to progress in your skills and abilities, an intemperate leader can be a disaster. He will try to tear down everything you've built.

A good leader is someone who draws upon your gift set and brings life to your talents. This kind of leader can have a tremendous influence upon you. When you've served under a harsh taskmaster, serving under a leader who brings out the best in you is like sunshine after a stormy day.

REMEMBER

Stay clear of an intemperate leader.

READ PROVERBS CHAPTER 16

fivestarman.com/day-259

Day 260: Stop Fussing

PROVERBS 17:14 (NLT)

Starting a quarrel is like opening a floodgate,
so stop before a dispute breaks out.

PRINCIPLE

A quarrel is the seed of strife, and strife is the manifested presence of evil.

Have you ever been around people who fuss all the time? It seems some people thrive on drama. Some families are always at it—fussing and cussing. That's not the atmosphere you want in your home. In fact, it is dangerous. A large dispute can break out from small fights.

Some might say, "Well, we enjoy a good fight now and then."

My wife and I established very early on that we wouldn't have a home filled with strife. We wouldn't jab at each other or fuss over small things. I know this is a rarity, but we simply will not raise our voices at each other. Don't get me wrong: We've disagreed on things, but we do not argue and fight to get our way.

One of the byproducts of not arguing and fussing in our home is that our children didn't argue with one another. They copied our behavior of having conversations rather than yelling.

REMEMBER

Stop fussing.

READ PROVERBS CHAPTER 17
fivestarman.com/day-260

Day 261: Friends

PROVERBS 18:24 (MSG)

Friends come and friends go,
but a true friend sticks by you like family.

PRINCIPLE

A friend is someone who shows up when everyone else has left.

The Hebrew root for the word *friend* indicates *those who flock together or graze together in a pasture.* It paints a picture of sheep out in the field bonding together while they're going about their business eating.

That's what friends do. They dine together, laugh, cry, and share experiences, as they go about the business of life. Friends can become closer than blood relatives. They can have more in common and more harmony than natural-born brothers.

However, not all friends are true and faithful to friendships. When things don't go their way, some will come and go. There seem to be two ways to weed out those who aren't true friends: Go through a crisis, and you may find your friendship list gets pretty small; or strike it rich, you may find there's an envious person questioning your worthiness. In either case, consider it a good thing that their true motives were exposed when they depart.

REMEMBER

When trouble strikes a friend, be one.

READ PROVERBS CHAPTER 18
fivestarman.com/day-261

Day 262: Disgraceful Children

PROVERBS 19:26 (NLT)

Children who mistreat their father or chase away their mother
are an embarrassment and a public disgrace.

PRINCIPLE

It takes discipline to discipline correctly.

It only takes one visit to Walmart to see how our society has lost its sanity regarding disciplining children. Children are ruling their parents. Disobedient, disrespectful, and insolent children are becoming much too prevalent. They are a byproduct of years of neglectful parenting.

Now the debate is about *how* we should discipline. A while ago, the old-fashioned switch from a tree put football player Adrian Peterson on trial for child abuse.

Here's what I know: If you love your children, you will discipline them and raise them to treat you and your wife with respect. Respect is fundamental in establishing them to live long, successful lives. And it takes discipline to discipline correctly.

REMEMBER

Don't allow your children to disrespect you.

READ PROVERBS CHAPTER 19
fivestarman.com/day-262

Day 263: Eyes To See—Ears To Hear

PROVERBS 20:12 (NLT)

Ears to hear and eyes to see—
both are gifts from the Lord.

PRINCIPLE

There's more to hearing than sound. There's more to seeing than sight.

"You have eyes—can't you see? You have ears—can't you hear? Don't you remember anything at all?" (Mark 8:18 NLT)

Someone once asked Helen Keller what could be worse than being blind. She replied "to have sight without vision."

The goal of ***The Daily Champion*** is to encourage you. It is to motivate you to continue your quest for authentic manhood. I realize the daily grind can be tough. I know the routine of life is boring. What we must do is perceive. We must seek a revelation of the deep passions that are within us.

I spoke with a leader awhile back. He is also passionate about helping men in their pursuit of authentic manhood, but our motivation will be short-lived if we rely only upon what we can see with our eyes. We need to perceive what is happening deep within us.

REMEMBER

Don't base your motivation on only what you can see.

READ PROVERBS CHAPTER 20
fivestarman.com/day-263

Day 264: Calling But No Answer

PROVERBS 21:13 (NLT)

Those who shut their ears to the cries of the poor
will be ignored in their own time of need.

PRINCIPLE

The manner in which you respond to others is the manner in which God responds to you.

Yesterday's ***Daily Champion*** talked about having ears to hear. Today, we need to see that our ears need to be attentive to the needs of others. This principle is amazing and challenging at the same time.

How do you respond when someone calls upon you? Is that the way you would want God to respond when you call upon Him?

Do you return calls promptly? Do you put people off when they have a need? Are you aware and observant of the needs of others? Do you respond to emails and texts without delay? Is your voicemail maxed out?

How do you like it when people cancel meetings and appointments? Do you do that to others? How do you respond to the needs around you?

REMEMBER

Listen! Is someone calling you?

READ PROVERBS CHAPTER 21

fivestarman.com/day-264

Day 265: Know Your Boundaries

PROVERBS 22:28 (NLT)

Don't cheat your neighbor by moving the ancient boundary markers set up by previous generations.

PRINCIPLE

We must honor those who established and defined the boundaries.

This precept establishes a code of honor regarding those who pioneered new ground—the generations who paved the way for us and laid down boundaries. There is much more to this precept than meets the eye. It's amazingly arrogant for a young and zealous generation to disregard previous generations.

This principle doesn't elevate tradition over progress; however, it does provide a cautious pause to keep us from acting willy-nilly with established boundaries.

Take the current agenda for those who want to redefine marriage—replacing a time-tested and biblically mandated union between a male and female. Move this ancient boundary stone, and the value of marriage will be lost. The destruction of society will follow close at hand. Moving the stone of marriage isn't progress. It's degradation.

When I was raising my children, I established boundaries to protect them from the dangers outside my reach. If their behavior or decisions took them close to those guardrails, I pulled them back. My actions communicated my love as I kept an eye on where their behavior would lead.

REMEMBER

Boundaries actually demonstrate our love and protection for the generations that follow.

➔ READ PROVERBS CHAPTER 22

fivestarman.com/day-265

Day 266: The Ways Of My Father

PROVERBS 23:26 (NIV)

My son, give me your heart
and let your eyes delight in my ways.

PRINCIPLE

When we follow God, we acknowledge that His ways are superior to ours.

You may remember, the Hebrew word for *heart* is *the seat of purposes, appetites, and emotions.* When you align your purposes to the Father, your cravings will thirst and hunger for Him, and your emotions will follow.

Men relate to others differently than women do. Women relate face-to-face sharing feelings, while men relate shoulder-to-shoulder, facing a challenge. That doesn't mean men aren't emotional. It means our emotions flow from our purposes.

That's why the foundational philosophy of ***FivestarMan*** is to speak to the heart of a man. When we focus on a man's purposes, he will cast off the things that would constrain him.

When we follow God's ways, we're acknowledging that His ways are superior to our ways. His purposes for us are better than whatever plans we could concoct.

REMEMBER

The heart of man is the seat of purposes.

READ PROVERBS CHAPTER 23

fivestarman.com/day-266

Day 267: The Protocol Of Prosperity

PROVERBS 24:27 (AMP)

[Put first things first.] Prepare your work outside
and get it ready for yourself in the field;
and afterward build your house and establish a home.

PRINCIPLE

Plant your fields. Build your barn. Enjoy the benefits.

There's a process involved in prospering. It involves "The Law of Seed." God gave us this law so we could satisfy our cravings in life. The ability to sow a seed for a determined harvest is an amazing gift.

However, "The Law of Seed" involves work. It's a fantasy to expect a future for which you haven't sown a seed to harvest. The real challenge of today's culture is that most people want to enjoy a harvest they haven't worked to reap.

Authentic manhood is motivated by a strong work ethic and a determination to honor the protocol of prosperity: seed + time = harvest. At the end of a good work day, we're able to sit down on the porch, look over our fields, take a glance at the barn, and have gratitude for our labor, being able to look back at our labor with joy.

REMEMBER

Honor the protocol of prosperity (seed + time = harvest).

READ PROVERBS CHAPTER 24
fivestarman.com/day-267

Day 268: Be Refreshed

PROVERBS 25:25 (MSG)

Like a cool drink of water when you're worn out and weary
is a letter from a long-lost friend.

PRINCIPLE

Speak kind and comforting words.

I came to Christ under the leadership of some wonderful people in a small town in Oklahoma. My work in a coal mine let me experience enough in a few years of young adulthood to know that I needed Christ. Reverend Charles and Sister Taylor were there, not only to lead me to the knowledge of Christ, but also to invite me into their home where I asked Brother Taylor a thousand questions.

Recently, I received a handwritten note from Sister Taylor. (I know it's old-fashioned to use the honorific term of "Sister," but she is fully due that title.) Her note shared how grateful they were for me and for the books I've written. Frankly, I was humbled by the very thought that they were proud of me. They knew me at my worst. I only hope I continue to show them my best.

Her words encouraged me and strengthened my resolve to press on for the mark of the high calling. I refuse to live beneath the dignity of the One who gave me life.

Is there someone you can write a note of encouragement to? Your words may be a cool drink of refreshment for someone else today.

REMEMBER

Speak kind and comforting words.

READ PROVERBS CHAPTER 25

fivestarman.com/day-268

Day 269: The Jokes Of A Madman

PROVERBS 26:18 (NLT)

Just as damaging
as a madman shooting a deadly weapon
is someone who lies to a friend
and then says, "I was only joking."

PRINCIPLE

We need to be sober-minded, using wisdom and protecting our friendships with integrity.

When I was fifteen, my family and four other families caravanned in RVs to tour the western states. I got to spend the night in a sleeping bag outside under the stars, and it was here that I determined to live my life differently than what had been modeled before me.

It was on this trip that I watched my mother's second husband, Ted, reveal himself as a buffoon. We were driving up to Virginia City, Nevada. RVs were detoured around the steep incline into the city. He lied to his friends on the CB radio, saying we had gone up the short, steep route and dared them to try it. It was a disaster. All four families got stuck.

After the tow trucks came, the only response from Ted was, "I was only joking."

No one was laughing. One RV almost blew an engine. Another's transmission was damaged. Another almost went off the road. It could have been deadly. This event severed some relationships.

It was that moment when I saw the stupidity of practical joking. This may sound harsh, but very few practical jokes are funny. Some are dangerously stupid.

REMEMBER

Don't be a madman.

READ PROVERBS CHAPTER 26
fivestarman.com/day-269

Day 270: Iron Man

PROVERBS 27:17 (NIV)

As iron sharpens iron,
so one man sharpens another.

PRINCIPLE

Manly relationships are forged through competition on the field of contest.

Authentic manhood relates to other men differently than what this culture espouses. Men relate shoulder-to-shoulder, facing a challenge on the field of contest. It could be a football field, a baseball field, or even a battlefield, but that is where men relate.

Iron doesn't sharpen by the caress, but by the clash. The rough edges of a man are sharpened when he is around other men. There is nothing like it. It's comparable to no other relationship.

I hope you have authentic manly relationships which encourage you and bring out the best in you. We've designed ***FivestarMan*** with the strategy to express the five purposes of authentic manhood so men can gain an understanding of their purposes and express them with a passionate pursuit.

We encourage men daily to do these things: engage other men weekly; get on the field of contest for an excursion each month; each quarter have a deep encounter with God; and do great exploits at least once a year.

REMEMBER

Other men will sharpen you.

READ PROVERBS CHAPTER 27
fivestarman.com/day-270

Day 271: Get-Rich-Quick Schemes

PROVERBS 28:20 (NIV)

A faithful man will be richly blessed,
but one eager to get rich will not go unpunished.

PRINCIPLE

Committed and persistent work pays off. Get-rich-quick schemes are rip-offs.

A ***FivestarMan*** is faithful. He is the kind of man who keeps his word. He has integrity. He is authentic. He has a strong work ethic.

Authentic manhood believes work is a moral good. There is a purpose behind work. In fact, we know God gave Man a vocation (a divine calling) before He gave Man the Woman.

A faithful man is in contrast to the eager-beaver who is running around, fluttering from one job to the next. Inconsistent, and wishy-washy, his goal isn't to work—it's simply to get riches.

Riches without purpose are disastrous. There are countless stories of people who received large sums of money, and it destroyed their lives. Let's not be shallow in our thinking to conclude it was the money that destroyed them. In reality, the lack of purpose did.

REMEMBER

Faithfulness brings riches for a reason.

READ PROVERBS CHAPTER 28
fivestarman.com/day-271

Day 272: Where Does Your Help Come From?

PROVERBS 29:26 (MSG)

Everyone tries to get help from the leader,
but only God will give us justice.

PRINCIPLE

Trust the One who gave you the dream to make it come true.

When you're passionate about something, it is very easy to begin to scheme a way to get it done. Many begin to look for shortcuts or an audience with someone who can make it happen for them. They plot and maneuver to present their case to someone important they think can help. Most of the time this plan is embarrassingly rejected.

I have seen it a thousand times. In fact, I've been tempted to consider trying to get my God-given ideas to someone so they can be accomplished without all of the struggles I've faced.

Consider this: If God wanted someone else to do it, He would have given it to them. But God gave the assignment to you. That means He will give you the wisdom to accomplish it. Don't try to curry favor with someone. Seek God, and He will direct your steps. It may be that God uses someone of means and connections to help, but let God do that for you. Don't collude with someone to get it done.

REMEMBER

The God who gave you the assignment will also give you the means and connections to get it done.

READ PROVERBS CHAPTER 29

fivestarman.com/day-272

Day 273: Small Wonders Of Wisdom

PROVERBS 30:24–28 (NLT)

There are four things on earth that are small but unusually wise:
Ants—they aren't strong,
but they store up food all summer.
Hyraxes—they aren't powerful,
but they make their homes among the rocks.
Locusts—they have no king,
but they march in formation.
Lizards—they are easy to catch,
but they are found even in kings' palaces.

PRINCIPLE

Wisdom can be found in small things.

We can learn wisdom simply by observing God's Creation. It's amazing when you think of it. Solomon understood a great many things about animals and birds, reptiles, and fish. Take the four small wonders Solomon points out in today's proverb:

Ants—They have the wisdom for savings (an emergency fund).

Hyraxes—A small animal more closely associated with an elephant, even though it looks like a rodent, a hyrax is wise with a strong fortress for protection.

Locusts—Although they're leaderless, they know how to work together to advance their communal cause.

Lizards—They're often invited to live in high-class palaces because of their benefit to the owners, eating insects and ridding the place of them.

REMEMBER

Don't underestimate the small things that are wise.

READ PROVERBS CHAPTER 30
fivestarman.com/day-273

Day 274: Where Does Your Help Come From?

PROVERBS 1:33 (NLT)

But all who listen to me will live in peace,
untroubled by fear of harm.

PRINCIPLE

Just because someone speaks fear doesn't mean you should listen.

With round-the-clock cable news scouring the world for disaster, it's pretty easy to drift into fear. I've had to become diligent to turn off the news and only catch up on it occasionally. I've made a conscious effort to turn off the news and turn on the audio of the Word of God. (I use YouVersion.) I've also gathered a mix of podcasts of good preaching.

Listening to the Word of God is more than just a good habit, because the Word of God is the source of all life. All things were made by the Word. It is like oxygen and water. You can't live without them. The Word is the source of those elements. That's how important the Word is.

"The Word gave life to everything that was created, and his life brought light to everyone" (John 1:4 NLT).

The light is what extinguishes the darkness. The fear that can come upon you by hearing so much bad press can be replaced by hearing the Word.

REMEMBER

Don't give your ears to all the voices that are speaking.

READ PROVERBS CHAPTER 1

fivestarman.com/day-274

Day 275: Wise Choices

PROVERBS 2:11 (NIV)

Discretion will protect you,
and understanding will guard you.

PRINCIPLE

Life is the combination of choices. Wise or foolish—decisions determine destiny.

As we've been reading Proverbs each day of the month, the benefit is that wisdom begins to watch over our decision-making. After thirty years of reading Proverbs each day, I can't tell you how many times the insight, understanding, and wisdom I've gained helped me make the right choices.

The Daily Champion has encouraged thousands of men who are now reading Proverbs each day. Wisdom is watching over each one as they navigate life.

How about you? Have you noticed yourself pushing a pause button on some decisions, while, at other times, you're getting a green light to move forward? That's wisdom at work. That's why it's so important to have the discipline to read a chapter of Proverbs each day, along with this encouraging word.

REMEMBER

Champions do daily what the average man does occasionally.

READ PROVERBS CHAPTER 2

fivestarman.com/day-275

Day 276: Friend Of God

PROVERBS 3:32 (NLT)

Such wicked people are detestable to the Lord,
but he offers his friendship to the godly.

PRINCIPLE

God has offered His friendship to man.

The word *detestable* is pretty strong isn't it? Some men find it hard to swallow—the idea that God looks at anyone as an abomination; yet, that's exactly what He does. He considers wicked people detestable.

But God also offers friendship to the righteous. Friendship is an incredibly intimate relationship. Can you fathom that God Almighty would seek that kind of relationship with us? When Jesus walked with man, you see Him expressing friendship.

"When Jesus saw their faith, he said, 'Friend, your sins are forgiven'" (Luke 5:20 NIV).

If your sins are forgiven, you're a friend of God.

REMEMBER

You're a friend of God.

READ PROVERBS CHAPTER 3

fivestarman.com/day-276

Day 277: Guard Your Heart

PROVERBS 4:23 (MSG)

Keep vigilant watch over your heart;
that's where life starts.

PRINCIPLE

Guard your heart above all else, for it determines the course of your life.

Lately, I've had some amazing revelation regarding the definition of the Hebrew word for *heart*. Go to our ***FivestarMan*** website and take a few minutes to read an article entitled, "How To Discover Your Purposes, Control Your Appetites, and Stabilize Your Emotions."

Solomon pinpoints the importance of the heart of man in today's proverb by saying it is the heart that determines the course of your life. Wow!

Obviously, we know the physical vitality of the heart, but the cognitive neuroscientist Dr. Caroline Leaf explains that your heart has a direct link to your brain. Your brain and heart have a kinetic relationship. Your heart has a "seat" of thinking. This "seat," or foundation, determines your passionate pursuit of authentic manhood. Pretty amazing isn't it?

Let's be vigilant to watch, guard, protect, and condition our hearts.

REMEMBER

Out of the heart flow the issues of life.

READ PROVERBS CHAPTER 4
fivestarman.com/day-277

Day 278: The Sad End Of A Misspent Life

PROVERBS 5:11 (NIV)

At the end of your life you will groan,
when your flesh and body are spent.

PRINCIPLE

The poisons of a rebellious life will bring a sad ending to a misspent life.

At ***FivestarMan***, we talk about the fifth purpose of authentic man, which is leaving a legacy with a philanthropic cause. Amazingly, few men live their lives with the goal of leaving a legacy. In fact, temporary and carnal thinking seem to rule most men's minds.

Solomon said God has placed eternity within the heart of man (Ecclesiastes 3:11). As we've been studying the Hebrew word for heart—the seat of purposes, appetites, and emotions—we can see that to think eternally is within the purposes, appetites, and emotions of each man.

That's what makes today's verse seem so disappointing. Many men live their lives in complete rebellion to the original intent of manhood. In their youth, they stand, stomp their feet, and resist the will of God. When they're old and weakened by poisons (e.g., alcohol, tobacco, drugs, sexual sins, bitterness, antipathy, etc.) their yellowed skin, rotted teeth, and bloodshot eyes reveal the groaning of their bodies.

I've known many men who lived the last season of their lives in regret. It's a sad ending to a misspent life.

REMEMBER

Set your course for eternity.

READ PROVERBS CHAPTER 5

fivestarman.com/day-278

Day 279: Get Up!

PROVERBS 6:10–11 (MSG)

A nap here, a nap there, a day off here, a day off there,
sit back, take it easy—do you know what comes next?
Just this: You can look forward to a dirt-poor life,
poverty your permanent houseguest!

PRINCIPLE

The greatest temptation in a man's life is comfort.

Men, we need to wake up! We have drifted into an apathy that is seriously dangerous.

"Suddenly, there was a bright light in the cell, and an angel of the Lord stood before Peter. The angel struck him on the side to awaken him and said, 'Quick! Get up!' And the chains fell off his wrists" (Acts 12:7 NLT).

The context of this verse is that King Herod began to persecute Christians. He had the disciple James put to death and then set his eyes upon Peter. Peter had been arrested and was about to face a mock trial and execution. However, believers began to pray and intercede for him. An angel, who was assigned to rescue Peter, showed up and awakened him out of his stupor.

As I travel each week to speak, my goal is to awaken men out of their stupor—to shake them—to sound the alarm and wake them out of apathy!

We're facing a real danger in our times. This isn't a time for fantasy games. We can't afford to slumber. Our nemesis hates us for what we stand for.

"So be on your guard, not asleep like the others. Stay alert and be clearheaded" (1 Thessalonians 5:6 NLT).

REMEMBER

Man of God, wake up!

READ PROVERBS CHAPTER 6
fivestarman.com/day-279

Day 280: Dead Meat

PROVERBS 7:22–23 (MSG)

Before you know it, he's trotting behind her,
like a calf led to the butcher shop,
Like a stag lured into ambush
and then shot with an arrow,
Like a bird flying into a net
not knowing that its flying life is over.

PRINCIPLE

A young man is never treated with more disrespect than when an adulteress sets her traps for him.

I don't like when a man plays the fool. It bothers me to see a young man being naïvely led astray by an adulteress. He doesn't know how vulnerable he is to her trappings. She leads him into a snare. The result is tragedy and death.

He's dead meat.

It is so frustrating to see a man treated like a piece of meat by a woman. He has no value beyond the consumption of her ruthless and evil desires.

Don't fall into this trap! Don't put your foot into her snare. Don't allow her hooks and knives to cut you up. You're too valuable. Your future is too promising to throw it away for this disgusting trick.

REMEMBER

Don't be a piece of dead meat.

READ PROVERBS CHAPTER 7

fivestarman.com/day-280

Day 281: Delight In Mankind

PROVERBS 8:30 (NIV)

Then I was constantly at his side.
I was filled with delight day after day,
rejoicing always in his presence,
rejoicing in his whole world
and delighting in mankind.

PRINCIPLE

Delight in mankind.

This is a remarkable statement that Wisdom is speaking concerning God's Creation, especially delighting in mankind. That's a contrast from what we mainly hear regarding mankind. Most of us struggle with delighting in people these days.

It's good for us to stop listening to the evil reports and read some good reports regarding mankind. It's easy for us to become calloused and cynical regarding humanity. But there is some good out there. Let's just keep our eyes open to it and acknowledge it when we see it.

Look at it this way: Maybe you're a craftsman and are able to create something with your hands. When you've finished a project, have you ever stepped back, looked it over and admired it—maybe, even delighted in it? That's what Wisdom does concerning the work of God, especially mankind.

REMEMBER

Take delight in mankind.

READ PROVERBS CHAPTER 8
fivestarman.com/day-281

Day 282: Don't Fool With Folly

PROVERBS 9:13 (NIV)

Folly is an unruly woman;
she is simple and knows nothing.

PRINCIPLE

There are some women it's best to avoid.

The authentic man is gallant toward women. We give attention and show respect toward all women in an honorable way.

However, there is a certain kind of woman—the Bible calls her, *Folly*—who is simple, brazen, boisterous, and morally loose. Some men are attracted to her, but she is an empty vessel of stupidity. You may think I am the opposite of gallant by being so blunt, but this woman isn't a lady. She's yielded herself to destruction. She is used by evil spirits to entrap men.

She is personified by the Sidonian woman Jezebel, the wicked wife of Ahab, the King of Israel. Again, her name means, *without cohabitation.* Although married, she does not submit to, nor honor covenant with her husband. She is unchaste and immoral.

Unfortunately, there are many women who have accepted the spirit of Jezebel. These women dishonor marriage and are loud and defiant.

Solomon's advice regarding Ms. Folly is to avoid her. Stay away from Madam Whore. You're not going to gain anything from this kind of woman. Your time with her is a waste.

REMEMBER

Don't fool with Ms. Folly.

READ PROVERBS CHAPTER 9

fivestarman.com/day-282

Day 283: Wealth Without Trouble

PROVERBS 10:22 (NKJV)

The blessing of the Lord makes one rich,
And he adds no sorrow with it.

PRINCIPLE

The wealth God brings into your life is a blessing.

If we're not careful, we can buy into the popular notion that wealth creation can only happen if you're doing something evil. Sure there are those who do evil and profit from it: drug dealers, sex traffickers, porn peddlers, those who charge usury; however, if we live righteously, those people will never make a dime off of us.

Biblical wealth accumulation is a reward of those who fear God and walk according to His ways. It is recognized as such a direct link to His blessing upon a person's life that we're warned not to take personal credit for it.

"You may say to yourself, 'My power and the strength of my hands have produced this wealth for me,' But remember the Lord your God, for it is he who gives you the ability to produce wealth...." (Deuteronomy 8:17–18 NIV).

When we remember God is the one who empowers us to prosper, greed and pride in wealth is a non-issue.

I've known wealthy people who were anti-prosperity because they didn't want to give God the credit for their wealth. They claimed that it all came from their hard work and abilities. That's foolishness.

REMEMBER

The wealth God brings into your life is a blessing.

READ PROVERBS CHAPTER 10

fivestarman.com/day-283

Day 284: Generosity

PROVERBS 11:25 (NLT)

The generous will prosper;
those who refresh others will themselves be refreshed.

PRINCIPLE

Generosity flows from a heart of gratitude.

I recently had dinner with a young entrepreneur who has done extremely well in the last few years. What's remarkable is that just a few years ago, he could hardly rub two nickels together.

We were eating at a local dive (a favorite of mine). The waitress was good and attentive but not outstanding. There was nothing worth noting about her service.

When it came time for the bill, we both reached for it as our normal custom of arguing over who would pay. This time, he won. He got out the amount of the bill plus a hundred-dollar bill and put it in the folder. We stood up to leave, and as the waitress took the folder toward the register, she looked stunned. She ran over to us and said, "You've made a mistake. Here. You left a hundred."

My friend, politely said, "No mistake. That's for you and your family."

You may think it was easy for him to be generous because he is wealthy. The fact of the matter is that he was generous when he didn't have money.

I've known men who weren't generous, even though they were doing well financially. They didn't have the joy my friend has. They counted the cost of everything. They seemed embittered even though they had money. They weren't happy people.

REMEMBER

Refresh others and you will be refreshed.

READ PROVERBS CHAPTER 11

fivestarman.com/day-284

Day 285: Diligent

PROVERBS 12:24 (AMP)

The hand of the diligent will rule,
but the slothful will be put to forced labor.

PRINCIPLE

The diligent put constant effort into accomplishing something. They are attentive and persistent in all they do.

The Diligent:

- **Become leaders**—"The hand of the diligent will rule, But the lazy man will be put to forced labor" (Proverbs 12:24 NKJV).
- **Obtain wealth and prosper**—"The soul of a lazy man desires, and has nothing; But the soul of the diligent shall be made rich" (Proverbs 13:4 NKJV).
- **Have a definite purpose and objective**—"Therefore, brethren, be even more diligent to make your call and election sure, for if you do these things you will never stumble" (2 Peter 1:10 NKJV).
- **Work even when it's inconvenient in order to reap the reward**—"Be strong, therefore, and let not your hands be weak and slack, for your work will be rewarded" (2 Chronicles 15:7 AMP).
- **Will be successful and stand before kings**—"Seest thou a man diligent in his business? he shall stand before kings; he shall not stand before mean men" (Proverbs 22:29 KJV).

REMEMBER

Diligence is a key to personal success.

READ PROVERBS CHAPTER 12
fivestarman.com/day-285

Day 286: Injustice

PROVERBS 13:23 (AMP)

Abundant food is in the fallow (uncultivated) ground of the poor, But [without protection] it is swept away by injustice.

PRINCIPLE

Injustice rules this world.

Have you read insurance documents and noted the phrase, "Acts of God" when referring to something disastrous? People often attribute untimely death, sickness, and calamity as "God's will."

We see the tragedies of this world and shake our heads. Some even shake their fists; however, these are not the acts of God—but the acts of god. I use the little "g" to distinguish between the One True God Almighty, and the god of this world—namely, Satan (2 Corinthians 4:4).

Some assign *ALL* acts to God's will, but today's proverb assigns the misfortune and disaster of the poor person's field to injustice. Injustice is an act of unfairness. It involves a more powerful opponent using excessive force to harm or violate another.

Obviously, this doesn't represent the character of God. The Psalmist declared, "The heavens proclaim his righteousness, for he is a God of justice" (Psalm 50:6 NIV).

We see injustice every day. This world is ruled by those who do injustice. Governments execute injustices toward the very people they are elected to serve.

Is there injustice in this world? You bet there is. It comes from the god of this world—not God Almighty, the righteous, holy, God of Justice.

REMEMBER

It's best to know whom to blame when bad things happen to good people.

READ PROVERBS CHAPTER 13

fivestarman.com/day-286

Day 287: Leadership Is Influence

PROVERBS 14:28 (MSG)

The mark of a good leader is loyal followers;
leadership is nothing without a following.

PRINCIPLE

A leader without followers is merely taking a walk.

By birth, men are leaders. As a man, you are positioned for leadership. You're given the authority for the position. However, if you're not a good leader, you will lose your followers.

Saul was given a position as the first king of Israel because he was a humble man; however, in the course of time, his position went to his head. He began to think of himself more highly than he should. The larger he grew in his head, the smaller his influence became in his kingdom. When the young shepherd boy named David arrived on the scene, men began to follow David, and women began to sing songs about him. Saul's insecurities caused him to lose his mind.

It's tempting for leaders to get too focused on the benefits of their position rather than humbly accepting the responsibility of leadership.

Men do this on a much smaller scale regarding their wives and families. They throw around their *position* as "the man of the house" without living up to the responsibilities of *being* the man of the house. They eventually lose the respect of their wives and experience the mockery of their children.

REMEMBER

With leadership comes the responsibility of the position.

READ PROVERBS CHAPTER 14
fivestarman.com/day-287

Day 288: What's On Your Playlist?

PROVERBS 15:15 (MSG)

A miserable heart means a miserable life;
a cheerful heart fills the day with song.

PRINCIPLE

Allow your heart to express music.

"Music is the art of the prophets that can calm the agitations of the soul." —Martin Luther

Men have an amazing connection with music. A song has the power to dig deep within the heart of a man and draw upon his purposes, appetites, and emotions. Some songs trace back to a particular incident in your past. They can stir the exact emotions you were feeling on a particular day. Within seconds, you're either smiling or weeping. Music can lift you up, build your courage, and arouse your emotions to incredible levels of excitement.

To be honest, I don't listen to a lot of music. My playlist only has a few songs. I'm not always playing songs in the background of my life. However, when I've had a tough day or two, I find myself wanting to turn on music that can cleanse my soul, a song to shift my thinking. Music is like washing your feet from the journey of life.

"Music washes away from the soul the dust of everyday life." —Berthold Auerbach

"Is anyone among you in trouble? Let them pray. Is anyone happy? Let them sing songs of praise" (James 5:13 NIV).

REMEMBER

There are times when you need to lift up your voice in a song.

READ PROVERBS CHAPTER 15

fivestarman.com/day-288

Day 289: The Seat Of Appetites

PROVERBS 16:26 (MSG)

Appetite is an incentive to work;
hunger makes you work all the harder.

PRINCIPLE

God gave Man a purpose in his work. He also gave Man the appetite to pursue it.

It would have been an exciting time for me, if I hadn't had been so afraid. My start into manhood came at graduation from high school. At that time, it was expected for me to simply go get a job and make a life.

I left home with $35 and a 1966 Chevy pickup. (It was an awesome classic short bed, black and chromed out). I bounced around in a couple of jobs until I landed my "dream job" in a coal mine. Working in the mine proved the starting blocks of my manhood. I worked alone, twelve hours a night, seven nights a week, eighty-four monotonous hours of pumping water out of the strip mine so the operators would have access to continue moving masses of Earth to unveil the coal.

The responsibility, the loneliness, and the isolation forged my manhood and my work ethic. I continue to draw upon those few years of experience that shaped my perspective.

I was so motivated because deep within me was an appetite. My stomach growled. I was hungry. If I didn't work, I didn't eat. It was that simple.

REMEMBER

The growling in your stomach is motivation.

READ PROVERBS CHAPTER 16
fivestarman.com/day-289

Day 290: Don't Say A Word

PROVERBS 17:28 (NLT)

Even fools are thought wise when they keep silent;
with their mouths shut, they seem intelligent.

PRINCIPLE

When you don't know, don't say anything. It's better to remain silent and appear wise than to speak and reveal folly.

Several years ago, I was involved in a real estate negotiation when this proverb became part of the deal. As the Lead Pastor, I was the point person when a neighboring business was interested in our property. They wanted to pick it up at a bargain-basement price.

Our church was growing fast and needed room to accommodate the growth. My architect disclosed to me that it would be impossible on that land.

When the company approached me with their offer, I was amazed. It was a good deal; however, wisdom whispered, "Even fools are thought wise when they keep silent." So, I kept quiet. I was a novice in negotiations. They were seasoned pros.

As I kept silent, the deal got better and better. Finally, when they became exhausted trying to persuade me to agree on the deal, I looked across the table and said, "Yes, we can make that happen."

We set a new benchmark in the community for real estate. Property values skyrocketed after our deal. My architect was thrilled. We purchased a prime piece of property, and the assets on our balance sheet soared.

I wasn't really that wise, but I kept my mouth shut, and it paid off handsomely.

REMEMBER

When you don't know, don't say anything.

READ PROVERBS CHAPTER 17

fivestarman.com/day-290

Day 291: Scandalous Behavior

PROVERBS 18:3 (NLT)

Doing wrong leads to disgrace,
and scandalous behavior brings contempt.

PRINCIPLE

Your gift may usher you into greatness, but a lack of character will escort you into obscurity.

It's now in the playbook for young upstarts to use scandalous behavior to get attention. The scandal is plotted and schemed to promote their personality. Character is no longer valued—becoming a caricature is. I find this embarrassing for them. Today, infamy has become equal to being famous. Unfortunately, their foolishness is being rewarded by this perverted culture.

It's one thing to see a former child star burst through puberty and manipulate their fans into their trickery. It is another for grown men to use the same tactics.

Frankly, it's a disgusting, sophomoric representation of manhood. Actors, music artists, politicians, and even some preachers are using scandalous behavior for personal gain. What is so disappointing is that many of these guys are gifted.

Your gift may usher you into greatness, but a lack of character will escort you into obscurity.

Let's represent authentic manhood with integrity. We don't need schemes to have influence. We do not want infamy. We want influence—influence based upon character and governed by conviction. That's what it means to be a ***FivestarMan***.

REMEMBER

Let's represent authentic manhood.

READ PROVERBS CHAPTER 18

fivestarman.com/day-291

Day 292: Loyalty

PROVERBS 19:22 (NLT)

Loyalty makes a person attractive....

PRINCIPLE

There's something wrong with your character if opportunity controls your loyalty.

I must admit this subject is a sensitive one for me. As most leaders have found through difficult experiences, people can be very fickle when it comes to loyalty.

I hate disloyalty. The spirit behind betrayal is the same adulterous spirit that seduces people into a false reality. They are delusional. They believe a lie by telling it. I've seen the darkness envelop them, work them like puppets, and speak words through them like a ventriloquist.

On the opposite end of the spectrum is the person who is loyal to their disadvantage. The person who will pay the price to guard their character, they're attractive people.

As a leader, I've learned my lesson. When I was young and naïve, I trusted people. When I became older and wiser, I tested them.

I worked for a leader who had been burned many times by disloyal people. This created a suspicious attitude in him toward all others. When he had a promotion in mind for someone, he would carefully orchestrate a situation to test their loyalty. If they failed, they never knew he had a better situation planned for them. If they passed, he would give them the huge opportunity.

Some leaders find this is a difficult concept to grasp; however, I recommend you study Matthew 25 and the "Parable of the Talents." Jesus taught qualification before promotion.

REMEMBER

Loyalty makes a person attractive.

READ PROVERBS CHAPTER 19

fivestarman.com/day-292

Day 293: Successful Plans Require Counsel

PROVERBS 20:18 (NLT)

Plans succeed through good counsel;
don't go to war without wise advice.

PRINCIPLE

Wisdom is found in the counsel of others.

One of the greatest leadership lessons I've ever seen is based on the counsel Moses' father-in-law, Jethro, gave when he saw a line of people standing day-in-and-day-out to get Moses' advice. Make no mistake about it: Moses was the one and only person who had revelation from God on holy behavior and conduct.

The people had been slaves for hundreds of years. They struggled with knowing how to conduct themselves in freedom. They had been controlled and manipulated, even tortured, to do exactly as they were told. When they were freed, they didn't know how to live in their liberty.

Jethro approached Moses and asked, "What are you really accomplishing here? Why are you trying to do all this alone while everyone stands around you from morning till evening?" (Exodus 18:14 NLT)

Then Jethro gave the most amazing advice to Moses regarding leadership and organizational flow charts.

Here's the takeaway from this proverb: No single person has all wisdom. We need to seek counsel to lead and be effective in our efforts. Moses had spent face-to-face time with God, yet when it came time for a leadership lesson, Jethro, his father-in-law, was the source of wisdom.

REMEMBER

Wisdom is found in the counsel of others.

READ PROVERBS CHAPTER 20
fivestarman.com/day-293

Day 294: The Pursuit Of Pleasure

PROVERBS 21:17 (MSG)

You're addicted to thrills? What an empty life!
The pursuit of pleasure is never satisfied.

PRINCIPLE

Out of the heart flow the issues of life.

Since the beginning, the addiction to pleasure has been one of the greatest challenges to authentic manhood. It comes from a perversion of the adventurous spirit within us.

Remember, out of our hearts flow the issues of life—our purposes, appetites, and emotions. These purposes are incredibly powerful for us. They motivate us and give us the excitement of fulfilling them. There is nothing more satisfying than fulfilled purpose. A cheap thrill cannot compare to it.

However, if we pervert the purposes that are deep within us, we find ourselves being driven in the opposite direction. Rather than our purposes dictating our appetites and releasing the excitement of emotions—we reverse the course. When we live for emotions, our appetites become insatiable and pervert our purpose, directing all our efforts toward the pursuit of pleasure.

"By faith Moses, when he had grown up, refused to be known as the son of Pharaoh's daughter. He chose to be mistreated along with the people of God rather than to enjoy the fleeting pleasures of sin" (Hebrews 11:24-25 NIV).

The conflict within Moses was either to enjoy the pleasures his privilege afforded him or to fulfill his purpose and realize his potential. Moses chose to live by purpose.

REMEMBER

We must put the issues of our hearts in the proper order. Our purposes dictate our appetites and release our emotions.

READ PROVERBS CHAPTER 21

fivestarman.com/day-294

Day 295: Competent Workers

PROVERBS 22:29 (NLT)

Do you see any truly competent workers?
They will serve kings rather than working for ordinary people.

PRINCIPLE

You can't hide skill. It always gets noticed.

A young entrepreneur and I were talking not long ago about his growing company. Do you know the greatest challenge his company was facing? Hiring skilled workers.

It's an amazing paradox. We have the lowest participation rate in the workforce. Millions are unemployed; yet, companies are begging for skilled workers.

My advice to this young business owner was based on the prayer Jesus recommended. "The harvest is plentiful, but the workers are few. Ask the Lord of the harvest, therefore, to send out workers into his harvest field" (Matthew 9:37-28 NIV).

I realize this is speaking of reaching people; however, the Lord can help a business owner find skilled workers, too. We can ask God to give us discernment to connect us to skilled workers.

Over the last thirty years, I've had anywhere from just a few employees up to hundreds to lead and manage. It has become a real matter of prayer for me to ask the Lord for skilled workers.

If you're a worker, ask the Lord to connect you to great leaders. You don't want to serve in obscurity. You want to serve the best, and you will if you develop your skills and do your work with excellence. You can't hide skill. It always gets noticed.

REMEMBER

Ask the Lord for connections.

READ PROVERBS CHAPTER 22
fivestarman.com/day-295

Day 296: Double Vision

PROVERBS 23:33 (NLT)

You will see hallucinations,
and you will say crazy things.

PRINCIPLE

We need to keep our minds alert.

We're living in serious times. The culmination of global events are aligning to become catastrophic if men do not rise to the challenge and take control. "…The kingdom of heaven has been forcefully advancing, and violent people are attacking it" (Matthew 11:12 NLT).

It is very important to remain sober-minded and alert. As a husband, father, and grandfather, I don't afford myself the license or luxury to lose it. I can't give myself over to uncontrolled thoughts, fantasies, double-mindedness, or hallucinations.

As James warned, "A double minded man is unstable in all his ways." (James 1:8 KJV).

In serious times we need serious men to step up to the challenge. Be the kind of man that is stable and strong. I have a good feeling you're taking things seriously, as well—otherwise, you probably wouldn't be reading ***The Daily Champion.***

REMEMBER

Keep your head.

READ PROVERBS CHAPTER 23

fivestarman.com/day-296

Day 297: The Law Of Order

PROVERBS 24:27 (NLT)

Do your planning and prepare your fields
before building your house.

PRINCIPLE

Our decisions either create order or cause disorder.

I've learned that I am uncomfortable with disorder. My creativity and work ethic suffers in an environment of chaos. Apparently, God feels the same way. The universe was chaotic until He said, "Let there be light." He pulled everything together, separated the waters, prepared the fields, and then prepared a place for mankind.

All throughout Scripture, and as evidenced in Creation, we see that everything with God's name on it has order, excellence, and precision. Anything associated with Almighty God was made with infinite detail and was designed to function perfectly and in order.

We can learn from the order God used to prepare for us.

- **He planned**—In fact, it's called predestination. He started with the end.
- **He prepared**—There is nothing missing in His Creation. I believe God is wise enough to put on deposit within His Creation more than enough to amply supply.
- **He is building a place**—Jesus said, "There is plenty of room for you in my Father's home" (John 14:2 MSG).

We should follow God's lead—Make plans. Get prepared. Then build.

REMEMBER

God is a God of order.

READ PROVERBS CHAPTER 24

fivestarman.com/day-297

Day 298: The Hedge Of Protection

PROVERBS 25:28 (NLT)

A person without self-control
is like a city with broken-down walls.

PRINCIPLE

Mastering one's self is the greatest defense.

The greatest threat to your own life and the protection of your family is the man you see in the mirror. Unfortunately, men can be their own worst enemies.

Self-control is so important for us that this attribute is included in the nine fruits of the Holy Spirit. If self-control is that important, we must give it some serious consideration and heed the warning that, without it, we're vulnerable to destruction.

The Apostle Paul says one of the signs of the End Times is that men are without self-control. He lists it with other damaging and abusive behaviors (2 Timothy 3:3).

One of the rights of passage into adulthood is when a young man is able to control himself and not act like a child—when he no longer talks like a child, reasons like a child, and emotionally reacts like a child. When a boy can conduct his behavior with self-control, he has matured.

Periodically, I will fast certain foods or habits to practice self-control. I want to submit my flesh to my determined will. It has helped me tremendously from time to time to give up for a season things that I may enjoy, such as, golf, coffee, or certain foods.

How well can you control yourself?

REMEMBER

You will never conquer the world without first conquering yourself.

READ PROVERBS CHAPTER 25

fivestarman.com/day-298

Day 299: Don't Start A Fire

PROVERBS 26:21 (MSG)

A quarrelsome person in a dispute
is like kerosene thrown on a fire.

PRINCIPLE

Don't allow a person to start a fire with strife.

I use social media platforms to promote the message of ***FivestarMan***. These platforms can be a tremendous help in spreading the message. We hear great feedback and testimonies from men who are stepping up to the cause of authentic manhood.

One of the pitfalls of social media platforms, though, are those who troll looking for a dispute. They are usually people of very little influence with their own platforms who want to use ours to spew their venom.

As tempting as it is to debate them, I've found it is best to cut them off quickly. I have a natural inclination to debate. I like the ping-pong of ideas and would welcome it on so many levels; however, on a public platform, it's not a good idea. The problem is the collateral damage it can have on others. It's like starting a wildfire and stoking it into a rage.

You may have a family member or coworker who is always stirring up strife by starting quarrels. The best thing to do is simply shut it down. Don't try to reason with them. Don't try to persuade them. They simply won't change.

REMEMBER

Don't allow a person to start a fire with strife.

READ PROVERBS CHAPTER 26

fivestarman.com/day-299

Day 300: Double Your Potential

PROVERBS 27:18 (NLT)

As workers who tend a fig tree are allowed to eat the fruit,
so workers who protect their employer's interests will be rewarded.

PRINCIPLE

When you are faithful to your present ability, you double your potential.

There's a dangerous attitude that has arisen in our nation. It pits workers against companies. The propaganda is the product of unscrupulous profiteers who stir up envy and hatred against "evil" corporations. They rail against capitalism, which is the most effective and biblical economic system in history.

In Matthew 25:14-30, Jesus used a remarkable story to teach the same principle today's proverb espouses.

Here are some take-aways from the "Parable of the Talents:"

- The employer gave to each employee the management of his own money, according to each one's proven ability.
- He trusted the employees to bring a return on his capital.
- The employee who started with five talents gained five more talents.
- The employee who started with two talents gained two more talents.
- The employer was happy with their faithfulness and shared the profits.
- The employee with one talent maintained the talent, but didn't risk losing it out of fear.
- The employee with one talent accused his master of having a demanding personality, slandering him to say he profited unfairly.
- The employer terminated the one-talent employee!

When you're faithful to your present ability, you double your potential. When you're unfaithful to your present ability, you lose the potential you once had.

REMEMBER

Look out for the one who is paying for your employment.

READ PROVERBS CHAPTER 27

fivestarman.com/day-300

Day 301: Grasping For Stuff

PROVERBS 28:25 (NLT)

Greed causes fighting;
trusting the Lord leads to prosperity.

PRINCIPLE

A grasping person stirs up trouble, but trust in God brings a sense of well-being.

Economics theories are constantly clashing against one another. Academia sits in their bubbles of conversation, espousing their theories at the luxury the endowment of millions affords them. Unfortunately, most people teaching economic theories have never actually worked at a job, much less created one.

The problem at the root of most conversations is greed. Greed is an insatiable appetite for money. It is closely aligned with covetousness, which is not only wanting what another person has, but wanting what they have at their expense.

"What causes fights and quarrels among you? Don't they come from your desires that battle within you?" (James 4:1 NIV)

Greed and covetousness come from a battle within, but they are manifested in outward hostility toward others. A greedy person stakes a claim to possessions they want but haven't earned. They claim that the system is rigged against them.

"You desire but do not have, so you kill. You covet but you cannot get what you want, so you quarrel and fight. You do not have because you do not ask God" (James 4:2 NIV).

Our advisor, Solomon, tells us that putting your trust in the Lord is what leads to prosperity. James confirms Solomon's wisdom by suggesting to simply ask God.

REMEMBER

Don't grasp for stuff. Ask God.

READ PROVERBS CHAPTER 28

fivestarman.com/day-301

Day 302: Mutual Disrespect

PROVERBS 29:27 (NLT)

The righteous despise the unjust;
the wicked despise the godly.

PRINCIPLE

The clash of culture is between the righteous and the wicked.

We're experiencing a cultural clash between those motivated to live righteous lives and those who are driven by forces of evil. We wrestle, not with flesh and blood, but with the influences of darkness. Make no mistake about it, evil exists, and it manipulates its will onto those who yield to it.

There is a spiritual law upon the Earth that no spirit can operate outside of flesh. In order to do his will, a spirit must have a person who opens themselves to its manipulation and control. The deeds of darkness are accomplished by the surrendered and those enslaved to sin.

The insidious nature of the wicked is an abomination to the righteous. We find its injustice disgusting and are repulsed by it.

Likewise, righteousness and moral integrity is disrespected by the wicked. They laugh and mock at those who choose to live within the guidelines of righteousness. The wicked find it gleeful to see the righteous hurt and abused for their faith.

We're not dealing with rational people. They're delusional. Evil.

REMEMBER

We wrestle not with flesh and blood.

READ PROVERBS CHAPTER 29

fivestarman.com/day-302

Day 303: Dignity

PROVERBS 30:29–31 (MSG)

There are three solemn dignitaries,
four that are impressive in their bearing—
a lion, king of the beasts, deferring to none;
a rooster, proud and strutting;
a billy goat;
a head of state in stately procession.

PRINCIPLE

There are two kinds of pride—both good and bad.

"'Good pride' represents our dignity and self-respect. 'Bad pride' is the deadly sin of superiority that reeks of conceit and arrogance." —John Maxwell

Have you been to the fitness center where the posers are flexing constantly in front of the mirrors? They strut their stuff and grunt loudly, dropping the weights at the end of their reps. It's hard to see manhood misrepresented in such a way.

On the other hand, some men need to step up their game and represent themselves with some dignity and self-respect. It may be in the area of their physical condition or in their clothing or in the way they carry themselves in public.

Having dignity isn't sinful pride. Having some self-respect isn't being showy or arrogant. As men, we need to have a good sense of self-worth without strutting our stuff in front of mirrors.

REMEMBER

Have some dignity.

READ PROVERBS CHAPTER 30

fivestarman.com/day-303

Day 304: She Brings You Respect

PROVERBS 31:23 (MSG)

Her husband is greatly respected
when he deliberates with the city fathers.

PRINCIPLE

It takes a Proverbs-1-through-30 man to have a Proverbs 31 woman.

Proverbs 31 has been promoted to women as the model of a godly wife and mother. The woman in this chapter of the Bible is described with such admirable qualities that she is certainly an attractive person. Any man would want to be married to this kind of woman. Some of us believe that we are.

However, let me also point out that Proverbs is a book written from a man to a man. So, the Proverbs 31 woman is married to a Proverbs-1-through-30 man. He is a man of wisdom. He is a faithful, hard working man. He is the kind of man who not only attracts a Proverbs 31 woman, but also he cultivates her remarkable gifts and draws upon them.

Before we read this Proverb and measure our wives in comparison to this woman, let's measure ourselves from the previous thirty chapters. Are we living up to the standard of authentic manhood, which our advisor teaches?

REMEMBER

Be the kind of man who attracts this kind of woman.

READ PROVERBS CHAPTER 31

fivestarman.com/day-304

Day 305: Comprehension

PROVERBS 1:2 (AMP)

That people may know skillful and godly Wisdom and instruction, discern and comprehend the words of understanding and insight.

PRINCIPLE

Proverbs help you connect the dots.

I get frustrated when men tell me that they do not like to read. Many publishers have told me that they've all but given up trying to sell books to men. It's a sore spot for me because it is dismissive to men.

As a young man, I struggled with reading and my poor education didn't help. My problem was comprehension, the ability to understand and perceive. I knew my life would be difficult if I didn't start living with wisdom.

My sister was dating a guy who seemed intelligent. He had a private school education; he was regularly exposed to executives who were in business relationships with his father, and he was an avid reader. In conversation, he mentioned the name of motivational guru, Zig Ziglar.

I immediately went to a bookstore and purchased a copy of Mr. Ziglar's book, ***See You At The Top.*** It was the first book I had ever read completely. It changed everything.

In that book, Zig recommended reading Proverbs each day, and promised that the reader would gain wisdom, insight, understanding, and comprehension. I didn't know that the Bible had such promises. Returning to my apartment, I pulled out the Bible my grandmother had given me and opened it up to find Proverbs.

I'm so thankful for that word of advice from my sister's male friend. It changed everything.

REMEMBER

Have some dignity.

READ PROVERBS CHAPTER 1

fivestarman.com/day-305

Day 306: Wise Friends

PROVERBS 2:16 (MSG)

Wise friends will rescue you from the Temptress—
that smooth-talking Seductress
Who's faithless to the husband she married years ago,
never gave a second thought to her promises before God.

PRINCIPLE

Relationships leave a residue with us for good or bad.

Unfortunately, there are married women who entered their marriage without commitment to their husband, nor to the Lord. Their vows were flippant and meaningless. A relationship with this type of woman leads straight to Hell. Her residue is destruction.

It's important to have wise friends who can help rescue you when you're facing temptation that comes through seductive, smooth-talking, faithless women. The residue of wise friends is protection.

A friend asked me to hold him accountable regarding a recurring temptation in his life. He was struggling. A few weeks later, after a few attempts to get a hold of him, I finally prevailed. I asked a couple of questions, and I realized that he wasn't transparent. He was spinning his answers and diverting from my probe. Finally, I said, "You know, when a friend asks you to hold him accountable, but then stops talking to you, there's probably a problem."

It's important to have wise friends who aren't afraid to speak into your life. They'll protect you from destructive forces.

REMEMBER

Relationships leave a residue. What kind of residue do you want?

READ PROVERBS CHAPTER 2

fivestarman.com/day-306

Day 307: The Blessed House

PROVERBS 3:33 (NIV)

The Lord's curse is on the house of the wicked,
but he blesses the home of the righteous.

PRINCIPLE

Your home should be and can be blessed.

I grew up in a tumultuous home filled with strife and disorder. Even as a child, I determined that, when I became an adult, I would not have a home with strife.

Very early in our marriage, my wife and I made a decision to have a home of peace. I remember the day we decided that we would not go to sleep with the house being unkempt or in disorder. After three decades, I can confidently say that was one of the best decisions we ever made as a young couple.

We feel extremely blessed in our home. We have a home of peace.

As a man, you can set the tone of the home. When you walk in from a difficult day of work, it can be a place of refuge and peace. It can be your place of confidence and security.

REMEMBER

Set the tone of the home.

READ PROVERBS CHAPTER 3
fivestarman.com/day-307

Day 308: Focus

PROVERBS 4:25 (NIV)

Let your eyes look straight ahead;
fix your gaze directly before you.

PRINCIPLE

Your life will always move in the direction of your focus.

"My father could look straight ahead but concentrate on something on the very edge of his vision, almost nearly behind him." —Dale Earnhardt, Jr.

There is something very wise about this statement about the famed NASCAR champion Dale Earnhardt. Being able to fix your eyes straight ahead, focused on where you are going, and, yet, having a sense of what is chasing you is an art.

That's something we need to master and hew in our skill set as men in the pursuit of authentic manhood. We must have a focus on where we're going, but also have the realization that we're being chased.

A man of broken focus is bound to fail. If we take too much time to look back or around and break our focus, we're doomed to hit the wall. Authentic manhood doesn't have time for trivial pursuits. We must take this role—this passionate pursuit—seriously.

We can certainly have good times and fun adventures, but make no mistake about it—the kind of man you want to be isn't going to happen by meandering through life.

REMEMBER

Keep your eyes fixed on the prize—authentic manhood.

READ PROVERBS CHAPTER 4

fivestarman.com/day-308

Day 309: Captivated By Love

PROVERBS 5:19 (NLT)

She is a loving deer, a graceful doe.
Let her breasts satisfy you always.
May you always be captivated by her love.

PRINCIPLE

Never belittle the woman who believed in you. Never admire the one who didn't.

Our advisor encourages us to consider the tenderness, gracefulness, and love of the wife of our youth. We should embrace her, even be captivated by her.

This advice is appropriate for us today because so many men seem to be casting off the wives of their youth for younger models.

It's a display of disloyalty for a husband to disregard the wife who believed in him when he was young and naïve to chase after a trophy wife after he has "made it."

It is beneath the dignity of manhood to attract trophy girls simply because we can buy them with success.

REMEMBER

Be a man who is captivated by the wife of your youth.

READ PROVERBS CHAPTER 5
fivestarman.com/day-309

Day 310: Worthless Liars

PROVERBS 6:12 (NLT)

What are worthless and wicked people like?
They are constant liars.

PRINCIPLE

You can never trust the words of a liar.

Our culture is consciously accepting lies from leaders of government and business. In fact, many leaders are using the art of lies (which is mendacity) to purposely deceive. Stockholders excuse fraud for profit. Politicians say they simply "misspoke."

God is not a man that He can lie. He doesn't have much patience for those who speak words that are untrue.

Unfortunately, the erosion of our culture is happening before our eyes, and it all begins with lying.

REMEMBER

People believe a lie by speaking it.

READ PROVERBS CHAPTER 6

fivestarman.com/day-310

Day 311: Listen To Me

PROVERBS 7:24 (NLT)

So listen to me, my sons,
and pay attention to my words.

PRINCIPLE

Faith comes by hearing; hearing comes by the Word.

If you're going to lead people, you must give them faith to follow. That means people need to hear from you for direction.

I can't recall not having chores to do as a child. We always had a list of things to do. Saturdays were times to wake up and get out in the field to work.

My mother's second husband wasn't a father to me, nor was he a good leader. He would cuss and carry on if I didn't do something right, even though he didn't tell or show me how to do it. It was incredibly frustrating trying to anticipate what I was supposed to know and do.

The Bible tells us not to exasperate children (Ephesians 6:4). To *exasperate* means *to arouse anger as a form of punishment*. It's abusive for an adult to use or manipulate anger to punish a child. It can cause tremendous damage to a young mind.

I've had many conversations with men who, even as adults, struggle with the side effects of their parents' or guardians' misuse of anger.

If you want someone to follow you, you need to give them faith to follow. In other words, teach and show them what to do. I've found that people willingly and enthusiastically follow a leader who gives them instruction and inspiration to follow.

REMEMBER

People need to hear from you.

READ PROVERBS CHAPTER 7

fivestarman.com/day-311

Day 312: Stop Hurting Yourself

PROVERBS 8:36 (NIV)

But those who fail to find me harm themselves;
all who hate me love death.

PRINCIPLE

Those who hate wisdom harm themselves.

When a man thinks he can navigate life without wisdom he hurts himself. It's amazing to see men think that they're smart enough or have had enough life experience that they don't need wise advice.

Those who despise wisdom are in love with death. In other words, they are so dark that they embrace the destructive force of stupidity. It's hard to believe that anyone would enjoy abuse, but that's exactly what some people want. It's not reasonable, but it's true. It's a spiritual disorder. It's irrational; yet, it is very common.

Don't turn away from Wisdom's voice.

REMEMBER

Stop hurting yourself.

READ PROVERBS CHAPTER 8
fivestarman.com/day-312

Day 313: Wisdom First Works

PROVERBS 9:10a (NIV)

The fear of the Lord is the beginning of wisdom….

PRINCIPLE

Wisdom is the principle thing. Start with wisdom.

We need to learn from God how He does things. His ways are higher than our ways. His thoughts are much more precise and defined than our thoughts (Isaiah 55:8–9). If we will not lean on our own understanding, and trust that God's ways are better than ours, we can expect the same results that God receives. Think about God's process.

God begins with wisdom. He established wisdom before anything else. This sounds elementary but is rarely used in man's thought processes. Men often think about a whole laundry list of things before they begin with wisdom.

I've spoken with a lot of aggressive entrepreneurs who had great ideas for businesses; however, when it came to implementing their ideas, they struggled to break the goal into doable steps.

God directs our steps. He also promises that if we lack wisdom, if we will ask Him, He will give us wisdom with generosity (James 1:5).

Rather than suffer the agony of defeat, why not rely upon the processes God has established?

REMEMBER

Start with wisdom.

READ PROVERBS CHAPTER 9

fivestarman.com/day-313

Day 314: Fears And Hopes

PROVERBS 10:24 (NLT)

The fears of the wicked will be fulfilled;
the hopes of the godly will be granted.

PRINCIPLE

Fears serve as warning signs. Hopes serve as directional signs.

One of the worst things about living a life of wickedness is the haunting that comes with it. Fears can be warning signs that forecast the future. Unfortunately, a lot of men don't read the signs. They worry about them, talk about them, fret over them, tossing and turning in bed, destroying their bodies with anxieties. Yet, when it comes to changing their ways they don't consider.

"In the day of prosperity be joyful, But in the day of adversity consider: Surely God has made the one as well as the other, So that man can find out nothing that will come after him" (Ecclesiastes 7:14 NKJV).

Solomon is saying that we shouldn't take our future for granted. We need to be thoughtful about our lives and examine the signs of adversity. If things are constantly going wrong, we should carefully examine our fears, words, and actions to see if we are on a path of destruction.

The good news is that the hopes of the godly will be granted. Hope is joyfully expecting the promises of God to come to pass. Hope has an assignment. Hope is a sign for the future and gives us directional intent.

REMEMBER

Put your hope in the Lord—now and always.

READ PROVERBS CHAPTER 10
fivestarman.com/day-314

Day 315: Your Gift Will Make Room

PROVERBS 11:26 (NIV)

People curse the one who hoards grain,
but they pray God's blessing on the one who is willing to sell.

PRINCIPLE

Your gift will usher you into greatness.

Joseph, a young dreamer, matured to become the Prime Minister of Egypt. You may remember that Joseph's path took him from the pit of rejection by his brothers, enslavement by Ishmaelites, indentured servanthood by Potiphar, imprisonment by false accusation, and then to promotion into the palace as second only to Pharaoh.

What escorted Joseph from the prison to the palace? It was his gift of interpreting dreams. Solomon says that your gift will usher you into greatness (Proverbs 18:16). However, a lack of character will escort you back into obscurity.

After Joseph had interpreted the dreams of Pharaoh, he was selected to oversee the financial management of the entire economy of Egypt. The Bible says he stored twenty percent of all grain that was harvested for seven years. The accounting became almost unimaginable; yet, within the next seven years, when everyone else was suffering from a drought, Joseph used his genius to amass the greatest wealth in the history of Egypt by selling the storehouse of grain back to the people. It was an incredible transfer of wealth.

The Egyptian people were extremely thankful that Joseph was in charge because he was willing to sell grain to them.

REMEMBER

Your gift will make room for you.

READ PROVERBS CHAPTER 11
fivestarman.com/day-315

Day 316: The Weight Of Worry

PROVERBS 12:25 (NLT)

Worry weighs a person down;
an encouraging word cheers a person up.

PRINCIPLE

Worry weighs you down. Encouragement lifts you up.

I've known people who consider worrying as a sign of their commitment and love. They express their love by how much they worry on your behalf. It seems that they're anticipating the bad for you.

Worriers are much like the mourners of Scripture. Mourners were people who traveled from death to death, bewailing for profit. They were compensated for bemoaning. These people were heavy—weighty in spirit.

At ***The Daily Champion*** we feel you have enough troubles and challenges to face so our goal is to instill courage.

As a young man, I went through a difficult time of worry that bordered on a deep depression. The amazing timing of it all was that my life was as good as I had ever had it. I couldn't understand. I awakened in the middle of the night with tremendous anxiety, walked outside and sighed out my prayers of depression.

I wanted to hear God's gentle sympathy. What I heard in my spirit was, "Get up, and get your fight back."

Amazingly, that word encouraged me. It instilled a cheerful resolve. I stood up, walked into the house, and went to sleep. Although great challenges have come, I haven't faced that battle since.

REMEMBER

"Take courage and be a man" (1 Kings 2:2b NLT).

READ PROVERBS CHAPTER 12

fivestarman.com/day-316

Day 317: Don't Refuse Loving Your Child

PROVERBS 13:24 (MSG)

A refusal to correct is a refusal to love;
love your children by disciplining them.

PRINCIPLE

Without guidance, your child will go wild. With guidance—directional intent—your child will have joy.

It is a scene that is repeated much too often—a young man gets involved with a crime and is injured, jailed, or worse—dead. The parents talk about what a good boy he was. The facts prove otherwise. He was involved in criminal activity for years, and it finally caught up to him.

What went wrong?

When parents don't discipline their children, they don't love them.

That sounds so contrary to what society would argue, but it's true. If a parent fails to lead and give their children directional intent, they are hopelessly lost.

"When people do not accept divine guidance, they run wild. But whoever obeys the law is joyful" (Proverbs 29:18 NLT).

We must give our children directional intent to secure a joyful and successful life.

REMEMBER

Don't refuse to love your child.

READ PROVERBS CHAPTER 13
fivestarman.com/day-317

Day 318: The Cancer Called Jealousy

PROVERBS 14:30 (NLT)

A peaceful heart leads to a healthy body;
jealousy is like cancer in the bones.

PRINCIPLE

Jealousy is like bone cancer.

There is a kinetic relationship between our emotional balance and the physical health of our bodies. It is not only a biblical truth, but a scientific fact. We must be aware and in control of our emotions.

When we understand our purpose, we dictate our appetites, and the expression of our emotions is in check. When these things are in alignment they work to our benefit. If they are reversed in order, they are disastrous.

Our advisor warns us about the cancer called jealousy. Jealousy is an unhappy feeling or a deep-seated antipathy toward someone else because we want what they own. It becomes an unsatisfied craving or appetite.

Even though Ahab was the King of Israel, he was jealous of a neighbor's vineyard and wanted to buy it. When the neighbor refused his offer, Ahab became disturbed to the point of physical sickness, and his wife committed murder (1 Kings 21:4–16).

Here's a man who perverted his purpose as a king and couldn't control his emotions. Ahab thought that his position privileged him to another man's possessions, a fundamental flaw in those who lead without purpose. Where the purpose is unknown, abuse is inevitable.

"Any authority that is used as a means to be served rather than to serve is satanic in nature." —Jeff Ables

REMEMBER

Keep the alignment of your purpose—appetites—emotions.

READ PROVERBS CHAPTER 14

fivestarman.com/day-318

Day 319: A Timely Word

PROVERBS 15:23 (NLT)

Everyone enjoys a fitting reply;
it is wonderful to say the right thing at the right time!

PRINCIPLE

One word from God can change your life.

My children never know what to get me for special occasions. They're at a loss when it comes to trying to figure out what to buy. When they ask in desperation, "Dad, what do you want?" I'll suggest that they just get a card and write a note.

I value words more than anything else.

Not long ago, I gave my son a card for a special day. He opened the envelope, barely read the words on the front, opened the card and noticed that I hadn't written anything other than my salutation. He looked up and said, "Where's the note?"

I had always written a note expressing my affirmation and encouragement in the inside of cards. This time I hadn't. He felt cheated.

Jesus valued words more than anything else. "These words you hear are not my own; they belong to the Father who sent me" (John 14:24b NIV).

Jesus not only spoke what He had heard from His Father, but He said the words in the way that His Father instructed Him to say them. He spoke words in a "fitting reply."

It's not only important to say the right words, but also to say them in the right manner.

REMEMBER

Choose your words carefully, and say them in the right manner.

READ PROVERBS CHAPTER 15

fivestarman.com/day-319

Day 320: Seeds Of Strife

PROVERBS 16:28 (NLT)

A troublemaker plants seeds of strife;
gossip separates the best of friends.

PRINCIPLE

When strife takes root, it will bring division.

We've talked about strife being the manifested presence of evil. We cannot underestimate the destructive power of strife. How does strife grow into such an evil force?

It begins with the seeds of gossip.

When the Early Church began to increase, they faced the possibility of strife entering into their fellowship. It all began with racial division with widows. The Grecian Jews began to complain against the Hebraic Jews because favoritism was in play with the distribution of food.

If this issue wasn't addressed quickly, the Early Church could face tremendous repercussions. There is a progression in division, and it begins with gossip.

Gossip matures to become strife. Strife becomes evil work. Evil work becomes manipulation. Manipulation becomes witchcraft. Witchcraft is the sin of rebellion. Rebellion is the sin of division.

We must be careful to uproot the seeds of strife before they take root.

REMEMBER

Uproot the seeds of strife before they take root.

READ PROVERBS CHAPTER 16

fivestarman.com/day-320

Day 321: The Banquet Of Bitterness

PROVERBS 17:1 (MSG)

A meal of bread and water in contented peace
is better than a banquet spiced with quarrels.

PRINCIPLE

Peace with a little is better than a banquet of bitterness.

The day of Thanksgiving is designed to be a day for Americans to pause and express our gratitude for God's faithfulness to us. It's also a great time for us to let those close to us know how much we appreciate them.

Unfortunately, some families gather for feasting, yet chew on each other's bitter morsels instead of gratitude for one another.

It would be better for them to stay at the home of peace, eating bread and drinking water, rather than have "all of the fixin's" of a big family meal.

I grew up around quarreling. It was exhausting. It was frustrating to go through the emotions of a holiday without the spirit and purpose behind it.

My wife and I decided early on that we wouldn't have that in our home. Our gatherings are times of joy, gratitude, and family celebrations. We've made the holiday season a time of worship. It is so exciting to have the family over to the house and express our gratitude for God and one another.

REMEMBER

Peace with a little is better than a banquet of bitterness.

READ PROVERBS CHAPTER 17

fivestarman.com/day-321

Day 322: What's In A Name?

PROVERBS 18:10 (MSG)

God's name is a place of protection—
good people can run there and be safe.

PRINCIPLE

As believers in Christ Jesus, we have access to invoke the most powerful name that is given to man—the Name of Jesus!

A name is used for the identification of a person. Historically, names were often assigned to individuals based upon their occupation or their residence. However, the person of Jesus exalted the name to be above all names.

"That at the name of Jesus every knee should bow, in heaven and on earth and under the earth, and every tongue declare that Jesus Christ is Lord..." (Philippians 2:10–11 NLT).

There is NO OTHER NAME that compares to Jesus. Jesus is more than a rabbi, a teacher, a prophet, or a historical person. Jesus is the Messiah, prophesied about with irrefutable evidence and incalculable odds of fulfilling the very precise and exact prophesies.

According to MIT the odds of Jesus fulfilling eight prophecies in the Bible are one in more than one hundred trillion; yet, Jesus fulfilled three hundred and fifty-three Old Testament prophesies.

But, the evidence that I rely upon the most is personal. It is evident in my life change. I am redeemed.

If you believe in your heart and confess with your mouth, Jesus is Lord, you are also redeemed. Run to the Name of the Lord, and be safe!

REMEMBER

The Name of Jesus is the place of protection. You can run to Him and be safe.

READ PROVERBS CHAPTER 18

fivestarman.com/day-322

Day 323: The Simple-Minded Learn From Pain

PROVERBS 19:25 (NLT)

If you punish a mocker, the simpleminded will learn a lesson;
if you correct the wise, they will be all the wiser.

PRINCIPLE

The simple-minded only learn through the pain of punishment.

It doesn't have to be this way, but many people are so dull to learn that the only lesson they will heed is when they experience pain. It's an endless cycle of stupidity and punishment.

The wise receive correction from the mistakes of others. The foolish only learn from pain.

I look for every opportunity to read biographies and learn from the life experiences of others. The men I read about become mentors to me. You will either gain wisdom through a mentor or through the experience of pain. Mentors are better.

REMEMBER

A wise person can learn from the mistakes of others.

READ PROVERBS CHAPTER 19
fivestarman.com/day-323

Day 324: Charming Snakes

PROVERBS 20:19 (NLT)

A gossip goes around telling secrets,
so don't hang around with chatterers.

PRINCIPLE

A gossip uses the magical murmuring of a snake charmer.

Historically, cities were built with high walls and strong gates. The elders of a city would gather at the gates to see who was coming to do business. The elders were the "gate-keepers."

In the early design of American cities, architects built cities around a square. The square became the center of commerce and conversation. Influencers would gather at the square to know what was happening.

In recent years, we have ushered in a remarkable new avenue to encounter people—social media has become our gate for discourse.

I embrace social media because it gives us an opportunity to enter people's lives in a way no other avenue would give us. I've personally seen positive things happen because of connectivity. In fact, ***FivestarMan*** is constantly using these platforms to raise the volume of authentic manhood.

However, as good as these platforms can be, they can also be horrific when misused. The most common misuse is gossip.

The word *gossip* is defined as *the magical murmuring of a charmer of snakes.* That's a spiritually descriptive picture of a manipulative person, whispering their damaging accusations against another. When people traffic in slander, they can cause irreparable harm to the person injured.

REMEMBER

Let's use our voices to raise the volume of authentic manhood, rather than use it to tear others down. Avoid godless chatter.

READ PROVERBS CHAPTER 20

fivestarman.com/day-324

Day 325: Get All The Help You Can

PROVERBS 20:18 (MSG)

Form your purpose by asking for counsel,
then carry it out using all the help you can get.

PRINCIPLE

To gain understanding of your purpose, you need good mentors and counselors.

When I first received the commission to build a movement to resurrect authentic manhood, I felt impressed to "focus upon men's purposes, and they will cast off the things that constrain them." When a man gains understanding of his purposes, his life becomes a passionate pursuit of authentic manhood.

During an interview, I was asked, "If you could have breakfast or lunch with three people from history, excluding someone from the Bible, who would you choose?"

My answer surprised my interviewer—I responded, "I have done that through reading biographies and books that men have written. I can have breakfast with the great investor, Warren Buffett. I can have lunch with Bill Gates. I can have dinner with the late, Steve Jobs."

Amazingly, I can do that for very little money. For a few dollars, I can purchase their books. I can gain the highlights of their entire life experiences with very little exchange on my part. I don't have to know them personally to receive the best that they offer. I can gain all their life lessons through books.

If you're going to fulfill your purpose, you will need counsel, but it doesn't all have to be face to face.

REMEMBER

Get all the help you can.

READ PROVERBS CHAPTER 21

Day 326: Don't Be Silly

PROVERBS 22:3 (NLT)

A prudent person foresees danger and takes precautions.
The simpleton goes blindly on and suffers the consequences.

PRINCIPLE

There are times that require a seasoned and serious man.

Go to any fitness center and you'll see the poser—the guy who can't walk by a mirror without flexing his "guns." He waddles to the water fountain convinced everyone is impressed with his muscles. Yet, all the poser does is train. He's not training for a purpose. He's not disciplining his body for a determined outcome. He simply wants to *look* like he could do something.

There are a lot of posers in life. Men who think their look alone will earn them a place in the victor's circle. They soon discover that's not how life works. Life, business, family, even our spiritual walk is a challenge. If we're going to win, we need to be conditioned for it. We need to be strong.

You're not conditioning yourself just to look good. You're preparing for the challenge, strengthening yourself so when crisis occurs—and it will—you are prepared.

And a reminder: When facing challenges don't attempt to draw your strength from your wife and kids. It's not their job to strengthen you. Go to God and let Him strengthen you so that you can turn to your family and say, "It's OK, we're going to get through this. Follow me."

REMEMBER

Don't shrink back in times of trouble. Be a man, and be prepared.

READ PROVERBS CHAPTER 22
fivestarman.com/day-326

Day 327: Staggering

PROVERBS 23:34 (NLT)

You will stagger like a sailor tossed at sea,
clinging to a swaying mast.

PRINCIPLE

A double-minded man is unstable, tossed by the wind and waves of the sea.

Our advisor warns us against those who are gazing upon wine; however, I also see the warning of how a double-minded man is unstable and confused. Someone who hasn't kept his wits about him is vulnerable and exposed to potential danger.

As men, we have a responsibility to be alert and sober-minded.

"In the same way, encourage the young men to live wisely. And you yourself must be an example to them by doing good works of every kind. Let everything you do reflect the integrity and seriousness of your teaching" (Titus 2:6–7 NLT).

We're living in dangerous times that require us to live wisely. We need to exemplify integrity and seriousness.

REMEMBER

Keep your wits about you.

READ PROVERBS CHAPTER 23
fivestarman.com/day-327

Day 328: The House Of Poverty

PROVERBS 24:31 (MSG)

They were overgrown with weeds,
thick with thistles, all the fences broken down.
I took a long look and pondered what I saw;
the fields preached me a sermon and I listened:
"A nap here, a nap there, a day off here, a day off there,
sit back, take it easy—do you know what comes next?
Just this: You can look forward to a dirt-poor life,
with poverty as your permanent houseguest!"

PRINCIPLE

The greatest temptation in a man's life is comfort.

The advisor takes a stroll to see the ruins of a home, farm, and vineyard that once thrived under the faithful care of the owner. Falling apart, the owner has taken time off, seduced by the comfort of the couch.

The Garden God planted for Adam was a storehouse of seed. God's first gift to Adam was the currency of seed. With seed man could dominate the entire Earth, transforming it into an amazing abundance of harvest. His resources would be unlimited.

However, Adam embezzled from God's property. Poverty was the result. Adam's failure caused the land to produce thorns and thistles, rather than fruits and vegetables. Fighting systemic poverty is the daily toil of mankind.

As we gain understanding of the deep passions of authentic manhood, we become proficient with the entrepreneurial drive that is within us. This drive gives us discernment and insight on how to continually produce and thrive against poverty.

REMEMBER

Our homes don't have to be subjected to systemic poverty!

READ PROVERBS CHAPTER 24

fivestarman.com/day-328

Day 329: Don't Stuff Yourself

PROVERBS 25:27 (MSG)

It's not smart to stuff yourself with sweets,
nor is glory piled on glory good for you.

PRINCIPLE

Show restraint.

If you've traveled outside of North America, you know how much abundance we have at our disposal. We've mastered the art of production and capitalism. It's a compliment to decades of innovation and competence in our work ethic; however, it also has caused a collateral damage of gluttony and narcissism.

I believe that a person with an abundance mentality shows restraint in his personal indulgence and balance in his personal identity, not thinking too much of himself and not stuffing himself with sweets.

As authentic men, we should strive for healthy balance. Knowing who we are in Christ will give us an assurance of identity. It will also give us security in our diets, knowing we don't have to indulge. There will be plenty tomorrow. We won't run out.

The people who left Egypt were given manna (the bread of angels) each day. The manna had a twenty-four-hour expiration time. The people had to develop a trust in God's supply, leaning upon His ability to meet their needs daily and having confidence that God held them in high estimation.

Let's take a lesson and show restraint in our foods and our egos.

REMEMBER

Show restraint, and don't stuff yourself.

READ PROVERBS CHAPTER 25

fivestarman.com/day-329

Day 330: The Boomerang

PROVERBS 26:27a (NLT)

If you set a trap for others,
you will get caught in it yourself.

PRINCIPLE

If your appetite is violence, you're eating from the wrong tree.

The Earth operates on "The Law of Seed." It is the currency of the Earth by which all men's currencies operate. God will not be mocked. A man can't turn up his nose toward this law. A man will reap what he sows. As good as this law is, it is also a law that works in the negative. If a man sows seeds to destroy another person, the harvest of destruction will return upon his head.

"Malice backfires; spite boomerangs" (Proverbs 26:27 MSG).

Don't plot and plan evil against someone and expect blessing to come upon you. If you live by the sword, you will die by the sword. If you dig a pit, you will fall into it.

If speaking a blessing invokes angels, speaking a curse entices demons. That's why Jesus said to bless your enemy—doing so brings the boomerang blessing.

REMEMBER

What you sow is what you'll reap!

READ PROVERBS CHAPTER 26

fivestarman.com/day-330

Day 331: Insatiable Hell

PROVERBS 27:20 (MSG)

Hell has a voracious appetite,
and lust just never quits.

PRINCIPLE

"Death and Destruction are never satisfied, and neither are human eyes" (Proverbs 27:20 NIV).

I have a confession—I've struggled with being a news junkie. I wanted to know what is going on around the world, so I listened to news talk radio, watched cable news channels, and flipped channels to other news broadcasts to see what I was missing.

Lately, I've pulled away from it all. I am glad that I have. The constant violence and threats of disaster are endless. It just doesn't get better.

Hell has a voracious appetite. It is insatiable. Hell wants all of the captives it can have and will never say, "Enough!"

I've had enough. I've decided to spend my drive times in prayer and praise. I leave the noise off while I'm studying and focused on writing projects.

My new practice keeps me from developing a harshness, bitterness, and cynical attitude toward our world and our future. Yes, we're still living in troubling times; however, I'm focused on the vision God has given me for the movement. Amazingly, the world still goes on without me knowing all of its troubles.

REMEMBER

Monitor how much focus you're giving to Hell.

READ PROVERBS CHAPTER 27

fivestarman.com/day-331

Day 332: Survivor

PROVERBS 28:26 (MSG)

If you think you know it all, you're a fool for sure;
real survivors learn wisdom from others.

PRINCIPLE

If you're the smartest man in the room, you need a new crowd.

My wife, Kay and I enjoy the reality show, ***Survivor***. Human nature is revealed—lying versus loyalty—integrity versus immorality. Add the incredible physical challenges and lack of food, and you've got an amazing dynamic at work among the contestants.

But let's enlarge our concept of the game called "Survivor." The Earth is a secluded island in the universe, and we're doing life with a population of unique characters, each with their own story and diverse in their moral compass, all navigating to get to the end.

It seems as if every season of ***Survivor*** there's a "know-it-all" on the island. The know-it-all boasts as if they're going to dominate everyone, only to find themselves blindsided by their ignorance—voted off the island.

I've seen this happen in life, as well. Those who are so arrogant to think that they are the smartest men in the room—they walk puffed up with the stride of self-assurance. However, before they know it, someone has outwitted, outplayed, and outlasted them.

The key to winning this reality game is to learn from previous players. Take the lessons others have learned the hard way and apply them to your game. That's wisdom.

REMEMBER

Look around you. Is there anyone you can learn from?

READ PROVERBS CHAPTER 28

fivestarman.com/day-332

Day 333: Mockers Stir Up A City

PROVERBS 29:8 (NIV)

Mockers stir up a city,
but the wise turn away anger.

PRINCIPLE

Mockers spew out their violence without regard for those injured.

When there is injustice, people have a right to protest peacefully and raise the volume of their voices to express their concerns; however, there are unscrupulous people who protest for profit. They're mockers.

When mockers stir up a city, they're not looking for the good of those who are rightfully protesting. They take advantage of other people's pains for their personal gain. They add insult to injury.

When a city is in turmoil, it takes a wise leader to speak with gentle wisdom to disquiet the mockers, heal the wounded, and bring justice to the injured.

REMEMBER

A gang of cynics can upset a whole city.

READ PROVERBS CHAPTER 29
fivestarman.com/day-333

Day 334: Bloody Nose

PROVERBS 30:32 (MSG)

If you're dumb enough to call attention to yourself
by offending people and making rude gestures,
Don't be surprised if someone bloodies your nose.

PRINCIPLE

You become a man when you no longer reason like a child.

There are a lot of guys who can't navigate life without looking for a fight. They're constantly calling attention to themselves by offending people. Make no mistake about it. These guys will get their due. Someone will be "bigger and badder" and will teach them a lesson.

These guys got their way throughout childhood by throwing temper tantrums. Now that they're older, they continue to use their childish fits.

The Apostle Paul tells us that when he was a child he thought like a child and reasoned like a child, but when he became an adult, he put away childish actions (1 Corinthians 13:11).

You become a man when you no longer reason like a child.

REMEMBER

Authentic manhood doesn't make rude gestures and offend people.

READ PROVERBS CHAPTER 30

fivestarman.com/day-334

Day 335: Complementary Parenting

PROVERBS 1:8 (NLT)

My child, listen when your father corrects you.
Don't neglect your mother's instruction.

PRINCIPLE

Parents have a complementary strategy to teach a child.

When God created the world, the only part of His Creation that made God pause and say, "It is not good," was when God saw Man alone. So God created Woman.

Adam and Eve had perfect complementary designs. Their complementary functions fulfilled the purpose to "be fruitful and increase."

Not only do the two become one to procreate—they also have complementary strategy to instruct their children. This is an extremely important part of the parental purpose that God established for us.

Every credible study confirms the importance of both a father and mother to raise a healthy, secure, and well-balanced child. Our culture is experiencing the collateral damage of divided families, causing tremendous societal ills.

My experience of being raised by my mother, without the influence of my father, played a significant role in my life. Fortunately, I was able to hear the Gospel, accept the redemptive work of Christ, and receive Him to become a child of God (John 1:12).

For those who are facing this very challenge, I want to encourage you. God can redeem your situation. He can give you a hope and a future.

REMEMBER

As parents, work together to teach and correct your children.

READ PROVERBS CHAPTER 1
fivestarman.com/day-335

Day 336: Highway To Hell

PROVERBS 2:18 (NLT)

Entering her house leads to death;
it is the road to the grave.

PRINCIPLE

Don't be seduced by proximity.

When a man, seduced by seductive words and the unreserved exposure of an immoral woman, is on the fast track to death and the grave, he is on the highway to Hell.

Few realize that the covenant breaker—the immoral woman—has allowed a seductive spirit to embody her to entrap vulnerable men. The seduction is a spirit that entices a man with the look of the eye, the whisper of words, and the caress of suggestion. Her craft is the capture. Her art is adultery.

It is, frankly, embarrassing when a man gives up the dignity of his manhood for her. His value plummets. His influence is wasted. The damage has ripple effects that last a lifetime.

I've seen the mighty fall. I've witnessed brilliant men pay the toll to ride this road. I've wept with men who gave up the woman of their dreams for the fantasy of a whore.

You're better than that!

Don't believe the lie that suggests all men do it. Don't buy into the scheme that sin is secretive. Don't be seduced by the spirit.

REMEMBER

Don't take the highway of the harlot.

READ PROVERBS CHAPTER 2

fivestarman.com/day-336

Day 337: Favor

PROVERBS 3:34 (NIV)

He mocks proud mockers
but shows favor to the humble and oppressed.

PRINCIPLE

Humility attracts the favor of God. God makes fun of mockers.

The first time favor is expressed in the Bible is when Abel gave the best portion of the first of his flock as an offering unto the Lord.

"...The Lord looked with favor on Abel and his offering, but on Cain and his offering he did not look with favor. So Cain was very angry, and his face was downcast" (Genesis 4:4–5 NIV).

Notice that the lack of God's favor had a profound impact upon Cain. His face was downcast, which means he was severely depressed. However, even after God's prodding him to do right, Cain mocked God, thumbing his nose upward. Cain's antipathy toward his brother drove him out of his mind enough to accept a murderous spirit.

The first murder ever committed was over an offering to the Lord.

As authentic men, our competition isn't with brothers, but with the men we were yesterday. Humility causes us to pursue excellence and honor toward God. God isn't going to show us favor at the expense of another. God's favor flows to every man who is humble toward Him.

REMEMBER

God shows His favor to the humble.

READ PROVERBS CHAPTER 3
fivestarman.com/day-337

Day 338: Watch Your Step

PROVERBS 4:26 (NIV)

Give careful thought to the paths for your feet
and be steadfast in all your ways.

PRINCIPLE

Walk confidently toward your destiny.

After an injury to my feet during an intense workout, I quickly learned the importance of watching my steps. My paths were carefully chosen to ensure my stability. One false step and pain would shoot up my leg with vengeance. The lesson will certainly stay with me.

The Bible strongly recommends that men watch their steps.

Here are a few examples:

- "My feet have closely followed his steps; I have kept to his way without turning aside" (Job 23:11 NIV).
- "My steps have held to your paths; my feet have not stumbled" (Psalm 17:5 NIV).
- "Righteousness goes before him and prepares the way for his steps" (Psalm 85:13 NIV).
- "I have considered my ways and have turned my steps to your statutes" (Psalm 119:59 NIV).
- "When you walk, you won't be held back; when you run, you won't stumble" (Proverbs 4:12 NLT).
- "The prudent give thought to their steps" (Proverbs 14:15b NIV).
- "To this you were called, because Christ suffered for you, leaving you an example, that you should follow in his steps" (1 Peter 2:21 NIV).

Let's be aware of our steps and walk accurately on the path, stable in our footing, assured in our motions.

REMEMBER

Walk confidently toward your destiny.

READ PROVERBS CHAPTER 4

fivestarman.com/day-338

Day 339: The Shadow Of Sin

PROVERBS 5:22 (MSG)

The shadow of your sin will overtake you;
you'll find yourself stumbling all over yourself in the dark.

PRINCIPLE

Evil deeds ensnare those who work evil.

The tactics, schemes, devices, and tricks a man plays to get ahead catch up to him. The very means that he uses to deceive will be used against him. Evil deeds ensnare those who work evil. They stumble over themselves in the darkness of their actions.

This principle is important to remember, especially when someone has targeted you with their schemes. It gives you the assurance that God's precepts that govern the universe and the moral code of conduct will not be broken. Remember, a man reaps what he has sown.

David may have taught this principle to his son Solomon. He wrote a lyrical, Messianic prophesy regarding the tactics of evil men.

"May their path be dark and slippery, with the angel of the Lord pursuing them" (Psalm 35:6 NIV).

The reference to the "angel of the Lord pursuing" is acknowledging the preeminence of God's established laws, precepts, and judgments. They will govern mankind's conduct.

REMEMBER

Don't use evil tactics and expect positive rewards.

READ PROVERBS CHAPTER 5

fivestarman.com/day-339

Day 340: Body Language

PROVERBS 6:12–14 (MSG)

Riffraff and rascals
talk out of both sides of their mouths.
They wink at each other; they shuffle their feet;
they cross their fingers behind their backs.
Their perverse minds are always cooking up something nasty,
always stirring up trouble.

PRINCIPLE

Foot shifting and gestures are signs that we should discern.

On a recent trip to Chile, my host shared with me that a relaxing gesture that I used while standing and waiting was considered offensive in their culture. Of course, I not only honored his suggestion to stop but have since quit the habitual use of that gesture altogether.

There is a science behind body language. The science doesn't have hard facts related to it, and it uses a lot of generalizations; however, many people interpret gestures as non-verbal communication.

Our advisor refers to those who are always double-speaking, saying one thing and then saying the opposite. But the perverse-minded also use body language as signs of their deceptions. Winking, shuffling, crossing fingers—they're cooking up something to cause trouble.

I am not suggesting that we jump to conclusions, but I encourage you to be aware of the movements of others while they're talking. Also, listen carefully to their words. Are they consistent? Do their words match their actions?

Those who pervert the truth with their mouth are often dramatic and overly expressive in their body language.

REMEMBER

Discern the signs around you.

READ PROVERBS CHAPTER 6

fivestarman.com/day-340

Day 341: How The Mighty Have Fallen

PROVERBS 7:26 (NIV)

Many are the victims she has brought down;
her slain are a mighty throng.

PRINCIPLE

A strong man can be brought down by weak agents.

Proverbs is the compilation of wisdom written by a man to men. When you repeatedly read Proverbs, you can see one of Solomon's major concerns for men was the Adulteress.

If we're not careful, we can become calloused and skip over the warnings. Much like a child when you've repeated your wisdom, they sigh with disbelief, "I know. I know. You've told me."

My sensitivity to adultery is much like my repulsion to cigarette smoking. I grew up in a household of chain smokers. The pungent, stale, and bitter smell of smoke was disgusting to me. The exposure to second-hand smoke developed an allergy in me. Cigarettes are an enemy that has killed many of my family members.

The same is true for adultery. My family was torn apart because of an adulterous affair. My childhood was marked by the absence of my father because of it. The repercussions have lasted a lifetime.

For me, adultery is an enemy that has destroyed many of my friends' lives. I'm not entertained by it. I'm not humored by it. I'm not sympathetic to it. I hate how it reduces a man to his lowest form.

These two agents of destruction have destroyed more men than all of the wars combined.

REMEMBER

Don't gloss over this warning.

READ PROVERBS CHAPTER 7
fivestarman.com/day-341

Day 342: You Have A Cause

PROVERBS 8:10 (MSG)

Prefer my life-disciplines over chasing after money,
and God-knowledge over a lucrative career.

PRINCIPLE

Life-disciplines and God-knowledge will get you where you want to go more than money and power.

As men, we are designed with an entrepreneurial drive, which empowers us to pursue the means to meet our needs, to grant the desires of our families, and to finance our purposes. However, it's not about cars, clothes, and cottages—it's about our cause.

As we pursue our purpose, we instill life-disciplines and apply God-knowledge to meet the challenge of our cause. As others chase money and climb ladders for success, we find our significance in a cause. Money isn't the goal, and titles aren't a prize.

However, money is a tool, and titles are positions of influence. It will take money to accomplish our purpose, and it will take titles for influence. So, don't go to the extremes on either side. Poverty certainly won't help your purpose. We've also been warned that riches can be distracting. Let's keep our eyes on the prize.

REMEMBER

You have a purpose to pursue. As you work disciplines and add knowledge, you'll get there.

READ PROVERBS CHAPTER 8

fivestarman.com/day-342

Day 343: Secret Food

PROVERBS 9:17 (NIV)

Stolen water is sweet;
food eaten in secret is delicious!

PRINCIPLE

Your appetite for secret food isn't about your stomach; it's about your heart.

It is subtle when it happens. You may have had a tough day. On your commute home you pull into a convenience store, fill up with gas, and walk in to pick up something to hold you over until dinner. There is almost nothing that is healthy to eat, so you grab some junk food. Typically, it's food that you were denied when you were young. Food eaten in secret is delicious!

Eating disorders are more often found in young ladies; however, as I've traveled around the country, it's obvious that men are suffering from dysfunctional diets. I suspect this is tied to emotional insecurities that they are unwilling to deal with on a serious level. I must admit that I've been guilty of allowing the stress of life to cause me to gain weight.

A while ago, I made an appointment with my physician to design a plan of action regarding my health. I changed my mindset regarding the purpose for food and exercise. I no longer eat for enjoyment or comfort. My exercise is for conditioning, not for weight loss.

I've learned to cast all of my cares upon the Lord. It can sound trite, but it is true. I've learned to lean in to the Lord for my comfort and emotional sustenance.

REMEMBER

Properly align your purpose by dictating your appetites.

READ PROVERBS CHAPTER 9

fivestarman.com/day-343

Day 344: Aspiration Or Ambition?

PROVERBS 10:28 (MSG)

The aspirations of good people end in celebration;
the ambitions of bad people crash.

PRINCIPLE

The end of the ambitious is horrific. The end of those who aspire end in celebrations.

There's confusion when it comes to the drive of the entrepreneur to achieve success. Some struggle with justifying their desire for increase with the religious idea of contentment. They believe they can either pursue God or greed, but never the two should meet. I've known men who would rather give up their pursuit of God so that they can earn a living and meet the needs and desire of their families.

This is unfortunate because it completely disregards the biblical narrative regarding the blessing that comes from the pursuit of God. It is clear that the aspirations of the righteous—the object of a strong desire to achieve something of significant value—end in celebrations.

It is also evident the ambitions of the wicked come crashing down. Ambition is an ardent desire for rank, fame, or power. Obviously, the motivations are distinctly different.

Having an aspiration is a pure motivation to pursue God and, as a byproduct, receiving the means to an end—ending in a celebration. On the contrary, an ambitious person is all about themselves, seeking titles, notoriety, and abusive influence.

We should aspire to fulfill God's plan and purpose for our lives, living for significance and leaving a legacy.

REMEMBER

Pursue God, and you'll end up at a party.

READ PROVERBS CHAPTER 10

fivestarman.com/day-344

Day 345: Domestic Violence

PROVERBS 11:29 (MSG)

Exploit or abuse your family, and end up with a fistful of air;
common sense tells you it's a stupid way to live.

PRINCIPLE

We should champion our lives in front of our families before all others.

The NFL announced rigorous standards for their players on the premise that playing in the NFL is a privilege that comes with responsibility. A new Special Counsel for Investigations and Conduct will have oversight of the high standards of conduct.

Recent news has exacerbated the already damaged public images of many NFL players. Now, what a player does in the privacy of his home is open for the scrutiny of the league.

At ***The Daily Champion***, we've talked a lot about "The Closet Principle"—what a man does in secret is what moves him in public. Isn't it interesting that a man can be a champion on the "field of contest" (e.g., the football field) and a loser in the passion of being gallant toward his wife?

As we pursue authentic manhood, we should strive to live exemplary lives in all five passions of authentic manhood. If anyone should think that we're champions, it should be our family. I would much rather be a champion to my wife, children, and grandchildren than to complete strangers in a stadium.

REMEMBER

Any man who raises his hand in violence against his family forfeits his manhood and will suffer the wrath of his stupidity.

READ PROVERBS CHAPTER 11
fivestarman.com/day-345

Day 346: A Diligent Man

PROVERBS 12:27 (NLT)

Lazy people don't even cook the game they catch,
but the diligent make use of everything they find.

PRINCIPLE

A diligent man takes care of everything his hand touches, making the most out of his possessions.

When I was in college, I took a step of faith by selling my car so that I wouldn't have a car payment. Amazingly, someone heard about it and offered to give me a car—a 1976 Chevrolet Chevette.

I was grateful for the gift and treated it with appreciation. At the time, I worked at a car wash. Every day, I washed it, waxed it, treated the tires, and sprayed "new car" air fragrance in the interior. That car turned out to be a great "get-around" car.

What you respect is what you attract; what you disrespect you will repel. What you have in your possession right now is either qualifying you or disqualifying you for more.

I see people who get a new car and treat it as if it's junk. It's not long until it loses its luster and shows disrepair. The value plummets, and they trade it in for another one. The cycle repeats itself.

It's a sign of respect and dignity to take care of what you have in your hand and under your leadership. Put anything or anyone in the hands of a diligent man, and he will take good care and show responsibility for it.

REMEMBER

You can't get a new car because your ashtray is dirty. Take care of your possessions.

READ PROVERBS CHAPTER 12

fivestarman.com/day-346

Day 347: The Gift Of Seed

PROVERBS 13:25 (NLT)

The godly eat to their hearts' content,
but the belly of the wicked goes hungry.

PRINCIPLE

An appetite for good brings satisfaction, but the belly of the wicked always wants more.

The first gift God gave to mankind was the gift of seed so that man could determine his diet, thus satisfying his personal cravings. This is a remarkable gift. We have the unique ability to have a craving and then sow a seed for a determined harvest to satisfy that craving.

I can't emphasize the importance of this enough. In fact, this one principle is the currency of the Earth. Seed is a currency. ALL currencies that man use are based upon this principle and remarkable gift.

Those who understand and apply the principle of seed are fully satisfied and content in life. Those who don't, go hungry. They will never be fulfilled.

REMEMBER

A man reaps what he sows.

READ PROVERBS CHAPTER 13

fivestarman.com/day-347

Day 348: A Nation Weakened

PROVERBS 14:34 (MSG)

God-devotion makes a country strong;
God-avoidance leaves people weak.

PRINCIPLE

"America is great because she is good. If America ceases to be good, America will cease to be great." —Alexis de Tocqueville

Americans are a resilient people that border on goodness. At times, we have the courage to rise against any who would desire to dethrone our way of life; yet, we are gradually giving up our freedoms for the seduction of security.

The security of the nation relies upon its devotion to God. When a nation chooses to avoid God, it is exposed to evil.

When President Bill Clinton redefined "sexual relations," yet was not held accountable for his actions, the damage rippled throughout the nation. Young people began to exchange sexual favors and call it "friends with benefits."

We've seen mendacity taken to a new level in politics. Historically, politicians have been known to speak untruths; however, the public rebuked and held charlatans accountable for such manipulation. Now, the public is choosing to believe the lies.

By not rebuking liars and removing them from office, the nation's young will grope in confusion and live in the fog of fantasies.

However, not so with your children. They will be taught of the Lord and they will experience great peace (Isaiah 54:13).

REMEMBER

As you lead your family with courage and character, they will rise above the evil around them and walk in victory.

READ PROVERBS CHAPTER 14

fivestarman.com/day-348

Day 349: Resurrected Life

PROVERBS 15:24 (NLT)

The path of life leads upward for the wise;
they leave the grave behind.

PRINCIPLE

If you're going to believe in something, believe in someone who can get you out of the grave.

The final enemy, the one who has conquered all mankind, the nemesis that defines the limits of all religions is Death. Who can beat Death?

The resurrection of Jesus Christ is evidence that He is the Son of God, the Savior of mankind, the first-fruits of the resurrection.

"And he was shown to be the Son of God when he was raised from the dead by the power of the Holy Spirit. He is Jesus Christ our Lord" (Romans 1:4 NLT).

Do you know that it is God's plan for men to experience resurrected life?

"The Spirit of God, who raised Jesus from the dead, lives in you. And just as God raised Christ Jesus from the dead, he will give life to your mortal bodies by this same Spirit living within you" (Romans 8:11 NLT).

The same power that raised Christ quickens our mortal bodies—meaning the life that we have now! Solomon suggested that the wise take the path that leads upwards—ascending and leaving the grave behind.

REMEMBER

Leave the grave behind.

READ PROVERBS CHAPTER 15

fivestarman.com/day-349

Day 350: Calloused Climbers

PROVERBS 16:29 (MSG)

Calloused climbers betray their very own friends;
they'd stab their grandmothers in the back.

PRINCIPLE

Some men have hardened their hearts and are so determined to get their way that they will do anything to anyone.

There are some very self-centered men out there. They will do anything to get ahead. They will use any tactic as long as they can get their way and accomplish their goals. It doesn't matter who gets in their way. They will stab their grandmothers in the back. Their only loyalty is to themselves.

When I was young, I naïvely considered that these people knew they were doing evil, and their consciences would correct them. Now I realize that they justify their actions and often believe that they are hearing from God and doing what He wants them to do.

"...The time is coming when those who kill you will think they are doing a holy service for God" (John 16:2 NLT).

It's pretty frightening to consider there are people who believe that they are hearing the voice of God to do evil toward you and consider it an offering to Him.

Their violence and antipathy come from a hardened and embittered heart. They're are unreasonable—even delusional in their conversations. They raise their voices, use strange language, and threaten. Their violence is without measure. They do not consider anyone innocent, they are ruthless beasts.

REMEMBER

Watch your back.

READ PROVERBS CHAPTER 16

fivestarman.com/day-350

Day 351: Words Matter

PROVERBS 17:4 (MSG)

Evil people relish malicious conversation;
the ears of liars itch for dirty gossip.

PRINCIPLE

Those who speak *to you* about someone will soon speak *about you* to someone.

When someone gossips and relishes malicious conversation, it's a sign of weak minds and insecure identities. That kind of language reveals darkness in a person's heart and displays an ignorance of the power of words. The tongue has the power of life and death.

Words matter.

The confession of three words can transform a person's identity from a sinner into a saint. Three words: "Jesus is Lord." Think about it—just three words!

If *any* of our words matter than *all* of our words matter. We need to be mindful of what we say, not only about ourselves but also about others.

Gossip is the use of words to destroy the influence and reputation of a person. It is worse than stealing money because money can be replaced. Words of gossip are feathers in the wind—you will never gather them back up.

REMEMBER

Don't assign your words to gossip.

READ PROVERBS CHAPTER 17
fivestarman.com/day-351

Day 352: Be Strong And Courageous

PROVERBS 18:14 (MSG)

A healthy spirit conquers adversity,
but what can you do when the spirit is crushed?

PRINCIPLE

Be strong, and show yourself a man.

As men we face challenges every day—marriage, children, work, temptation, cultural challenges—it takes a lot of courage to live out authentic manhood. Courage is an attribute that empowers men to stand up against the odds aligned against them.

"... Be strong and courageous. Do not be afraid; do not be discouraged, for the Lord your God will be with you wherever you go" (Joshua 1:9 NIV).

When Moses passed the baton to his protégé, Joshua, the loyal servant-leader needed to be strengthened. God directly commanded Joshua to be strong and courageous, to resist fear, to be encouraged because God would be with him.

As your steps are ordered each day and you walk out authentic manhood, you must be strengthened. That's our hope for you.

As we come to the final days of ***The Daily Champion,*** I hope you've been strengthened and encouraged to be strong and courageous. As you've read the chapter of Proverbs each day, I know that you've gained wisdom. You've done something very few men have ever done—to walk with God in the daily commute.

REMEMBER

Be strong, and show yourself a man.

READ PROVERBS CHAPTER 18

fivestarman.com/day-352

Day 353: God's Purpose Prevails

PROVERBS 19:21 (MSG)

We humans keep brainstorming options and plans,
but God's purpose prevails.

PRINCIPLE

The quickest way to succeed in life is to know the purposes of God and to take action upon them.

The primary purpose of Proverbs is to communicate life experience and wisdom for living, so as to spare us the expense of pain. We encourage you to seek counsel and recommend that you look for mentors; however, you must remember that the greatest wisdom comes in knowing the purposes of God. What is His original intent for mankind. More specifically—what is His purpose for you?

I meet men who are constantly pursuing new ventures and schemes. They boastfully talk "blue sky" vision and huge numbers; all the while they are unfaithful in the little things. They hit it big one time, and they think it is beneath them to get into minutia.

I've known entrepreneurs who, had they spent time in direct pursuit of their business rather that talking about it all the time, they might actually have made a living and accomplished their dream.

If you're going to succeed, you must explore the purposes of God and get involved in them.

What is my purpose in business? What should I focus on? What must I do today that will get me one step closer to my goal?

What is my purpose as a husband? Where am I leading my family? Does my wife know my family vision? Is she in agreement with me?

REMEMBER

Don't be distracted by boastful talk.

READ PROVERBS CHAPTER 19
fivestarman.com/day-353

Day 354: Love Wins

PROVERBS 20:28 (MSG)

Love and truth form a good leader;
sound leadership is founded on loving integrity.

PRINCIPLE

Leadership founded on love and truth is secure.

Very few leadership books talk about the two most significant characteristics of a good leader. They are love and truth. If a leader wants to secure his position, he will do it by loving integrity.

Unfortunately, love is often misunderstood to be simply a feminine attribute. Men are often reluctant to demonstrate love, but are shameless to let you know what they know.

Look at this description of love, and apply it to your leadership for your family, business, or civic cause:

> Love never gives up. Love cares more for others than for self.
> Love doesn't want what it doesn't have. Love doesn't strut,
> Doesn't have a swelled head, Doesn't force itself on others,
> Isn't always "me first," Doesn't fly off the handle,
> Doesn't keep score of the sins of others, Doesn't revel when others grovel,
> Takes pleasure in the flowering of truth, Puts up with anything,
> Trusts God always, Always looks for the best,
> Never looks back, But keeps going to the end (1 Corinthians 13:4-7 MSG).

REMEMBER

Secure a win in your leadership by loving truth.

READ PROVERBS CHAPTER 20

fivestarman.com/day-354

Day 355: The Passionate Pursuit Of Authentic Manhood

PROVERBS 21:21 (NIV)

Whoever pursues righteousness and love
finds life, prosperity, and honor.

PRINCIPLE

Whoever goes hunting for what is right and kind finds life itself—glorious life!

When a man discovers and gains understanding of his purposes, his life becomes a passionate pursuit of authentic manhood. Our goal at ***FivestarMan*** is to be a voice and become a movement to raise the volume for authentic manhood.

What is the outcome of a man who passionately pursues authenticity of manliness? The rewards are piled upon him—life, prosperity, and honor. His life is all that God originally intended for him. He has vigor and strength. His journey goes well with him, and he can fulfill his purpose and live out his days. He will be held in high regard both in this life and in the life to come.

Isn't that the kind of life you want to live as a man?

REMEMBER

Passionately pursue righteousness and love.

READ PROVERBS CHAPTER 21
fivestarman.com/day-355

Day 356: Generous Hands

PROVERBS 22:9 (MSG)

Generous hands are blessed hands
because they give bread to the poor.

PRINCIPLE

I've never asked God to meet a need in my life when He didn't show me someone whom I could meet the need in their life.

When generosity is practiced, the generous person becomes a conduit of blessing for everyone they meet.

I remember when God first impressed upon me to become a generous person. It started by his challenge to stop thinking about what I didn't have and to start thinking about what I did have to give. When I determined to become generous in my heart, my resolve was put to the test.

One day, I was praying about a great need I had while I was driving to an appointment. At the very moment that I closed the prayer, I looked up and saw someone in need. I felt impressed to give what seemed to me to be a large amount of money to that man.

To be honest, I felt a twinge of sorrow when I handed the money to him, but I didn't hesitate.

Within a couple of minutes, my assistant called to tell me that someone had just dropped off an offering at the office. It was exactly what I had asked God for.

REMEMBER

The generous person is blessed, meaning he will have more than enough to continue to be a blessing to those who are in need.

READ PROVERBS CHAPTER 22

fivestarman.com/day-356

Day 357: One Happy Parent

PROVERBS 23:15 (MSG)

Dear child, if you become wise,
I'll be one happy parent.

PRINCIPLE

There is nothing greater than seeing your children walk in wisdom.

Recently I read something my daughter wrote on her blog. She masterfully expressed how she stepped out in faith to be entrepreneurial, rather than to get a job working for someone else. She defined her goals, set her work hours, turned off the phone, and scheduled email replies and customer service. To say I was happy is an understatement. I became one happy parent because she demonstrated incredible wisdom beyond her years.

My son recently made a huge life decision that required much prayer and careful consideration. He strategized plans and worked hard toward his goals. Now, he and his wife have a thriving businesses. I was filled with happiness to see my son make wise decisions.

I don't want to leave out my first daughter and her husband. They have taken a tremendous step of faith in launching a new company, finding craftsmen with a work ethic to keep up with the demands. Adding so many workers and two shifts to fulfill orders is real pressure. However, they've responded with wisdom and are working a plan to take care of their business.

Please understand, I am not boasting in pride. I am dancing with joy. I'm one happy parent because my children are walking in wisdom.

REMEMBER

You'll be one happy parent by raising your children to make wise decisions.

➔ READ PROVERBS CHAPTER 23

fivestarman.com/day-357

Day 358: When Your Enemy Falls

PROVERBS 24:17 (NIV)

Do not gloat when your enemy falls;
when they stumble, do not let your heart rejoice,
or the Lord will see and disapprove
and turn his wrath away from them.

PRINCIPLE

If speaking a blessing invokes angels—speaking a curse entices demons.

When someone has willfully and strategically set their sights on you to become your enemy, it is very tempting to gloat a little when evil happens to them.

Our advisor challenges us to go completely against our nature on this one. He suggests that we refrain from gloating or rejoicing over their stumbling and failures.

Jesus said, "Bless those who curse you. Pray for those who hurt you" (Luke 6:28 NLT).

If speaking a blessing invokes angels—speaking a curse entices demons. Demons are merciless. They are horrific and filthy. You don't want their schemes and plots working against anyone.

We do not wrestle with flesh and blood, meaning the real enemy we're struggling with is the spirit behind the person's actions. How do we rebuke the spirit without harming the person? We do what Jesus did: We destroy the works of evil by speaking a blessing upon those who mistreat us.

Ask God to turn your enemy's attention away from you and back toward Him. That's what Solomon suggests. God is trying to get their attention. By praying for your enemy, you're heaping coals of fire upon their heads for their purification, not their destruction.

REMEMBER

Bless those who hate you, hoping to turn their attention toward God.

READ PROVERBS CHAPTER 24

fivestarman.com/day-358

Day 359: The Gate Of Authority

PROVERBS 25:28 (NLT)

A person without self-control
is like a city with broken-down walls.

PRINCIPLE

You are the gate of authority to your home.

With the position of leadership in your home comes tremendous responsibility for you to have self-control. We know that as the gate of authority, whatever comes, comes through us. A great example of someone who knew this was Job.

"I made a covenant with my eyes not to look with lust at a young woman" (Job 31:1 NLT). Job understood that his lack of control would open the door to his nemesis, the adversary. The adversary only has the power to destroy if we lack the control of our gates—the eye gate being one of the most important.

It is especially difficult in our day when hamburgers can't be sold without a double entendre. If a company must use vulgarity to sell their food, then they need a better recipe.

If a seductive commercial comes on the screen, or a woman walks in the room, or an ad on a website is trying to get your attention, bounce your eyes away. As simple as this sounds, it works.

Some men will suggest, "It doesn't hurt to look."

Jesus answered that emphatically. "But I tell you that anyone who looks at a woman lustfully has already committed adultery with her in his heart" (Matthew 5:28 NIV).

REMEMBER

You're the gate of authority. The gate you open is the one the enemy will access.

READ PROVERBS CHAPTER 25
fivestarman.com/day-359

Day 360: Lies And Flattery Are Hurtful

PROVERBS 26:28 (NLT)

A lying tongue hates its victims,
and flattering words cause ruin.

PRINCIPLE

The delusional believe a lie by speaking it.

Have you ever been the recipient of excessive and insincere praise? You know that the person pouring it out is using deceptive words for their gain. Frankly, it's not only deceptive, it's disgusting behavior.

Satan is called the father of lies (John 8:44). Think about that. He was the first personality to pervert truth for personal gain. Now, he masters mendacity (the art of lying). Those who practice perversion, lies, and flattery are using his schemes and devices for their personal gain.

In the case of Satan, his lies originated because he wanted to exalt himself and usurp the authority of Almighty God. As preposterous as it sounds, that is precisely what happens to the delusional mind. Lying thoughts become "truth" to them. They believe a lie by speaking it.

Know this—if someone uses flattery, they have ruin in mind for you. People lie because they hate you. Often, there is something you have that they want.

One of the passions of a ***FivestarMan*** is to be faithful in character. We need to walk and talk with integrity. We never use flattery for personal gain.

REMEMBER

Speak the truth in love.

READ PROVERBS CHAPTER 26

fivestarman.com/day-360

Day 361: The Test Of Flattery

PROVERBS 27:21 (NLT)

Fire tests the purity of silver and gold,
but a person is tested by being praised.

PRINCIPLE

The purity of human hearts is tested by giving them a little fame.

The flatterer has selfish gain in mind when they pour flattery on you. They will just as quickly turn their flattering praise into gossip and slander.

But the mendacious person isn't the only one tested with flattery. You will be tested when you are on the receiving end of such praise.

Your adversary will use these tactics to get to the very core of your belief system. Who are you? He goes directly to your identity and either mercilessly tears you down or excessively builds you up. In either case, he wins by making you ineffective in identity.

Jesus faced both of these temptations. "If you are the Son of God, throw yourself down." In other words, if you think you are who you say you are, test God. When that failed to move Jesus, the devil turned it around and lavished everything to suggest, "You can have all of this if you will simply bow before me!"

Jesus defeated the temptation of the devil and went in the power of the Holy Spirit from that day forward.

Every man is tested by those who beat him down with their insults and slander and by those who heap praise upon him for selfish gain.

REMEMBER

The only opinion we should concern ourselves with is the acknowledgment of God.

READ PROVERBS CHAPTER 27

fivestarman.com/day-361

Day 362: Not All Prayers Are Heard

PROVERBS 28:9 (MSG)

God has no use for the prayers
of the people who won't listen to him.

PRINCIPLE

Praying is a conversation with the Almighty. It's important to listen to Him.

None of us like to suffer fools—biblically defined as self-confident, boastful, know-it-alls. The Hebrew word for *fool* is pictured as Orion, the giant constellation, described to be impious and boastful. Job is asked by the Lord, "Can you loosen the belt of Orion?" (Job 38:31 NKJV).

When a fool comes up to you for a conversation, it's difficult to be polite and maintain decorum. Their arrogance is detestable. The conversation is always dominated by their mouth and never balanced with the use of their ears.

God doesn't suffer fools either. They may posture themselves as religious, but their prayers are not heard because they come only to speak and not to listen.

Listening is an active and positive action that requires as much thought as articulating a masterful speech. Listening is a sign of respect to the speaker. It demonstrates humility like almost nothing else. When most people have kneeled in the posture of humility, they still would rather speak than listen.

REMEMBER

If we want our prayers to be heard, we need to be prepared to hear.

READ PROVERBS CHAPTER 28

fivestarman.com/day-362

Day 363: Terrorism

PROVERBS 29:25 (AMP)

The fear of man brings a snare, but whoever leans on, trusts in, and puts his confidence in the Lord is safe and set on high.

PRINCIPLE

If we allow men to cause us fear, we will become paralyzed into inaction.

A terrorist's weapon is fear, causing others to capitulate to irrational demands. Terrorism is the art of war for the ignorant and the coward. Radical leaders recruit the disenfranchised from society and use them for their advantage. How do we respond?

My neighbor had a reputation of being a bully. For some reason, others put up with his foolishness. I was away on a trip when he bullied my young son. When my wife came out, he turned his drunken mouth, spewing cuss words toward her.

When I returned, I approached him at a calm and confident pace. "Dennis, you will never speak to my family again. If you ever do, I will deal with you man-to-man. Do you understand me?"

He snuffed his alcoholic breath to say, "And you call yourself a Christian?"

"Yes, I do. And my theology will allow me to defend my family and beat you to a pulp!" I replied.

For weeks after, Dennis would scurry into his home whenever he saw me.

Terrorists get what they want by intimidation. However, if we stand up to their tactics, they will crawl back into their caves.

REMEMBER

Stand up, put your shoulders back, look them in the eye, and be men!

READ PROVERBS CHAPTER 29

fivestarman.com/day-363

Day 364: Stirring Up Anger To Punish

PROVERBS 30:33b (NIV)

... So stirring up anger produces strife.

PRINCIPLE

Using anger as a form of punishment is stirring up a pot of pain.

Corporal punishment has been in the news of late. The debate continues on the merits of spanking versus other forms of punishment. I can see the pros and cons of each side of the debate; however, there is one form of "discipline" I find more insidious and damaging to mental and emotional stability than any other—namely, exasperating your child.

As a reminder, *to exasperate* means *to arouse anger as a form of punishment.* It is so damaging that the Bible warns fathers never to use it.

"Fathers, do not provoke your children to anger by the way you treat them. Rather, bring them up with the discipline and instruction that comes from the Lord" (Ephesians 6:4 NLT).

Our advisor also warns us that stirring up anger will produce strife, rather than obedience. The danger of this anger is that it manipulates and uses a person's emotions to cause them pain.

I've said before that strife is the manifestation of Satan. Evil lives where strife resides. You see the repercussions of strife during the evening news. Someone ends up hurt or even dead because of strife.

Do not provoke your children, rather discipline them by teaching them the precepts and principles of the Word of God. Rather than provoking them to anger, why not provoke them to good works? (Read Hebrews 10:24.)

REMEMBER

Don't stir up evil emotions.

READ PROVERBS CHAPTER 30

fivestarman.com/day-364

Day 365: Praise Your Wife

PROVERBS 31:30 (NIV)

Charm is deceptive, and beauty is fleeting;
but a woman who fears the Lord is to be praised.

PRINCIPLE

A husband should praise his wife.

Most people think praise is meant for God only. I would argue that *worship* is reserved for God only. However, we are encouraged by our advisor to praise a woman who fears the Lord.

The words of a husband have cultivating power for his wife. His words act like seeds sown into the ground. If a husband doesn't sow good seed, he can't expect a good harvest.

I've known men who play sophomoric games with their wives. Some men toy with jealousy, thinking it will keep their wives on their toes. Others are demanding and demeaning, treating their wives more like servants. I've also known men who control their wives with money.

After carefully observing these men, I've never known any of them to have a thriving marriage, nor one that lasted long term.

Even as a young man I knew that I would have a different kind of marriage. I wanted a woman I could trust; someone who would partner in life with me; someone who loved God and unreservedly loved me.

Remember: A woman who wants to become a Proverbs 31 woman needs to be married to a Proverbs-1-through-30 man.

REMEMBER

Speak kind and comforting words to your wife. Give her the praise she deserves.

READ PROVERBS CHAPTER 31

fivestarman.com/day-365

60683953R00205

Made in the USA
Columbia, SC
17 June 2019